You Are Here:

Essays on the Art of Poetry in Canada

YOU ARE HERE

ESSAYS ON THE ART
OF POETRY IN CANADA

JAMES POLLOCK

The Porcupine's Quill

Library and Archives Canada Cataloguing in Publication

Pollock, James, 1968 –
You are here : essays on the art of poetry in Canada / James Pollock

ISBN : 978-0-88984-357-8

1. Canadian poetry (English) — History and criticism. I. Title.

PS8143.P65 2012   C811.009   C2012-904926-3

1   2   3   4   •   14   13   12

Published by The Porcupine's Quill, 68 Main Street, PO Box 160,
Erin, Ontario NOB 1TO. http://porcupinesquill.ca

Readied for the press by Carmine Starnino.

Represented in Canada by the Literary Press Group.
Trade orders are available from University of Toronto Press.

We acknowledge the support of the Ontario Arts Council and the Canada Council for
the Arts for our publishing program. The financial support of the Government of
Canada through the Canada Book Fund is also gratefully acknowledged.

Acknowledgements

I am grateful to the editors of the following journals in which earlier versions of most of the essays collected here previously appeared. They are listed below with their original titles.

Arc Poetry Magazine: 'Hine Recollected', 'Karen Solie's Triple Vision'

Books in Canada: 'What to Pack'

Canadian Notes & Queries: 'The Art of Poetry', 'Cursing with a Broken Art', 'The Magic of Jeffery Donaldson', 'Still Out in Left Field'

Contemporary Poetry Review: 'Black and White Magician: The Poetry of Jeffery Donaldson', 'Anne Carson and the Sublime'

Literary Review of Canada: 'Choosing the Best Canadian Poetry', 'RE: "A Response to James Pollock's 'Choosing the Best Canadian Poetry' by Fraser Sutherland"'

Poetry Reviews.ca: '*Decreation: Poetry, Essays, Opera,* by Anne Carson', '*The New Canon: An Anthology of Canadian Poetry,* edited by Carmine Starnino'

The New Quarterly: 'Eric Ormsby: Sympathetic Magic and the Chameleon Poet'

Riddle Fence: 'Critical Mess'

Special thanks to the editors of *The Page: Poetry, essays, language, ideas* for linking online to 'Anne Carson and the Sublime' at *Contemporary Poetry Review*.

Table of Contents

To Charles Taylor

In the moment before his transformation, each poet has seemed to be living in a backwater, a province or enclave that time has forgotten.... History passes by such places, and the poets who live there are doomed to a hollow in time. Yet all at once, in the rush of initiation, the situation reverses.... [Their provinces] turn into prototypes of Jerusalem and Rome.

— Lawrence Lipking, *The Life of the Poet*

Preface

When I lived in Toronto in the late eighties and early nineties I rode my share of public transportation, and I often found myself perusing the glowing, back-lit advertising signs in subway stations and bus stop shelters. I vividly recall a campaign for a local cough medicine called Buckley's Mixture. Apparently this witch's brew contained no alcohol, sugar or pleasant flavour of any kind. The ads varied — one invited readers to 'Open wide and say "@#$%&*!"' — but all ended with the same slogan: 'It Tastes Awful. And It Works.' What a brilliant intuition, I thought. To sell medicine in puritan Toronto, you emphasize how bad it tastes. The campaign was a spectacular success.

Unfortunately, the same attitude prevailed in poetry.

In my undergraduate literature classes at York University I luxuriated in Homer, Chaucer, Shakespeare, Milton, Whitman. As a neophyte writer, however, I was also eager to discover what my compatriots were writing, and so, during my almost daily explorations of the campus bookstore, I would spend some time digging into anthologies of Canadian poetry and fiction, and the new issues of Canadian literary journals, and whenever a visiting writer gave a reading on campus, I was there. The hype was loud. Margaret Atwood was a world-famous writer; bpNichol was the greatest living member of the Canadian avant-garde. But as I read around, searching for a great Canadian poet, as I sat in the audience listening to Atwood's mildly amusing monotone wit, and Nichol's feral grunting and snarling and endless puns, it began to dawn on me that something was terribly wrong. These poets — not just Atwood and Nichol, but the names I stumbled across in anthologies and journals — were not very good. A lot of them were astonishingly bad. And yet they were being published and celebrated, it seemed, everywhere. I had to face the truth: their poetry tasted awful. But I'd be damned if it didn't seem, as far as their reputations were concerned, to work.

Two main kinds of poetry were being published in Canada at the time.

One was a rough, dull, plainspoken lyric poetry in casual free verse, either autobiographical or mythically didactic: Atwood, Al Purdy, George Bowering. The other was a loopy avant-garde composition whose main qualities were tedium and incoherence: Nichol, Fred Wah, Steve McCaffery. This second group differed from the plainspoken free-verse poets in part by surrounding their writing with a lot of pretentious theoretical bombast, and they seemed to go on forever repeating the same experiments that avant-gardes in Europe and the United States had been conducting for decades, without very interesting results.

On some days it made me depressed, on others furious. During my excursions downtown, I would often see a miserable-looking guy standing outside Sam the Record Man on Yonge Street. He was always holding a small stack of stapled chapbooks with one propped up on top so you could read the cover, announcing its title in big black handwritten letters: *Shit*. I never saw anyone slow down to take a closer look. It was the mirror image of the avant-garde literary magazine I'd encountered in the university library from a generation earlier, with its stupefying anagrammatic title, *Tish*. There you have it, I said to myself: the two main pipelines in the sewer of Canadian poetry.

Fortunately, it was partly an illusion. There were some gifted Canadian poets, including my teachers at York, Don Coles and Elisabeth Harvor, but most of them were forgotten or ignored. I'd never heard of Daryl Hine, for example, or Richard Outram, or Robert Allen. I felt claustrophobic. Here I was living in the largest city in Canada, reading some of the greatest literature of the Western world, and yet the provincial isolation of my own literary neighbourhood was overwhelming. If I was ever going to be a writer, I felt, I would have to leave.

So I moved to the United States for graduate school — this was twenty years ago now — started publishing poems and reviews, got married, and took a job as a professor in the American Midwest. But I never forgot my Toronto claustrophobia. And over time, in thinking about the art and theory of poetry, I began at last to understand the causes of that literary malaise.

One crucial factor was the xenophobic literary nationalism of the time, which, while mitigated somewhat, still runs deep in certain quarters even now. That attitude is one of the main targets of this book.

But there was, and is, a deeper problem: a lack of clarity in our thinking about poetry. The final essay here is an effort to address this problem head-on by considering the question of poetic value.

It's true that much has changed for the better in Canadian poetry in the last twenty years. A healthy crop of excellent new poets has emerged in Canada. And a few good new poet-critics have begun not only to respond to these poets, but also to undertake a desperately needed revaluation of the past. This has resulted, for example, in Evan Jones and Todd Swift's extraordinary revisionary anthology, *Modern Canadian Poets*, a review of which I have included here. As a devoted reader of Canadian poetry, I am encouraged by these developments. But a great deal still remains to be done.

This book — a collection of reviews and essays written over the last seven years — springs from two desires. First, to reconnect Canadian poetry to the larger context of poetry as an art. Second, to situate some of our poets on the map of world poetry — a map which, like one of those incomplete globes from the sixteenth century, still leaves this country largely uncharted.

My title — taken from a poem by Jeffery Donaldson called 'Bearings' — alludes to Northrop Frye's remark that, for Canadians, the question of identity isn't so much 'Who am I?' as 'Where is here?' My conviction is that where we are as a literary culture has a great deal to do with our relationship to elsewhere. If this book helps readers begin to answer that question about Canadian poetry and the particular Canadian poets I discuss herein, it will have done its job.

I am indebted to Loras College for a reassigned time award and a sabbatical, both of which gave me time to write some of the essays in this book.

Many thanks to the editors who edited and published earlier versions of many of these essays, including Ernest Hilbert at *Contemporary Poetry Review*, Anita Lahey at *Arc Poetry Magazine*, Amanda Jernigan at *The New Quarterly*, Moira MacDougall at *Literary Review of Canada*, Alex Good and Zachariah Wells at *Canadian Notes & Queries*, Eric Barstad at PoetryReviews.ca, Mark Callanan at *Riddle Fence*, and Carmine Starnino at *Books in Canada*. I am grateful for their invitations to write about subjects I might otherwise have overlooked, and for the freedom they often granted me to choose my own; and I am especially indebted to them for the ample space they so often gave me in their pages.

Much gratitude to Carmine Starnino, in particular, who invited me to put this collection together for The Porcupine's Quill. His brilliant editing has made this a much better book.

Special thanks to my former teachers Edward Hirsch and David Mikics, who urged me more than ten years ago to write a book on Canadian poetry. My thanks as well to my colleague Andrew Auge for his encouragement. And I am particularly grateful to the poets who responded so graciously to my essays on their work; they helped convince me of the value of criticism to a poet, and thus went far to encourage my completion of this book.

I owe a debt of gratitude to my parents and siblings for their support and encouragement over many years. A big thank you to my son for sharing me with these essays. And gratitude beyond words to my wife and editor, Stormy Stipe, who was the first to read every word.

PART I

Daryl Hine Recollected

'Criticism,' writes Helen Vendler, is 'the revenge of the student who once, perforce, sat silent while things that seemed untrue were said unrebuked, and poets who loomed large in the mind were ignored in the classroom.' So many untrue things have been said for so many years about Canadian poetry, and not just in classrooms, that it is hard to know where to begin to take one's revenge, if that is the right word. But fortunately the recent publication of Daryl Hine's *Recollected Poems: 1951–2004* (2007) gives us a chance to reassess our most unjustly ignored poet, and to fill in — or begin to fill in — one of the most forlorn and gaping holes in our literary history.

There are, as far as I can tell, five reasons for Hine's neglect. First, our poetry's puritanical devotion to sincerity and personal authenticity. At a time when many poets are loyal to the facts of their own perception and experience — even, or especially, when such facts conflict with the claims of art — Hine has been a shameless, even ruthless, artist. For Hine, the purpose of poetry is not self-expression, or even self-fashioning, but pleasure. As he puts it in the introduction to this career-spanning selection of poems, with its characteristically punning title, 'For me a poem is a verbal object capable of giving a specific kind of aesthetic pleasure in itself. As such it is like a painting or a sculpture.' This aestheticism has manifested itself in Hine's work in a variety of ways — each of them, alas, another brick in the wall obscuring Hine from critical view in this country.

For example — and here is the second reason for his neglect — Hine practises a brand of classicism which, for all its mastery, could not be less fashionable. He studied classics and philosophy at McGill, and comparative literature at the University of Chicago, and has published five fine volumes of translations from ancient Greek and Latin, including Hesiod, Theocritus, the so-called Homeric Hymns, and some of the lesser-known poems of Ovid. In all but the most cosmopolitan milieux, such interests would be unusual, rarefied even. But in Canada, outside of university classics departments, they are positively esoteric. (By contrast, consider Anne Carson's translations of widely read poets like Sappho, Aeschylus, Sophocles and Euripides; where Carson's is a Romantic classicism of the sublime, Hine's classicism is secular and Hellenistic — and the same may be said of his own poetry.)

The third strike against him in Canada has been his highbrow homosexuality. *Puerilities,* for instance, is his translation of pederastic lyrics from the Greek Anthology. Such books don't go over well in a country where a lot of male poets are very touchy about their straight sexuality, leading them to suppress any whiff of refinement that might waft from their pages — a fear which used to lead many of them, not so long ago, to pad their book-jacket bios with evidence of manly labours.

Fourth, there's his highly sophisticated prosodic imagination. Nothing has proven more off-putting to plainspoken free-verse poets and the avant-garde alike than Hine's formalism (though apparently Canadian formalists have never heard of him; you will find nary a poem by Hine in the anthology *In Fine Form: The Canadian Book of Form Poetry,* though for some reason you will find bpNichol and Fred Wah.) In his introduction Hine suggests his formalism is simply an aspect of his poetic temperament, 'not a matter of deliberate (let alone political) choice, but an involuntary and, to me, natural style of composition, as natural if not normal as my sexual predilection.' One imagines him saying this with a wry smile; it may come naturally to someone who has been writing this way for more than fifty years, but it is impossible to read Hine without feeling one is in the hands of a technical virtuoso.

And finally there is the matter of Hine's long-term residence in the United States during an era of fervent nationalist anti-Americanism in Canada. While many Canadian writers of his generation were feverishly devouring (not to mention penning) nationalist manifestoes like *Lament for a Nation* and *Survival,* Hine was busy teaching comparative literature at the University of Chicago, the University of Illinois, and Northwestern, publishing his books primarily with American publishers like Atheneum and Knopf, and serving as editor, from 1968 to 1978, of the storied American literary journal *Poetry.* Over the years he received a number of awards from American institutions, including Guggenheim and MacArthur Fellowships and a medal from the American Academy of Arts and Letters. He also attracted enthusiastic critical responses from American poetic luminaries, including poet-critics like Richard Howard, John Hollander and Anthony

Hecht. (Hine himself, who was born and grew up in British Columbia, points out in his introduction to the present book, which was published in Canada, that his 'alien residence' in the United States was never a matter of 'national preference', but of personal circumstance, and adds that he always remained a Canadian citizen.)

In short, one could hardly have invented a poet less likely to be celebrated in Canada in the second half of the twentieth century. It should go without saying that, aside from his formal mastery, none of these things is relevant when it comes to judging the quality of his poetry. But alas, such a thing does not go without saying.

There is more variety in Hine's oeuvre, even aside from his published prose and translations, than I can possibly do justice to here. He has written in nearly every form, from epigrams and sonnets to extended sequences and book-length narratives, and in every kind of verse, from free verse to anapestic metre. He has written elegies, love poems, *artes poeticae*, satires, travel poems, diaries, dramatic monologues, homages, meditations, confessions, arguments, riddles, alphabets — you name it — and has written on an extraordinarily wide range of subjects, from tidal waves to high art, from Oscar Wilde to serial killers. It is impossible for a single essay to cover Hine entirely.

Open his *Recollected Poems* at random and you will find him practising a certain recherché etymological style, suffused with paronomasia. That is to say, he loves puns that, by summoning the ghosts of root meanings, often though not always from the graveyards of dead languages, split words and phrases into the vehicles and tenors of metaphor. It is a style which to the uninitiated can appear merely abstract and *non sequitur*, but which is in fact richly figurative. Consider, for instance, this delightfully witty sonnet in praise of sex, entitled 'Phoenix Culpa':

Adam again as his namesake nude
Awoke out of the water where his sex,
Shrunken, wrinkled to a bud,
Sprung from the fork between his sapling legs.
Eve rose to meet him. Naturally blood
Flowed in reunion; flesh like artefacts
Melted. What unimaginable good —
Family ruin, innocence in rags —

Depended on their lapse they could not know.
Then how did the revolting senses guess
That in despite of death delight would grow
Immense out of proportion to distress,
Because, though the head of state had vetoed No,
Sensibly the members voted Yes?

As usual with Hine, it takes an alert reader to enjoy all the things that are going on here, and I have space only to address a few. The title is a pun on the Latin phrase *Felix culpa,* or 'fortunate fall,' a traditional name for the Christian doctrine of original sin, that is, the first disobedience of Adam and Eve — which is fortunate because, for all its evil consequences ('Family ruin, innocence in rags'), it makes Christ's salvation necessary. The phoenix is the mythical bird that dies in fire on the top of a tree and rises again from the ashes. And Hine is using both myths, one biblical, one classical, as tropes for an imagined tryst.

But notice how this Adam's body, with its 'sapling legs', is itself the Tree, though whether of Life or the Knowledge of Good and Evil he does not say. (Trees and woods are central images in Hine, signifying here the body, and elsewhere the unconscious, the imagination, the realm of the dead, and the material of art). Notice the etymological pun, in the fifth line, on the Semitic root of Adam's name ('*dm,* red ground, akin to *dam,* blood); and consider the way the word 'artefacts' in line six reminds us with its etymological roots that the flesh of Adam and Eve is fashioned by the hand of God. Notice moreover the astonishingly paronomastic final lines: the 'senses' in line ten are certainly 'revolting' only in the political sense, and the members of parliament sensibly voting 'Yes' are tropes for the sexual organs ('members') whose sensual affirmation is orgasmic. The 'head of state' in line thirteen is at once the mind, the king, and God, whose veto, in every case, is overridden by the voting members of the legislative body.

There is a great deal more to say about this delicious poem, but this is enough to give a sense of Hine's unusual method of figuration. The key that opens the door of many a Hine poem is to recognize that he treats words as living beings. For him a pun is not an occasion for a bad joke, or the belabouring of some theoretical idea, but an uncovering of a metaphor lying asleep in the language. In reading him one would do well to keep an etymological dictionary handy. In this way, Hine resembles James Merrill, to whom Hine dedicated his fourth collection and more than one poem, and, among younger Canadian poets, Jeffery Donaldson.

And it's not just words he loves; Hine is also one of those rare poets for whom the whole history of Western poetry is present and available for plunder. I have mentioned some of his translations from ancient Greek and Latin, but it's also instructive to know that he wrote his dissertation on the Latin poetry of the sixteenth-century Scottish humanist George Buchanan, and that he has written a memorable sonnet in homage to Luis de Góngora, the late sixteenth- and early seventeenth-century Spanish baroque poet, in which he praises his 'unequalled' conceits. If there is something distinctly baroque or Elizabethan in Hine's brand of pun, the same is true of his fondness — as in 'Phoenix Culpa' — for metaphysical conceits.

The effect of all this ready access to poetic tradition can be astonishing. Consider, for instance, his poem 'The Trout', which also appears in *Recollected Poems*. The poem engages with the Romantic tradition of using animals, and especially birds, as avatars for the poet, in a line that stretches from Shelley's 'To a Skylark' and Keats's 'Ode to a Nightingale' all the way to such modern poems as Karen Solie's 'Thrasher'. In Hine's extraordinary version, however — which also uses the Romantic image of mountain-climbing as a symbol of the spiritual journey — we have, instead of a singing bird, a musical fish:

My watery prison shatters in a prism
As I flounder up the fatal falls'
Arpeggios of air, a cataclysm
Of cataracts and broken intervals.

Still in the murk of motionless canals
I dreamt away my staid maturity
Till stirred by that immortal voice which calls
From the heights of the mountains to the depths of the sea.

I lean on air as prisoners on time
Not to let them down. My impetus,
In the interest of my kind sublime,
Appears in person merely perilous:

To climb the stair of stone where I was spawned,

Where ponds are oceans and the rapids give
Gasps of an unreachable beyond
I try, I fail, I wriggle loose, I live

Drop by drop against the stream I am,
And in death's shallow waterfall belong
Forever to the torrent and the dam
As defunctive music and recurrent song.

Spilt in sperm the mating pair ignore,
Caught in each other's scales as in a net,
I hung about above the ocean floor,
Part of the liquid pattern of the carpet,

Suspended like a living bathysphere,
Or upwardly mobile in a somersault,
Leaping to measures I can hardly hear,
I flop and I return to the assault,

A prelapsarian memory in man
And bird and beast, a universal wish
For the unforgiving world where life began
And your cold-blooded avatar, the fish.

What makes this poem so beautifully strange is, among other things, its combination of high Romantic diction, images, and themes, with a baroque or metaphysical double conceit, in which the trout is not only 'your cold-blooded avatar', it is also a musician, flying through 'arpeggios' and 'intervals', imagining itself dying in the waterfall's 'defunctive music and recurrent song', recalling its parents mating, 'caught in each other's scales', and then trying again, 'leaping to measures I can hardly hear'. To this is added Hine's characteristic punning (on 'scales' for instance, and 'flounder' in the first stanza). And the whole thing is made stranger still by being addressed to us by the trout, who sounds like nothing so much as a singing fish in a very sophisticated animated film. What other word is there for the effect of all this but 'postmodern'?

But if that word suggests superficiality, as it may to some readers, then it isn't quite right either, since there are hidden depths in the poem, too. Notice, for instance, the first line in the fifth stanza, where the syntax implies both that the fish is itself a kind of stream struggling against itself ('I live/ Drop by drop against the stream I am'), and, moreover, that the fish is in some sense wrestling with God (as in 'I live/ Drop by drop against the stream I AM'). I could say much more about this poem, particularly concerning its masterful deployment of prosody and syntax and its various sonic effects — try reading the poem aloud and hear for yourself — but this is enough, I think, to suggest some of the things Hine, with his extraordinary absorption and deployment of poetic tradition, is capable of.

Hine's lyric masterpiece is a group of twenty sonnets called *Arrondissements*. (That this powerful sequence is never included in anthologies or critical treatments of the so-called 'Canadian Long Poem' is unforgivable, though, alas, hardly surprising.) The title refers to the twenty districts of Paris, where Hine lived for some time in the late '50s or early '60s. Each sonnet is concerned somehow with one of these districts, whether with an experience the poet had, or something he encountered there. The final, climactic, sonnet is about a visit to Oscar Wilde's grave in the famous Père Lachaise cemetery:

Death's exclusive suburb, where the doors
Open upon empty anterooms,
Welcomes a few tardy visitors
Cryptically on morbid afternoons.
The bogus nineteenth century adores
More or less in mournful undertones,
What our sophisticated taste deplores,
Dramatic last words and attractive glooms,
Among marshals, musicians, courtesans and bores,
Ranked according to profession, who presumes
To flout society's posthumous laws?
Statuettesque among the solid tombs
Above our witty saint's dishonoured bones
Oscar's ithyphallic angel soars.

'Ithyphallic', which means literally 'having an erect phallus', is a technical name for a certain ancient Greek metre used for hymns devoted to the fertility god Priapus, and this makes the final image of the poem a celebration simultaneously of Wilde's sexuality and his literary art. Wilde's flouting of social convention during his lifetime, replicated in his monument which flouts the 'posthumous laws' and Victorian taste of the graveyard, corresponds to his critical attacks on literature, especially realistic literature, which tries to teach moral lessons. (The soaring Brutalist angel on Wilde's tomb was condemned as indecent at one point, and covered with a tarpaulin by the French police.) And thus Wilde is an 'angel' and, from Hine's perspective, 'our witty saint,' both because he was a gay martyr, and because he was a champion of precisely the kind of witty and sophisticated epicurean aestheticism for which Hine stands himself: the sort that takes pleasure in etymological puns on 'suburb' (literally 'under the city'), for instance, not to mention 'ithyphallic'. Wilde is also a saint for Hine because he was, in the end, an expatriate; Hine doesn't mention Wilde's epitaph, but it seems relevant here given Hine's recurring concern — in the title of his sixth collection, *Resident Alien,* for instance — with his status as a kind of exile from his native country. Here is the epitaph:

> And alien tears will fill for him
> Pity's long broken urn,
> For his mourners will be outcast men
> And outcasts always mourn.

One imagines Hine standing before Wilde's monument, reading these lines as a command from the Muses to write his elegy for Wilde, and realizing that of all the places he had visited and lived in Paris, this was the one closest to his own poetic heart.

One of the pleasures of reading Hine's *Recollected Poems* is in discovering the revisions he has made to a considerable number of his lyrics. Except for one wince-inducing botch ('Withdrawal Symptoms' appears in a much worse version now called 'Withdrawal'), these revisions are considerable improvements, although it must be said they are not always sufficient to salvage the weaker poems, especially the early poems from Hine's first three collections of the 1950s. Of these revisions I am especially moved by his changes to the poem formerly called 'The Copper Beech', and now renamed 'The Copper Maple'. In the original version, which appeared in *Minutes* (1968), the setting is Stonington, New York. The poem ends like this:

It is enough

To know (and this is surely recognition)
That the world is spherical and perfect.
Now I wish to introduce the copper beech
We saw on our walk, English and native here as I am,
Whose shade is not the green of contemplation
But the imagination's rich metallic colour
Wherein, under libido, we live.

The tree is as 'native here as [the poet is]' — which is to say, not in the least. (In 'Memo to Góngora', Hine says of that poet's 'native land' that it 'is a tongue when all is said that's done', and the same is true of Hine.) The poet identifies with the tree, moreover, not only as an exile, but because it is a symbol of the libidinous imagination and not, as in Marvell, of a merely contemplative 'green thought in a green shade'. He is a poet, in other words, not a philosopher.

In the new version entitled 'The Copper Maple', we are in Evanston, Illinois, the suburb of Chicago where Hine has lived for more than thirty years, most of them with the late American philosopher Samuel Todes. Here is the new ending:

Sufficient the momentary recognition
Of the world as anomalous and perfect
As this emblematic copper maple,
Alien yet rooted here as we are,
Whose shade is not the green of contemplation
But imagination's fierce metallic colour,
Bronze, an aegis under which we flourish.

There is no better example of Hine's ruthless disregard for superficial autobiographical authenticity — when it conflicts with the demands of the imagination — than the radical revision he has made to this poem. Not only is his new version set in a different city, but now its central image has changed, and so has its significance. The copper maple is unmistakably emblematic, not only of exile and the imagination, but also of Hine's status as a long-term resident of another country, a Canadian poet 'alien yet rooted' in Evanston, Illinois. Moreover, the maple's colour is no longer 'rich' and libidinous, but 'fierce'; it is a 'bronze aegis' like the powerful shield or breastplate of Athena, which makes this a startlingly military act of flag-planting in the name of the country of the imagination. The final word, 'flourish', refers, in context, to the productivity of the poet and the philosopher at the height of their powers, though as always in Hine, it embodies several etymologically figurative meanings as well: that the poet and his companion are thriving like flowers under the protection of the shielding tree of imagination; that these flowers wave dramatically, like banners, in the 'lyrical tempests' of inspiration mentioned in an earlier stanza of the poem; and, to return to the military imagery, that they make a kind of ceremonial music, like a military fanfare or flourish blown on a trumpet beneath the aegis. For Hine the distinctions between abstract and concrete diction, and between literal and figurative language, are almost meaningless; the word 'flourish' here at the end of this poem is all of these things at once.

To develop this kind of skill as a poet requires a long apprenticeship, and so it is not surprising to find that Hine's early work is very uneven. Indeed, *Recollected Poems* offers up rather too many bad poems. In this category I would include most of the poems from the 1950s, like 'Villanelle: Under the Hill', whose dud of a first line, 'The gates flew open with a pretty sound', is repeated mercilessly. Of these already elaborately formal poems one is tempted to demand more matter and less art, but the truer request would be for better art. They are the work of an extraordinarily gifted and very young poet, but even the revisions Hine has made for this new selection can't save most of them from being ultimately incoherent, as in, for instance, 'Lines on a Platonic Friendship'. On the one hand, this poem contains some good, memorable lines: 'Rephrasing silence till the silence fits,' for instance, and 'Where the print ends like a wave upon the page.' On the other, it contains much jejune fluff like this: 'You will search the skies to bring me down/Because I shall escape to other suns/Reflected in a geographic calm.' The contrast is so stark one wants to cut the good lines out and leave them alone on the page like the fragments of an ancient manuscript.

It must also be said that some of Hine's later poems are bad, too, though for a different reason. In three long poems, namely 'Yucatan' (formerly called, rather nauseatingly, 'Vowel Movements'), 'Linear A' and

'Lectio Difficilior', there is a kind of maniacal virtuosity, an almost frightening prodigality of technique combined with an emptiness of significance
that is just tedious (although the first two stanzas of 'Yucatan' are superb; if
only the poet had stopped there). Hine is at his best when he balances his
formal virtuosity with strongly felt human experience, however displaced
into myth or metaphor. When he treats his poems as elaborate language
games that must be completed at all costs, however, they impress us as
mere *tours de force*.

As for *Recollected Poems* as a book, I have mixed feelings. It contains more
of Hine's best poems than any other single volume, and many interesting
and sometimes radical revisions which are nearly always improvements. As
such it is indispensable. And yet, as I have said, it contains too many mediocre and bad poems, and worse, it leaves out nineteen of Hine's finest lyrics,
which remain scattered in out-of-print volumes: poems like 'Lady Sara Bun-
bury Sacrificing to the Graces, by Reynolds', 'The Man Who Edited *Mlle*',
'Doctor Faustus's Welcome Home', 'If Life is the Question is Death the
Answer', and 'Bluebeard's Bungalow'.* (A list of Hine's best poems should
also include his imperfect but delightful narrative masterpiece, the book-
length autobiographical poem entitled *In and Out: A Confessional Poem* (1989).)

Most troubling, however, is the matter of the book's unsatisfactory
organization. Instead of a standard ordering of the poems into sections
according to the volumes in which they originally appeared, the book is
divided into four thematic parts: basically, art, love, places, and time. And
within each section the poems are arranged according to some thematic
pattern rather than chronologically. At moments this can seem like a good
idea. Hine argues in his introduction that a chronological arrangement
would have been misleading, and I concede that in some cases it is interesting to see what Hine considers to be the dominant theme of a poem. But in
general I disagree. Ultimately the effect is just disorienting; one jumps from
an exquisite mid-career poem to a bad early or mediocre late one and vice
versa so often that it is impossible to keep from looking ahead at the

---

* My other missing favourites are 'Noon', 'Man's Country', 'Barakat', 'Untitled', 'Sap-
phics', 'Suttee', 'Alcaics', 'Samson', 'Unhappy Returns', 'Coma Berenices', 'A La Page',
'Withdrawal Symptoms', 'In Memory M.D. 1872–1962', and 'Les Rendezvous des
Gourmets'.

composition dates to see what kind of thing is coming next. (As a rule of thumb, anything from the sixties, seventies or eighties is likely to be good; as for the fifties, look out.) The confusion is compounded by the fact that the table of contents, misnamed an 'Index of Titles', is buried near the back of the book between a section of sketchy and incomplete 'Notes' and a relatively useless 'First Line Index', making it frustrating to locate particular poems. Why not just supply a table of contents at the beginning and a true, alphabetical index of titles and first lines at the end? And if there are going to be notes, why not make them usefully comprehensive?

What one wants next is a careful selection of all the very best short poems and sequences — eighty in all by my count from Hine's career to date — arranged in the order of their appearance in their original volumes, so that one can get a sense of the shape of each collection, and follow the development of Hine's imagination over the course of his mature career. Such a book will, if and when it appears, make Hine's exemplary worth as a poet impossible to ignore any longer. For now we will just have to make do with his indispensable *Recollected Poems*.

Dennis Lee:

Cursing with a Broken Art

One would rather read a good book than a bad one, naturally; and yet, even bad books may be instructive if we read them carefully enough to see why they are bad. Sometimes they contain enough good passages to allow us to imagine the good books they might have been had their authors made better choices, and this too may be instructive. Two such books are Dennis Lee's *Un* (2003) and *Yesno* (2007). Together they form a sequence of 101 brief lyrics in ten sections, five sections per book. For some reason the sequence itself is untitled, so I will refer to it simply as 'the sequence'.

Before I make my case for its shortcomings, which are profound, I want to spend some time acknowledging Lee's fairly complex intentions. For one thing, the language of these poems is strange, and Lee makes it clear that he wants it to be. Here is a brief *ars poetica* entitled 'slub':

> I want verbs of a slagscape thrombosis.
> Syntax of chromosome pileups.
> Make me
> slubtalk; gerundibles; gummy embouchure.

Allow me to unpack Lee's portmanteaus here. The title, 'slub', means either 'a thick nub in a piece of yarn', 'a twisted thread', or, as a verb, 'to twist slightly', which suggests Lee wants to write a kind of bunched, twisted language. He wants his verbs to be clotted (as in thrombosis) and piled up (as in a decimated landscape of slag heaps). He demands a language full of edible gerunds ('gerundibles'), that, when spoken, will make your mouth (your 'embouchure') feel like it's chewing gum. And if we pay attention to this poem's method, we can see he is striving to achieve these effects by means of truncated syntax, violently mixed metaphors, and, above-all, neologisms, including invented compounds ('slubtalk') and portmanteaus ('slagscape', 'gerundibles'). Despite the precise meaning of his title, it's also notable that he is not twisting his language 'slightly', but a great deal.

Lee's invented and condensed diction makes for a self-consciously artificial and literary language, a broken anti-language which is often very different from ordinary human speech. In one poem, entitled 'inlingo', he
describes his language as a 'scraggy lingo', a '[f]ractal untongue'. One thinks
of the language of Hopkins, Joyce, cummings and Celan, the nonsense of
'Jabberwocky' and the futuristic languages in *A Clockwork Orange* and *1984*.
But Lee's reasons for using such a language are different from these other
writers' reasons; Lee's sequence is a prophetic vision of the death of nature,
and he calls his language a kind of agonized physical response to this vision,
which causes him 'to/stammer the uterine painscape/in pidgin apocalypse', asking, 'how now not/gag on the unward, the once-upon, us-/proud
planet'?

Moreover, for Lee it is not just the Earth that is dying, but the very language we use to name and describe it. This is true, in particular, of language
systems, including orthodoxies and ideologies; for instance, in the poem
entitled 'ologies', he writes that 'Ologies foundle. Oxies disselve.' That is to
say, I suppose, that ideologies founder in the same moment they are
founded (though that doesn't account for the 'dle' in 'foundle', does it), and
that orthodoxies dissolve of themselves. In any case, these systematic
'wordscapes' soon become mere 'relics & runes'. Furthermore, individual
words themselves are also dying: 'The unredeemable names,' Lee writes in a
poem called 'hiatus', 'devolve in their/liminal slouch to abyss.'

This crisis of language is where Lee the poet comes in: 'I gather the
crumbs of hiatus,' he writes in the same poem, 'The blank where *evil* held.
The hole called *beholden*.' Even though these 'names' are 'unredeemable',
nevertheless Lee sees his poetry as a salvage operation. He gathers the
crumbs of language in order 'That phantom glyphs resound, that/lacunae
be burnished./That it not be leached from memory: once,/earth meant
otherly.' Why, we may well ask, does he clot and twist his language if he
intends to salvage it? Lee answers that this violence springs from hope: 'If
hope disorders words, let/here be where,' he writes in a poem called
'galore'. He means to regenerate language through a kind of creative
destruction. He wants to 're-/tuit sheer carnival logos. Where/nouns
ignite/moves in the dance they denote:/moniker lifelines.' Furthermore,
in a poem entitled simply 'song', Lee tentatively imagines that such a regen-
erated language, such a 'carnival logos', might somehow produce a regeneration of nature as well:

Song sinister. Song
ligature; now
sing.
Are there honks, are there glyphs, are there
bare alingual grunts that
tonguefastly cleave to the judder of
habitat mending? The static of unsong un-
sung?

Lee's two great subjects here are nature and language, both of which, as I
say, he considers to be dying and in need of regeneration by means of a dis-
ordering of language. But notice how he describes his imagined regener-
ated carnival lingo: honks, glyphs, 'alingual' grunts. For Lee the problem
with language seems to be that it is too far from nature, that is, too far from
the honks and grunts of animals. He is saying: if only we spoke, or rather
sang, like the animals, then perhaps nature would be healed. No doubt he's
right; if there were no human language, and therefore no human culture,
the Earth would not be suffering the damage human beings have inflicted
upon it. However, neither would there be any poetry. Honks and grunts
would seem to be a disastrous ideal for a poetic language.

Of course, what matters is what Lee's actual language achieves in practice. Unfortunately, too often Lee's poems are simply overwhelmed by neologisms; he lets his linguistic invention take over until the poem is reduced
to gibberish. Consider the lyric entitled 'flux':

As stuttle inflex the genomes.
As bounty floundles.
As coldcock amnesia snakes thru
shoreline/sporelane/syngone —
       hi diddle
template, unning become us,
palimpsest gibber & newly.

I spin the yin stochastic, probble a
engram luff, & parse haw
bareback the whichwake, besoddle a thrashold flux.

Could anything be more self-indulgent? There are two kinds of difficult poetry: the kind that, in the words of William Blake, 'rouses the faculties to act', and the kind that turns the brain to porridge. This poem is the latter. Unfortunately there are way too many poems like it in this sequence.

Even when Lee chooses to write in English, moreover, he is often recklessly imprecise in his use of words. This is true even when he is describing his own language, as in this passage from a poem called 'biscript':

> Wildword the bounty extant.
>
> Is earthscan in biscript, is
> doublespeak goners-&-*hail*. Still itching to
> parse with a two-tongued heart, shambala
> scrapings.

The term 'doublespeak' here, like 'biscript', refers obliquely to the title of the book in which this poem appears, that is, *Yesno,* a compound word meaning both affirmation and negation at once, and hence also, in the vernacular, 'goners-&-*hail*' — that is, death and birth. Lee's 'doublespeak', then, both affirms and negates, a meaning which may be deduced from its context in the poem and in the sequence. But the problem is that 'doublespeak', as we all know, already means something, namely, 'language deliberately constructed to distort or disguise its actual meaning' for sinister political purposes. How can he expect his readers to ignore that fact? Even if we grant Lee the right to re-coin the word 'doublespeak' for his own purposes, the effect is unintentionally ironic, since Lee's language is, we realize, nothing if not 'deliberately constructed to distort or disguise its actual meaning'. A more accurate word for what Lee apparently intends to say here would be 'double*think*', meaning, to quote Orwell who invented the term in *1984,* 'the power of holding two contradictory beliefs in one's mind simultaneously, and accepting both of them', although for Orwell it is a power one acquires only through strenuous totalitarian brainwashing. (To be fair to Lee, there are analogous ideas, including Keats's 'negative capability' and Heidegger's '*Gelassenheit*', that have much more positive connotations, though 'doublespeak' brings Orwell more readily to mind.)

In any case, I raise this issue because it turns out that Lee does this sort of thing a lot in this sequence; that is, he uses words loosely to mean something rather different from what the words ordinarily mean. This might not be a bad thing, necessarily, except that usually his use of a word in this way is far from an improvement. Take the word 'shambala' in the third stanza, above. Shambala is the name of a Bantu language spoken in Tanzania. But Lee uses the word loosely as a kind of exotic synonym for 'language'. This strikes me as an irresponsible way for a poet to use words, one that demonstrates a lack of respect for their precise meanings. Far from regenerating words, it empties them of their particular meanings and associations, and turns them into abstractions.

I assure you these are not isolated examples. Here, for instance, are the opening lines of the first poem in *Yesno*, entitled 'if': 'If it walks like apocalypse. If it squawks like Armageddon.' Lee is using the terms 'apocalypse' and 'Armageddon' here as, again, exotic but interchangeable synonyms for 'the end of the world.' It is as though he wrote the poem with a thesaurus open on his desk but his dictionary forgotten on the shelf. There is no hint in this poem of the root sense of apocalypse as an uncovering or revelation, or of Armageddon as a mountain battlefield. The words are stripped of their particular meanings, their rich histories and associations, and reduced to their lowest common denominator, an abstraction: end of the world. This is the way bad journalists use words, not good poets. And as if that weren't disheartening enough, in this passage the words are yoked absurdly, by echoing a cliché, to the image of a waddling and quacking duck, a simile that only degrades them further.

Here is one more example of Lee's carelessness with words, a poem called 'chumps':

Here's to destiny chumps for a change.
Rogue arthurs; geek
parsifals; flammable joans of *salut*. To
insurrection gandhis.

Who but a bupkus
quixote would tilt at the corporate windmills?
Who but a blunderling
underling hoot at the emperor's shanks?

This is, on its face, the most allusive poem in the entire sequence, but I get the feeling Lee merely looked up 'hero' in Roget and plugged in the names he found there. (In my copy, sure enough, there's Joan of Arc, Don Quixote and the Knights of the Round Table.) The adjectives he uses render the names nearly meaningless and interchangeable. What is a 'rogue arthur'? A 'geek parsifal'? An 'insurrection gandhi'? Why not an 'insurrection Arthur', a 'geek gandhi', expressions equally absurd? The only way this poem makes sense is if we mentally plug the words 'hero' or 'heroine' in wherever Lee gives us a proper name. Again, he is ignoring the particular meanings of his words, their histories and associations, and using them as if they were abstractions. It's true that Lee is intentionally subverting the myths of these figures; what he is celebrating is blundering heroes. But it's not the subversion I object to; it's the lumping together. That is, I object to Lee's using words as empty and interchangeable symbols, like coins, instead of treating them like living things.

And this brings me to the central problem with Lee's language. Generally speaking, it does not appeal to the imagination. It is abstract. For the most part it lacks vivid images. His sequence purports to be a prophetic elegy for nature, but it offers very few images from the natural world. (For all its indignation at the extinction of species, for example, only two or three poems actually name any of those species, and even then they are only names, not images of particular living things.) Here is an example of what I'm talking about, a poem called 'whatcan', in full:

What can, cog-
nostic with earthwrack, be
(who?ishly) known to co-
here, co-now with the
ratiosacral flex of
original yes?

This is truly bad writing. Leaving aside the insufferable preciosity of some of its neologisms ('who?ishly' and 'co-now' are just embarrassing), the essential problem here is, as I say, that it doesn't even try to appeal to the imagination, not to mention human feeling. It is just a philosophical question stated as obscurely and self-indulgently as possible.

Another major weakness has to do with the slightness of far too many of the poems, or 'blurts' as he so accurately calls them, which read not like poems so much as notes for poems. Several trail off into inarticulate silence with an ellipsis. And many are made up entirely of inert sentence fragments. Consider the following little poem about the first cloned sheep, called 'dolly', which I quote in full:

> Cloned pastoral.
> Data made fleece.
>
> Wisdom sub-
> rupted; brain on a breakaway nobel bender.

This reads to me like the barest wisp of an idea for a poem, scribbled down as though on the back of a napkin in limp fragments conducive to rapid notation. There is almost no human feeling, except perhaps a sneer, and very little in the way of vivid imagery. The joke in the second line, 'Data made fleece', which is a parody of the biblical phrase 'The Word made flesh', is promising, especially given that Christ is the Lamb as well as the Good Shepherd, but as it stands it is just a joke, and, like this poem, needs considerable development.

What about Lee's larger ambitions for his sequence? He claims he wants 'To/praise with a broken art'. I think I've given you enough of a taste of his broken art; as for his impulse to praise, I simply find it difficult to believe. Many of the poems in the sequence are ferocious satires aimed at humanity and language in general. For Lee, human beings — not just some human beings, but all of us, you included — are 'shat/flecks in the alley disjecta; snot/lobs on the valence of now'. Lest you suspect me of quoting him out of context, here is one of Lee's misanthropic poems, entitled 'fold', quoted in full:

> You fold you are
> folded, late-breaking primate, and
> brought to who-knew.
> Fold you are
> null again, nil again, knell again — one-swat no-
> see-um & whose. You
> fold you are un:
> stud of no

throne no dominion, kingshit of doodly.
Frag in the mean of let-be.

I can't help but hear the voice of E. J. Pratt's great Panjandrum when I read this poem: 'The ALL HIGH swore until his face was black./He called him …//Third cousin to the family of worms'. Pratt is satirizing the misanthropy of fascism (I quote from 'The Truant', which was an indignant response to the German bombing of London), but Lee's sequence is evidence that such dehumanizing may be found among the far left, as well. As for Lee's satire, unlike Pratt's it is not apparently meant to reform anything; rather, his vision of humanity is both nihilistic ('And are creatures of/nothing', he begins one poem, 'I noth you noth we/long have we nothed') and annihilating ('Destructible mother', he says to the earth, 'survive us/widewinnow our folly'). He imagines a future in which someone may 'celebrate an aevum cleansed of us', we whom he calls elsewhere 'the iffy human smear./Anthropox rising'. In a particularly revolting phrase he calls the coming destruction of humanity a 'pogrom absolute', although at least in the poem in question he opposes this vision with a 'Plea pleading, pretty-/please pleading' 'that/all my truths be false'. But even here the plea is mocked by the very language he uses to express it.

Lee also unloads several rounds of curses at language, which you will recall he claims to want to save. Here, for example, is his poem called 'word':

Lost word in the
green going down,
husk of a logos,
crybaby word, out
dragging your passel of absence —
little word lost, why in the
demeaninged world would I
cradle your lonely?
You, little murderer? You, little cannibal dreg?!

Lee is here content to heap abuse upon the little lost word imagined as a child, a 'crybaby word' whom he refuses to 'cradle'. (The echoes of William Blake's 'Little Boy Lost' and 'Little Girl Lost' could not be more ironic.) He goes so far as to accuse the child-word of murder, righteously certain that the deaths of nature and of language ought to be laid at the lost feet of language itself, the 'little cannibal'. As a humanist I find it difficult to sympathize with the self-loathing of a poet inclined to abuse both his own species as a whole and the medium of his art. The man is entitled to his opinions, of course, but I find it disingenuous that he claims to be praising and salvaging when he's mostly just cursing. Ironically, this last poem is actually one of the most rhetorically interesting in the sequence, largely because it addresses the word directly in a way that lets us hear the poet's voice for once. But the tone of the final line can only be described as paranoid and hysterical.

Finally, I'm afraid the sequence as a whole has little discernible structure. As Lee puts it himself in one of his poems,

Blah, blah was easy, we
diddled the scrutable chunks;
whole hog was beyond us.

There are recurring themes and topics (elegies for the planet, attacks on humanity, language, and technology, poems describing the sequence's poetic project), but after several readings their order of recurrence still seems to me effectively random, and the division of the sequence into sections feels arbitrary.

There *is* a sense of an ending, however, though not a good one: the last two poems in the sequence suddenly take on the tone of an editorial, in order to draw an easy moral at the end. If the planet is to be saved, Lee says in a poem called 'or what', it will be done 'by the law by the lab by the ballot' when we find our manly 'hometruth cojones'. And in 'tale', the final poem, he imagines a happy ending for the planet, however unlikely:

Yet a rescue appeared, in the
story a saviour arose. Called
limits. Called
duedate, called countdown ex-
tinction/collide. Called, eyeball to ego:
hubris agonistes.

As recommendations for solving our environmental problems, however vague, these are on the right track, as I think most people would agree. But let's face it: as poetry they are merely abstract commonplaces couched in odd language.

Fortunately, not all the poems in the sequence are bad, and it is instructive to see how the better ones differ from the others. The best poems, as it turns out, are not satires but elegies. Here is an elegy for the orthodoxies of religion, entitled 'gone':

An earth ago, a
God ago, gone
easy:

a pang a lung a
lifeline, gone to
lore.

Sin with its
numberless, hell with its
long long count:

nightfears in
eden, gone eco gone
pico gone home.

I find this interesting, first of all, because of its rhythms; it is free verse in the best sense, highly rhythmical for all its irregularity. I'm moved by the ambivalent feeling in the poem: the poet doesn't miss the 'nightfears in/ eden' of sin and hell, assuredly, and yet he does miss the 'lung', the 'lifeline' that has been lost, in no small part because the death of nature seems to be connected to the death of God: 'An earth ago, a / God ago....' Notice, moreover, how light this poem is on the 'fractal untongue', as if Lee were exercising a kind of classical restraint in that regard; I like the way the poem engages with large ideas in the simplest possible diction. Aside from 'eco' (as in ecology) and 'pico' in the last stanza ('pico' being Italian for 'little', and perhaps suggesting the Italian Renaissance humanist Pico Della Mirandola as a representative of human culture), and the easy compound of 'nightfears', the poem is free of neologisms of any kind. True, the syntax is terse and fragmented, but sentence fragments seem appropriate for this brief poem of death and loss. Above all, notice the way the poem engages with the myth of a lost Garden of Eden, which is the most powerful myth in our culture for the loss of an ideal natural world. Imagine what Lee's sequence might have been if it had made a genuine engagement with that myth, however displaced, more central to the imaginative structure of his sequence as a whole.

Another fine poem is 'lullabye', an elegy for the world imagined as having been destroyed by nuclear war. Here is the poem:

Lullabye wept as asia
buckled,
rockaby einstein and all.

One for indigenous,
two for goodbye,
adam and eve and dodo.

Fly away mecca,
fly away rome,
lullabye wept in the lonely.

Once the iguanodon,
once the U.N.,
hush little orbiting gone.

Again, it is partly the perfectly modulated rhythm I am drawn to here, this time the regular rhythm of a song. It was a brilliant idea to treat this subject in a dark, elegiac parody of a lullaby. Another of the poem's pleasures is the way it brings together specific disparate things from nature and culture: Adam and Eve and the dodo, the iguanodon and the U.N. And as for the language, there are certainly echoes here of cummings, as in the use of the adjectives 'lonely' and 'orbiting' as nouns. But Lee is restraining his neologisms here as well, and what a relief. Above all, notice again how the poem engages forcefully with the myth of a lost Eden, which gives it an imaginative power that is totally absent from far too many of the poems in the sequence.

Finally, consider a poem called 'Dixie' from *Yesno*:

Cold kaddish. In majuscule winter,
whistle down Dixie to dusk;
coho with agave to dust.

Bison with orca commingled —
whistle down dixie. With
condor to audubon dust.

52 pickup, the species.
Beothuk, manatee, ash:
whistledown emu.

Vireo, mussel, verbena — cry
bygones, from heyday to dusk.
All whistling down dixie to dust.

The majuscule winter, that is, winter with a capital W, is, I take it, an imagined nuclear winter, or by extension a metaphorical winter of mass extinc-
tions. The poem calls itself a prayer for the dead ('kaddish'), but in fact it is
an elegy whose pathos arises from its refrain. To whistle 'Dixie' is, according
to the idiom, to engage in unrealistic fantasizing instead of taking action,
which makes this a political poem, but one, you will notice, that avoids edi-
torializing altogether, and is therefore much more effective as poetry than
Lee's other explicitly political poems, such as the final two in the sequence
which I described above. If there is praise here it is in the deftly varied nam-
ing of the soon-to-be-extinguished species (and in the case of the Beothuk,
the already extinguished tribe); in fact, this poem names more plants and
animals than all the rest of the poems in the sequence combined. And the
off-rhyme of 'dusk' with 'dust' throughout does much to darken the poem's
sometimes jocular tone (as in the line '52 pickup, the species'), so that the
joking comes across as heartbroken, for once, rather than merely mocking.

There are some other things to admire in the sequence, brilliant lines
that flash from the ore of otherwise unsuccessful poems: '[A]nd/debit,
debit, debit moans the moon', Lee writes in a poem called '*boom!*', and for
an instant my imagination soars. Similarly, in a poem entitled 'stinct', I am

thrilled by these lines: 'Clamber down babel, climb down to the/nearaway country of homewhere', in no small part because they engage with the other major myth that ought to be central to the imaginative structure of the sequence, given Lee's concern with language, namely the myth of the Tower of Babel. What these good passages have in common with the sequence's best poems is a vivid appeal to the mythical imagination. To me, these, and a few other passages like them, are the traces of strong choices the poet might have made central to his enterprise, but, alas, did not.

Where did Lee's project go wrong? I suspect it had something to do with his misunderstanding of one of his key poetic models. The only other poet who is named in the sequence is Paul Celan, in the title of an elegy for that postwar European master (although Lee characteristically obscures his subject by calling the poem 'ancel', the Romanian form of Celan's original last name Antschel — Celan being an anagram of Ancel). Here is the poem:

> Deathbreath of the unbeholden.
> Mouth of the lorn.
> Mining for syllable
> rectitude, you struck clean seams of
> lesser, of lesion, of
> pitted implacable least.
> Homefree at last in a whiteout of shock & Seine.

This is very revealing. In Lee's reading of Celan, what he says first is not that Celan was speaking for the Jews killed by the Nazis, which he was, but, more abstractly, that he was speaking on behalf of 'the unbeholden' and 'the lorn', both of them vague adjectival nouns Lee uses elsewhere in the sequence to describe the dying earth and its dying species. Clearly he sees his own project as analogous to Celan's. But what really interests him is Celan's language, which he reduces to a matter of declension from 'lesser' to 'lesion' to 'least'. There is indeed a superficial similarity between Lee's neologisms and truncated syntax and some of Celan's language in his later work, although Celan deploys it with much more restraint than Lee, a key point as I have argued above. And Lee's poems in this sequence are certainly brief like Celan's. But what Lee misses in Celan is far more important than what he notices: I'm talking about the powerful recurring metaphors and symbols, the intensely vivid appeal to the imagination, the formidable introspection, the anguished human feeling, the profound engagement with Jewish mythical tradition, the wrestling with God in the name of an insulted and traumatized human dignity. That he misses these things is evident not only in this little elegy, but in the sequence as a whole, which was apparently inspired by Celan — though let us say 'nominally inspired', for the differences between them are vast.

Anne Carson and the Sublime

Anne Carson is considered an avant-garde writer because of her formal experiments and generic innovations. The label clearly makes some sense, at least superficially: think of her genre-bending first book of prose poems entitled *Short Talks*, for example, or the arbitrarily punctuated early sequence *The Life of Towns*. But when we realize that the formal method in the latter is evidently borrowed from Gertrude Stein's poem 'She Bowed to Her Brother' (1931), it seems more accurate to speak of its place in a certain kind of formal tradition. It is a modernist tradition, to be sure, and no one would deny that Carson feels modern. But in various ways, she is also a thoroughly, even radically traditional writer.

A superb translator from the ancient Greek, Carson was for many years a professor of classics at McGill, and in her own writing she returns often to the ancient roots, the classical and biblical origins of Western literature. These obsessions, combined with her interest in certain great innovators of the twentieth century like Stein, Beckett and Celan, help make her, at her best, truly original. Merely to rank her with 'the triumphant march of the avant-garde', in Zbigniew Herbert's sardonic phrase — cultural amnesiacs endlessly shooting at the easy target of novelty — is to miss completely what is most interesting and valuable in her work. In fact, Carson has always been a writer in the tradition of the sublime, a tradition stretching back through modernism and Romanticism to Homer, Sappho and the Bible. And never more so than in her recent book, *Decreation: Poetry, Essays, Opera* (2006).

The book explores, from a wide variety of perspectives, the theme of the sublime annihilation or decreation of the self. Carson borrows the term 'decreation' from the French philosopher and mystic Simone Weil, for whom the purpose of such an act of self-effacement was to get out of the way of God, to let God's will prevail over one's own. Any student of religions will recognize this as a very old idea. But one way of understanding Carson's focus on this theme is to think of her place in literary history; as a poet writing self-consciously after the heyday of confessional poetry, and one strongly influenced by the anti-subjective element in modernism, she is concerned with finding ways to displace the self from the centre of her work. Not, mind you, in order to replace it with the cold, inhuman babble of Language, but rather to make way for 'spiritual matters'. And this, as I say, places her squarely in the Romantic and modern tradition of the sublime. 'Not I,' writes D.H. Lawrence, in his 'Song of the Man Who Has Come Through': 'Not I, not I, but the wind that blows through me.' The main difference is that, where English Romantics like Shelley speak of 'wind', and modernists like Rilke and Lorca speak respectively of angels and *duende,* Carson concerns herself with the even more traditional sources of sublime power, the 'gods' or, in this book, 'God', and to this extent she resembles poets like Hölderlin and Hopkins. (Though in practice she does symbolize God more than once in the image of the wind, a figure that goes back at least to the Book of Job.)

As its subtitle indicates, *Decreation* is not only a collection of lyric poems, but a book of new writing in a wide variety of genres. Besides thirty-four short lyrics, four essays, and an opera libretto, the book includes a screenplay, the text of an oratorio, a cinematic shot list, a long ekphrastic poem, and something that reads like a series of study questions, complete with answers. But the book's intellectual centres of gravity are its four essays, each of which takes a different perspective on sublime experience. The particular subject of each of these essays is explored further in one or more other works that surround, or rather orbit it in the book, like moons around a planet in the solar system of the sublime. For example, the essay entitled 'Foam (Essay with Rhapsody): On the Sublime in Longinus and Antonioni', is followed by a group of lyric poems called *Sublimes,* and then by another sequence of poems on sublime subjects called *Gnosticisms.* Similarly, the essay entitled 'Decreation: How Women Like Sappho, Marguerite Porete and Simone Weil Tell God' is followed by the libretto, entitled 'Decreation: An Opera in Three Parts', whose main characters include Marguerite Porete and Simone Weil. The effect is rather like reading Yeats's *A Vision* together with his poems of the same period, or Dante's *Vita Nuova,* or Blake's *Marriage of Heaven and Hell;* prose and verse illuminate each another, often brilliantly, from a variety of perspectives.

The four essays on the sublime are erudite personal essays in the tradition of Montaigne, and, at the same time, incisive works of thematic literary criticism: they consist of surprising, associative arguments, supported by deft and wide-ranging quotation, acute readings of particular works of literature, and occasional incandescent descriptions of Carson's childhood memories. And although Carson keeps her personal feelings on a tight leash, one always senses from the passion of the writing that the subjects of these essays are of urgent spiritual and aesthetic significance to the writer.

The first essay in the book, 'Every Exit is an Entrance (A Praise of Sleep)', is concerned with the therapeutic consolation of the uncanny, the sublime, or the supernatural, and especially with the power to be gained from the extraction of some secret, hidden content from sleep. By extension, it is also about gaining access to what is real, to Kant's thing-in-itself, which is likewise secret or hidden. Carson clearly owes much to Freud here — whose book *The Uncanny* is one of the great contributions to the theory of the sublime — not to mention the larger Romantic tradition of the interior quest romance, but this is not a purely intellectual exercise for her. As an example from her own life of a 'supremely consoling' contact with the uncanny secret content of sleep, she describes the following childhood experience:

> My earliest memory is of a dream. It was in the house where we lived when I was three or four years of age. I dreamed I was asleep in the house in an upper room. That I awoke and came downstairs and stood in the living room. The lights were on in the living room, although it was hushed and empty. The usual dark green sofa and chairs stood along the usual pale green walls. It was the same old living room as ever, I knew it well, nothing was out of place. And yet it was utterly, certainly, different. Inside its usual appearance the living room was as changed as if it had gone mad.

After recalling her surprising childhood interpretation of this dream-vision ('I explained the dream to myself by saying that I had caught the living room sleeping'), Carson goes on to explain why she finds it so consoling, tracing her theme dazzlingly through the works and ideas of Plato, Aristotle, ancient Greek inscriptions, Kant, Keats, Lacan, Tom Stoppard and, especially, Homer, Virginia Woolf and Elizabeth Bishop, elucidating certain works of these authors in ways that have the power to change one's reading of them forever. It's a brilliant critical performance.

The second essay, already mentioned, entitled 'Foam (Essay with

Rhapsody): On the Sublime in Longinus and Antonioni', is about the 'excit-ing', 'dangerous' and sublime act of ... quotation. (Carson is nothing if not a scholarly poet.) As she puts it, 'the Sublime is a documentary technique'. After quoting Longinus' discussion, in *On the Sublime*, of a passage from the Greek orator Demosthenes, Carson invites us to feel the power of quotation as something extraordinary:

> Longinus' point is that, by brutal juxtaposition of coordinate nouns or noun clauses, Demosthenes transposes violence of fists into violence of syntax. His facts spill over the frame of their origi-nal context and pummel the judges' minds. Watch this spillage, which moves from the man who hits, to the words of Demos-thenes describing him, to the judges hearing these words, to Longinus analyzing the whole process, to me recalling Longinus' discussion of it and finally to you reading my account. The pas-sionate moment echoes from soul to soul.

Carson is a classical scholar with the soul of a Romantic, and she writes with the passion of a master teacher, inciting, inflaming her students to experi-ence the text with both heart and mind. (No surprise, then, to find that Car-son has dedicated her book to her students.) As this example demonstrates, Carson is also a critic with a poet's passion for technique, a quality she shares with the best poet-critics of our time. This is not her only theme here: the essay is also about the psychology, the joy and the 'structure' of the sublime ('the alternation of danger and salvation'), as well as the guilt of the sublime soul, which knows how to value the passionate moment, but for whom sublime threats may come from within as well as without. But ultimately the essay is an *apologia* for one of Carson's recurring personae: the passionate professor of classics.

The concept of the sublime was used in the eighteenth century pri-marily to describe certain aesthetic experiences of nature, and accordingly, Carson's third essay, 'Totality: The Colour of Eclipse', considers the sublime experience of the total eclipse of the sun. She describes it thus: 'You are now inside the moon's shadow, which is a hundred miles wide and moves at two thousand miles an hour. The sensation is stupendous.' Carson takes her bookish examples this time from Archilochus, Pindar, Dickinson, Woolf and Annie Dillard. Surprisingly, she finds the experience of watching eclipses is often associated in these writers with copulation, marriage, questions and doubts about marriage, and, less surprisingly, with a feeling of wrongness; in a metaphor borrowed from her own essay in praise of sleep, she compares seeing an eclipse to 'waking from a dream in the wrong direction and finding yourself on the back side of your mind'. Taken by itself, this is the slightest of the four essays — nature isn't really Carson's forte; however, when read together with the other three, its images and ideas help to link all four pieces in marvellously suggestive ways. For instance, although she never makes the link explicit, the image of a total eclipse of the sun is perhaps her most powerful metaphor for her central notion of 'decreation', which may be understood as a kind of eclipse or annihilation of the self.

This brings me to the last and longest essay, the four-part 'Decreation: How Women like Sappho, Marguerite Porete and Simone Weil Tell God', which, even more than the other three essays, is the intellectual heartland of the book. She begins with a stunningly original and profound reading of Sappho's famous fragment 31, the poem spoken by a jealous lover, beginning 'He seems to me equal to gods that man ...'. I urge you to read her analysis for yourself; I'll just say that ultimately she reads the poem as an ecstatic lyric about the 'theology of love', one which asks a profound 'spiritual question': *What is it that love dares the self to do?'* According to Carson, the answer in the poem is *'all is to be dared ... Love dares the self to leave the self behind.'* Carson, whose brilliant translations of Sappho's collected fragments, *If Not, Winter,* was published in 2002, and whose first book, *Eros the Bittersweet,* contains much passionate and insightful discussion of the poet, deserves her growing reputation as one of the most exciting guides to Sappho's work.

Part two of the same essay considers a thirteenth- and fourteenth-century French mystic named Marguerite Porete whose *Mirror of Simple Souls* Carson describes as 'a theological treatise and ... handbook for people seeking God', and also 'a book about the absolute daring of love'. Porete's central doctrine, as Carson describes it, is that 'the soul can proceed through seven different stages of love, beginning with ... "boiling desire",' until it achieves 'an ecstasy in which the soul is carried outside her own Being and leaves herself behind'. Like Sappho, Porete describes this ecstatic experience in terms of a love triangle, although this time the triangle consists of God the Spouse and the two parts of Porete's divided self; as Carson explains, 'she projects jealousy as a test of her ability to de-centre herself, to move out of the way, to clear her own heart and her own will off the path that leads to God.'

In part three, Carson brings in the work of Simone Weil, who also 'wanted to get herself out of the way in order to arrive at God'. Weil called her program for doing this 'decreation', 'to undo the creature in us'. She too imagines a love triangle, here involving God, herself and all of creation: she is a third wheel between two lovers, God and the earth, and wants to disappear. As she says, 'If only I could see a landscape the way it is when I am not there' (169). The implication is that this would give her access to reality, to the thing-in-itself. Moreover, Porete and Weil agree that such a sublime experience of self-annihilation would be one of tremendous joy.

Carson does an important critical service in this essay by restoring three notable women to the Romantic tradition of the sublime — a tradition often thought of as dominated by men — and by reminding us that this tradition is not confined to recent centuries, but is rather a mode of writing that has had adherents in every age; her essay is a subtle but powerful rejoinder to glib critics who dismiss this tradition as outdated, or inherently male, or both. In this way, Carson is defining a tradition for herself, and clearing a space for her own work as a poet.

(It occurs to me, moreover, that one can locate a central aspect of Carson's elusive Canadian-ness in this project: her concern with the feminist reform of this European tradition contrasts strikingly with, for example, Whitman's wholesale rejection of it in *Song of Myself*. In other words, she adopts a rebellious and reforming Canadian attitude toward the tradition very different from Whitman's revolutionary American one. Of course, one might argue that Pound and Eliot did a similar thing in their criticism, clearing a space for their own work by recovering certain half-forgotten European traditions; but then, they were precisely the two American modernist poets who strove most ardently to leave the United States behind.)

There is, however, a contradiction in Sappho, Porete and Weil, Carson argues, that arises from the fact that they are writers: they create a 'big, loud, shiny centre of self from which the writing is given voice', and yet they 'claim to be intent on annihilating this self while continuing to write'. To resolve this contradiction, each one 'feels moved to create a kind of dream of distance in which the self is displaced from the centre of the work and the teller disappears into the telling.'

Simone Weil, for example, 'arranged for her own disappearance on several levels', including self-starvation. This was related to Weil's economic and spiritual diagnosis of the human condition: 'Man's great affliction,' she wrote, 'is that looking and eating are two different operations.' Therefore, her 'dream of distance' is precisely a resolution of this affliction: 'Eternal beatitude is a state where to look is to eat.' Because food reminds us so powerfully of our physicality, 'she creates in her mind a dream of distance where food can be enjoyed perhaps from across the room merely by looking at it, … where the lover can stay, at the same time, near to and far from the object of her love.' But as Carson reminds us, 'eternal beatitude is not the only state where to look is to eat. The written page can also reify this paradox for us. A writer may *tell* what is near and far at once.'

Certainly this is true of Carson's own writing. She gives us just one brief personal story in this essay devoted to the works of others — 'I remember a little book of *The Lives of the Saints* that was given to me about age five. In this book the various flowers composing the crowns of the martyrs were so lusciously rendered in words and paint that I had to be restrained from eating the pages' — but we are, nevertheless, always aware of her fervent personal stake in what she is writing. She may be discussing writers distant from herself in time and place, but in these essays she almost always seems to be writing about herself as a writer, and, moreover, whispering her discourse urgently in our ears.

In Marguerite Porete, as in Carson herself, the dream of distance seems to involve time as much as space, but for Porete 'the writer's dream of distance becomes an epithet of God'. Porete calls God 'the divine Lover who feeds her soul with the food of truth', and, more to the point, 'the excellent FarNear'. In an act that Porete describes as both a kind of copulation and a kind of feeding, God 'ravishes' the soul in the moment of its annihilation, and fills it, through an 'aperture', with a glimpse of its eternal 'glory'. God must come 'Near' to perform this act, but remains 'Far' in time, apparently, because he only gives the soul a glimpse; that is, eternity itself will have to wait. By contrast, as Carson points out, Simone Weil considered prayer to be primarily an experience of spatial contradiction; nevertheless, its effect for her was similarly ecstatic.

This brings Carson back, as the essay ends, to Sappho, whose prayer to Aphrodite, fragment 2, she reads as another dream of distance. The poem is a calling hymn, 'an invocation to God to come from where she is to where we are'; as Carson says, such a hymn typically names both places, and then the invocation decreases the difference between them, 'an impossible motion possible only in writing'. Moreover, Carson's analysis of exactly how Sappho does this with her syntax is, as usual, superb.

All four of these essays are ultimately about displacing the self to make way for the sublime. The subjects of the first two, sleep and quotation, are nothing if not ways of getting the self out of the way, and the subject of the third, the total eclipse of the sun by the moon, is the book's great metaphor for this act. The fourth essay, besides performing the important literary-historical services I have described above, illuminates the spiritual motivation for, and aesthetic consolation of, sublime writing in ways that have seldom been rivalled. After reading them three or four times, I am convinced these essays contain some of the most original and insightful critical writing about the sublime since Freud.

What remains is to consider how well Carson puts her theory into practice in her less discursive writing. Certainly her theory teaches us how to read her poetry. When one re-reads the entire book after finishing her essays, the deeper structure of the book as a whole becomes immediately clear. On the ordinary level of genre, the structure is this: the first hundred pages contain all the poems and the first two essays; this is followed by three experiments in other genres, namely the oratorio, the Q&A and the screenplay; then the book finishes with the last two essays and the opera, with a brief cinematic shot list for coda. But on a spiritual and aesthetic level, the book's structure is this: like Sappho, Porete and Weil, Carson begins, in her lyric poems, by consenting to love's absolute dare and, in search of a sublime experience of decreation, progressively displaces herself from the centre of the writing, using every technique of depersonalization at her disposal, from quotation, imitation, parody, and critical analysis of others, to various kinds of dramatic technique, including experiments with screenplay and libretto. One is reminded of T. S. Eliot's desire to 'escape from personality' and his deployment of many similar methods, especially quotation, parody, criticism, dramatic monologues, and, ultimately, poetic drama.

However, as Carson reminds us, 'to undo self one must move through self' because the self is 'the parchment on which God writes his lessons'. (The phrase is Porete's.) This is why Carson opens her book with a series of personal lyrics. Her subject is her response to the illness of her ageing mother, whom she calls 'the love of my life'. It is this love that ignites and instigates the book's burning spiritual quest for decreation.

The first item in the book is 'Sleepchains', a small, beautiful lyric about setting out on such a quest, which I quote here in its entirety:

> Who can sleep when she —
> Hundreds of miles away I feel that vast breath
> Fan her restless decks.
> Cicatrice by cicatrice
> All the links
> Rattle once.
> Here we go mother on the shipless ocean.
> Pity us, pity the ocean, here we go.

Like her heroines, Carson begins her book with a dream of distance. Her anxious insomnia, 'hundreds of miles away' from her sick mother, is interrupted — an interruption enacted in the syntax, the anacoluthon or grammatically incomplete first line — by the physical sensation of some 'vast breath', the breath of God, one supposes, 'fan[ning]' the 'restless decks' of her mother imagined as a ship, as if the mother were not far away at all, but indeed very near. And yet the breath and the rattling it produces serve by the end of the poem to call the speaker to travel, to close the distance between herself and her mother, to begin the journey toward her mother and God, and this presupposes the great distance between them described in the second line of the poem. Nevertheless, whereas at the beginning of the poem the speaker uses two singular pronouns to indicate herself and her mother, 'I' and 'she', by the end they are united in 'us' and 'we'. Both the mother and the 'vast breath' are 'FarNear' indeed.

Despite its brevity, this poem is characteristically allusive. The compound title, 'Sleepchains', recalls Paul Celan, a poet for whom serious playing with spiritual paradoxes of nearness and distance, presence and absence, is central to his work. (Carson has written well and at length about Celan in her book *Economy of the Unlost*.) The poem's key image of a vast breath moving over the ocean echoes the beginning of the book of Genesis, in fact the very passage that Longinus quotes as a supreme example of the sublime style. And anacoluthon, the poem's opening scheme, is sometimes described by rhetoricians as a 'distancing' technique, because it directs the reader's attention to the writing as writing, and away from whatever object is being described, which makes it particularly appropriate for this writerly dream of distance. Such are the allusive pleasures of reading this learned poet at her best.

The poems that make up the rest of the opening sequence, entitled *Stops*, are, unfortunately, not always up to this standard. Of its fourteen lyrics, I count just four or five that are as good as anything Carson has done in this mode, including, besides 'Sleepchains', the following poems: 'That Strength', 'Nothing For It' and 'Her Beckett'. The others are decidedly less successful, though some of them are better than others. Here is one of the lesser poems, though not the worst, called 'Beckett's Theory of Comedy'. It's the last one in the sequence:

> Picking gooseberries, she said.
> O is shown moving to the window.
> Should traps be not available.
> Or they kneel throughout the play.
> That lifelong adorer!
> Same old coat.
> No verticals, all scattered and lying.
> *Tomorrow noon?*
> Goes back up the path, no sign of you.
> [Pause.]

It isn't that this is incomprehensible; the lines read like spliced passages from a Beckett play — they may in fact all be quotations from his plays, I haven't checked — and the point is clearly that the author's life with and without her mother resembles such a play. (Anne Carson herself is clearly 'That lifelong adorer!') But the literary game here feels too clever, too derivative, too dependent on stylistic imitation to have much emotional impact, at least on this reader. That's the aesthetic problem. The spiritual problem is that it leaps ahead to a kind of false decreation of the self, adopting Beckett's language without really moving through or displacing the self as a character in the poem.

A much more successful poem in both respects is a moving lyric called 'Nothing For It', which reads like a later episode of the spiritual quest romance begun in 'Sleepchains':

Your glassy wind breaks on a shoutless shore and stirs around the rose.

Lo how

before a great snow,

before the gliding emptiness of the night coming on us,

our lanterns throw

shapes of old companions

and

a cold pause after.

What knife skinned off

that hour.

Sank the buoys.

Blows on what was our house.

Nothing for it just row.

I like Carson's economy of language in this poem, the surprises that result from her syntactical elisions and interruptions, her scattershot rhymes and sharp enjambments, and her vivid and suggestive images. But what I admire most is the poem's emotional force, its feeling of balancing on the edge of despair and stoical perseverance. The wind which in 'Sleepchains' is a gentle 'vast breath', has now become an annihilating 'glassy wind', a 'knife' that 'skinned off / that hour' and 'Sank the buoys' and now 'Blows on what was our house'; and yet the speaker is determined to go on. The poem recalls Beckett's line: 'I can't go on. I'll go on.' And how much more emotionally powerful this remembrance of Beckett is than the explicit imitation of the playwright's language in 'Beckett's Theory of Comedy'. Having said this, I must say I find the form of this poem, with its centred lines à la Microsoft Word, and its melodramatic seventh line — 'and' — to be more or less arbitrary, and that is disappointing in a poem that is otherwise so good.

The next sequence of lyrics, *Sublimes,* suffers from a similar unevenness. I count just three poems out of twelve as first-rate, namely 'And Reason Remains Undaunted', 'Stanzas, Sexes, Seductions' and, with some hesitation, 'Guillermo's High Symphony'. 'And Reason Remains Undaunted' begins casually with a conventionally Wordsworthian search for the sublime in nature, but then veers off surprisingly into a wild series of adjectives and adjectival phrases to describe 'the many methods of moving green', never to return to the poem's original 'walk'; it is a brilliant specimen of the list or catalogue poem, making full use of the catalogue's disjunctive power, and, because it consists of adjectives instead of the usual nouns, it feels utterly fresh. 'Stanzas, Sexes, Seductions' is a witty and sad poem about sex and death: 'Who does not end up/a female impersonator?' the poem asks wryly, only to wipe the smile off our faces in the next lines: 'Drink all the sex there is./Still die.' This poem is notable also for its summary of the aesthetic impulse behind the quest for decreation and sublime experience:

> My personal poetry is a failure.
>> I do not want to be a person.
>>> I want to be unbearable.

When she puts it this way she reminds us of Eliot again. But she also raises the question of whether her personal poetry is in fact a failure.

My sense is that some is and some isn't. Certainly Carson's early narrative poem from *Glass, Irony and God*, 'The Glass Essay', which is both one of Carson's most personal poems, and, as it happens, a poem about her relationship with her mother, is one of her very best. But restricting the question to the poems in the present volume, the picture is mixed; when her personal poems are not successful it is generally because they overpower the limits of the lyric in the name of formal or rhetorical experimentation. Carson's continual playing around in this sequence with poems that blend lines from different voices, including quotations from other writers — a technique she has used many times before — fits intellectually into her program of displacing the self from the centre of her work, but in her hands it just doesn't produce very good poems. Here is a sample, from a poem called 'Blended Text':

You have captured:	*pinned* upon
my heart:	the wall of *my heart* is your love
with one glance:	as *one*
with one bead:	as *an exile of the kings* of royalty

And so on. That this cliché-ridden jumble ('You have captured:/my heart:/with one glance') is bad poetry is self-evident, and so the less said about it the better. But one has to wonder about any experimental technique that produces phrases as inane as '*the kings* of royalty'. Flannery

O'Connor once wrote that a writer is free to try and get away with whatever he wants, but that it had been her experience that there wasn't much one could get away with. The sooner Carson abandons this sort of thing, the better, though I won't hold my breath.

The third sequence of poems in the book, *Gnosticisms,* is, on the whole, much more successful. Take, for example, this fierce little *ars poetica* about writing the sublime called 'Gnosticism III':

> First line has to make your brain race that's how Homer does it,
> that's how Frank O'Hara does it, why
> at such a pace
> Muses
> slam through the house — there goes one (fainting) up the rungs
> of your strange BULLFIGHT, buttered
> almost in a nearness
> to skyblue
> Thy pang — Pollock yourself!
> Just to hang on to life is why

I find this weird little poem exhilarating, both in the way it follows its own advice with onrushing syntax and headlong lineation, and in the way it deploys mythic imagery in contemporary language in a way that reminds me of certain poems by P.K. Page. (I'm not crazy about 'BULLFIGHT', though, which relies on typography for a cheap effect when it ought to rely on its word choice.) And here is its companion poem, 'Gnosticism VI', about *reading* the sublime:

> Walking the wild mountain in a storm I saw the great trees
>   throw their arms.
> *Ruin!* they cried and seemed aware
>
> the sublime is called a 'science of anxiety'.
> What do men and women know of it? — at first
>
> not even realizing they were naked!
> The language knew.

Watch 'naked' (*arumim*) slide into 'cunning' (*arum*) snake in
    the next verse.
And suddenly a vacancy, a silence,

is somewhere inside the machine.
Veins pounding.

This, the culminating poem in the sequence and the last short lyric in the
book, is the most powerful depiction of an experience of decreation among
the book's lyric poems. Notice how deftly Carson moves from a sublime
Romantic landscape in the first couplet to Freudian analysis in the second,
and then to Longinian quotation and explication of a biblical text in the
third and fourth. It is the act of reading which triggers the ecstatic moment
of decreation, the displacement of the reader's self, and leaves behind 'a
vacancy, a silence' where a ghost used to be inside the body's 'machine'. But
the act of reading is itself erotic; the climax of the poem is a kind of serious
etymological joke about a naked sliding into 'cunning', and this moment of
very scholarly pornography is precisely the trigger for the ecstatic experience of decreation. If only every short poem in Carson's book were this
good.

At 245 pages, and with works in seven or eight distinct genres, *Decreation* is
an impossible book to do justice to even in a long review like this. Carson's
screenplay on the subject of Abelard and Heloise, her question-and-answer
session on a film production of Samuel Beckett's silent play (or dance) called
'Quad', the text of her oratorio in homage to Gertrude Stein, her cinematic
shot list for a silent film, and her decidedly anaphoric poem on a picture by
Betty Goodwin, are all interesting experiments, though some are more
interesting than others. But I want to turn instead, however briefly, to the
most ambitious work in the book, its grand finale, the sixty-five-page opera
libretto entitled *Decreation: An Opera in Three Parts*.

    The three parts are unified in theme but otherwise distinct; it may be
best to think of it as a trilogy of short operas. Part One dramatizes the story
of the god Hephaistos who discovers his wife Aphrodite in the act of
adultery with Ares, the god of war, and fails in his attempt to exact
revenge. Part Two deals with the trial of Marguerite Porete by the Inquisi-
tion on charges of heresy, and her death by being burned at the stake.

And Part Three concerns the life, thought and death of Simone Weil.

I have not seen the opera performed, although the 1999 production at the University of Michigan was apparently a success. But it must be said that it helps tremendously to understand the libretto if one has read the essay 'Decreation' immediately beforehand, and indeed that essay appears directly before the libretto in the book. I can only imagine how mystified an audience might be without the benefit of this introduction. This is not to say they would not enjoy the production, but simply that they might well leave the theatre scratching their heads about the relationship among the opera's three parts.

That said, the libretto is charming, moving and profound. I was surprised at how funny it is, even on the page, and a good production would no doubt amplify this quality many times over. The scenes that deal with the thought of Porete and Weil are not at all static or dry, as one might fear, but superbly dramatized and emotionally engaging. And the tragic scenes of Hephaistos's failure, Porete's immolation and Weil's life-ending stay in the hospital are all deeply affecting.

As a drama, the libretto is this book's apotheosis of decreation, a fully realized 'dream of distance in which the self is displaced from the centre of the work and the teller disappears into the telling'. The unevenness of the lyrics at the beginning of the book, as I have said, arises from their straining to transcend the limits of the short lyric in ways — such as the use of multiple voices and blended texts — that are far more appropriate for drama, and so it is not surprising that this is the direction Carson is headed in as she comes to the end of her book. As far as I know, this libretto is her first original published and produced dramatic work, but I would not be surprised if Carson continues to write in dramatic forms in the future. (She has already published translations of plays by Sophocles and Euripides.) If she does continue in this line, it would make *Decreation* an important turning-point in her career.

☆

The Magic of Jeffery Donaldson

Jeffery Donaldson never writes — or at least, never publishes — bad poems. Not everything in his three books to date is excellent, but all of it is technically accomplished, erudite and interesting. At their worst his poems can be wilful, that is to say, written too much by the conscious mind and not enough by the gods. A few of his poems, while largely quite good, suffer from the ordinary faults of good poems — an extraneous stanza, say, or a lapse of poetic logic — and one may hope for revisions of these someday. But what most concerns us as readers is Donaldson at his best, and here we can be grateful indeed, because he has written, so far, a score of excellent poems, poems that will last. And of these, nearly half a dozen are among the finest poems ever written by a Canadian poet.

Donaldson is a professor of poetry and poetic theory at McMaster University in Hamilton, Ontario, and also a literary critic and scholar, co-editor for instance of a superb collection of essays on Northrop Frye's late work entitled *Frye and the Word: Religious Contexts in the Writings of Northrop Frye*. He has published on Auden (the subject of his dissertation), Rilke, James Merrill, Geoffrey Hill, Mark Strand and, above all, Richard Howard, and these scholarly interests have strongly informed his poetry.

As a poet, Donaldson is a learned sorcerer; when he was a student at the University of Toronto he apparently kept a quotation from Goethe's *Faust* tacked on the wall above his desk: 'Settle your studies! and sound the depths/of that thou wilt profess.' There are two sides to this wizard, however. One is a Faustian necromancer, the author of brilliant but often *voulu* dramatic monologues that evoke the spirits of the illustrious dead. Only two or three of these monologues are ultimately convincing, although — no small thing — one of them is a masterpiece. The other is a young Prospero, wielding the white magic of lyric poetry; this is Donaldson at his best. And fortunately, he has none of Ben Jonson's charlatan alchemist Subtle in him; he is a true poet, not a faker.

Over Donaldson the necromancer it is Richard Howard, modern

master of the dramatic monologue, who has exerted the strongest influence, symbolized by Howard's having written an introduction to Donaldson's first book of poems, *Once Out of Nature* (1991). Of the forty poems in both that volume and Donaldson's second book, *Waterglass* (1999), fully a dozen are dramatic monologues very much in Howard's line of work; most are either spoken by, addressed to or otherwise concerned with certain illustrious European writers, artists and musicians from the nineteenth and early twentieth centuries, including J. M. W. Turner, Pierre Bonnard, Gustav Mahler, Claude Monet, Rainer Maria Rilke, Martin Heidegger, Osip Mandelstam, Gustav Klimt and Sigmund Freud, although there is also one devoted to Vitruvius, the ancient Roman architectural theorist. And yet James Merrill has been nearly as influential in these poems as Howard; in an essay on Merrill that refers to that poet's necromancing epic of the Ouija board, *The Changing Light at Sandover*, Donaldson seems to be speaking for himself as well as Merrill when he writes that poetry 'establish[es] ... our connection with all the elusive voices that change us and make us who we are, lost loved ones or the wholly other company on that side of the proscenium arch in which we feel ourselves continually instructed and renewed.' For Donaldson the necromancer, poetry is a 'mystic theatre of the word', as he puts it elsewhere, where one's artistic progenitors, the sources of the self, may be kept alive, or resurrected.

Like Howard and Merrill both — and Daryl Hine, the Canadian poet he most resembles — Donaldson is a poet of considerable erudition and remarkable technical virtuosity; his poems are written in beautifully modulated verse, shapely stanzas and varied, often complex syntax. Like these poets he is acutely aware of the dead metaphors buried just beneath the surfaces of words, and like them he resurrects these dead metaphors tirelessly, even borrowing his models' favourite rhetorical and prosodic resources to do so, especially ambiguous enjambment and paronomasia (that is, etymological puns). Consider this passage, for example, from the poem 'A Floating Garden at Giverny'; the lines are spoken by one of Claude Monet's pallbearers, who is describing what it was like to lift the dead painter's coffin:

> We stood inside
> out of the cold and lifted the whole man.
> Not quite equal to it, his body tipped

in the coffin, restless in the ascent,
the assumption we had so awkwardly
held out to him, impatient for the grave

he would — how many times! — roll over in.

Delightful, isn't it, the way Donaldson brings this cliché, this dead
metaphor about 'rolling over in one's grave', back to life by making it
almost physical again, like the body tipping in its coffin. A similar delight
accrues to the way the poet uses the word 'assumption' in the fifth line of
this passage, which, while not a cliché, has nevertheless hardened into an
abstraction in our everyday speech; Donaldson uses it here in its more concrete, though defunct, theological sense ('to take up into heaven') as well as
in its modern economic sense ('to take possession of, to make one's own'),
and both meanings shed light on what is happening here: the painter's pallbearers are certainly in a sense leading him to heaven, but, as disciples of
the great man — younger painters and patrons of the art — they are also
asserting their rights of artistic inheritance. Another example: in the phrase
'restless in the ascent' in the fourth line, the word 'ascent' is also a pun on
'assent'; that is to say, Monet's corpse is physically restless from being lifted
up, indeed, but the man's spirit also feels, we may imagine, a bit uncomfort-
able at having so thoroughly won the assent of his artistic heirs. There are
more threads to unravel in this little text, but what I've said here should suffice to convey Donaldson's method.

Or rather, Howard's method. I am afraid I get the feeling too often in
Donaldson's monologues that I am hearing the voice not of Mahler or Vitruvius, but of Richard Howard. The stylistic mannerisms he takes out of
Howard's mouth include, besides a near-constant onslaught of paronomasia, the following: the exclamatory interjection ('the grave/he would —
how many times! — roll over in'), the superfluous deployment of italics
('Since for ourselves, decisions/are never *made,*/just entertained'), and a
self-conscious lingering over the propriety of a word ('That's the right
word,/I hope, *involvement*'). The speakers of these three examples, taken
from three different poems, are, respectively, Monet's unnamed pallbearer,
Gustav Mahler, and an anonymous patient of Sigmund Freud. That they all
sound remarkably alike, and remarkably like Donaldson's poetic master, is a
serious fault, given that our poet, I presume, is trying to bring these figures

to life as individual characters. Consider, by way of comparison, the different styles of Robert Browning's jealous Duke of Ferrara in 'My Last Duchess' on the one hand, and the envious monk in his 'Soliloquy of the Spanish Cloister' on the other: the former is all urbanity and *sprezzatura*, the latter nothing but sarcasm and curses.

The example of Browning raises another difficulty with Donaldson's dramatic monologues. As the critic Robert Langbaum argues in *The Poetry of Experience: The Dramatic Monologue in Modern Literary Tradition*, dramatic irony is of the essence in this genre; it is crucial for there to be at least some tension between our identification with the speaker and our judgment of him or her. Langbaum analyzes examples by Browning, Tennyson and Eliot, among others, to make his case. But Donaldson is, generally speaking, not interested in dramatic irony; he is writing about his intellectual and artistic idols. Frankly, it makes me wonder why he doesn't choose genres more suitable to his attitude: the ode, perhaps, or the homage, even the elegy.

This is not to say that his dramatic monologues are never successful poems. Two or three are very well done, including 'At Toblach' in his first book, an imagined piece of correspondence by Gustav Mahler, and 'The Last Session' in his second, a fictional transcript of a session of psychoanalysis spoken to Sigmund Freud by an unnamed patient. That the patient is unnamed helps the poem tremendously.

And one of the monologues, as I say, is a masterpiece. I'm talking about the poem on Monet from which I've quoted above, 'A Floating Garden at Giverny'. I want now to take a look at it as a whole, and put my finger on what makes it so good. The first thing to notice is that, as in the Freud poem I just mentioned, the speaker is not the famous personage himself, that is, not Monet, but rather one of his anonymous disciples; and here, given Donaldson's admiring attitude toward Monet, we may assume that the speaker of the poem is a stand-in for the poet. If this pallbearer still sometimes reminds us of Richard Howard, at least we are not asked to imagine his voice in the throat of Claude Monet. Moreover, the metaphorical identification of speaker and poet suggests that what the pallbearer is doing — that is, raising Monet up, taking him up into heaven, and at the same time taking possession of him — is a metaphor for what Donaldson himself is doing in this poem: that is, raising the painter from the dead, and staking a claim on his inheritance. In other words, the poem is a delicious allegory of itself.

That would be enough to make any poem interesting, but there is something even more significant going on here. For one thing, the poem uses conventions more often associated with the pastoral elegy than the dramatic monologue. Thus the speaker tells the story of Monet's funeral procession, and how, once the pallbearers have lifted the coffin, the painter's wife Blanche suddenly decides to replace its grey pall with her husband's beautiful bedspread,

> all embroidered
> with blossoms, the drawn, free-floating yellow
> and orange of waterlilies, seamless
>
> and stemmed in a water stitched of whole blue
> silk, itself threaded by appearing
> shadows of cloudy white on gold.

Moreover, when the pallbearers carry the coffin outside into the garden, where winter has left 'the rose-beds and the rows of bell-flowers / razed to the earth', the new pall is transformed beautifully into the Impressionist floating garden of the poem's title:

> But as we stepped
>
> down, we felt an opulence bearing with us
> in the bright pall, whose needled green and gold
> flared clear an instant in the frosted air,
>
> its colours as the daylight fell in sheets
> stirred a little, rose, lengthened and dissolved
> in luminous folds that moved....

This is beautiful writing, and the image itself is beautiful. But it is only when we recognize that these embroidered flowers are the flowers of pastoral elegy, as in, for example, Milton's 'Lycidas', or Whitman's 'When Lilacs Last in the Dooryard Bloom'd' — the latter another poem about a funeral procession for the poet's hero — it is only then that the originality of Donaldson's poem suddenly becomes clear. For his flowers are explicitly the flowers not of nature but of Monet's art. ('Once out of nature', writes Yeats in 'Sailing to Byzantium', in the passage which provided Donaldson with the title for the book in which this poem appears, 'I shall never take my bodily form/From any natural thing.') And this is what enables 'A Floating Garden at Giverny' to achieve a genuinely plausible and moving elegiac consolation, which is something English-language poets have been struggling to do convincingly for more than a hundred years: a consolation not of heaven but of art. Although it is framed as a dramatic monologue, the poem is most effective, ultimately, as a gorgeous, vivid, and moving ceremonial elegy in the pastoral tradition. That this is the first poem in this poet's first book is astonishing. But its success has to do essentially with its lyrical qualities; the fact that it is a dramatic monologue is almost beside the point.

Which brings me to Donaldson's white magic, his lyrics proper, to which I turn with a great deal of pleasure. There are twenty-four of them in his first two books, and of these, fully a dozen or so are excellent; and three of these are, as I have said, some of the best Canadian poems ever written. (There are more in *Palilalia* (2008), Donaldson's third collection, but since that book is in some ways a departure, I want to treat it separately.) The finest are 'Bearings', from the first book, and, from the second, 'Feddy Doe' and 'Above the River'. The rest of the excellent: 'Rented Space', 'The Man Who Drew Days', and 'By Word of Mouth: At the National Portrait Gallery, London', all from *Once Out of Nature*; and from *Waterglass*, 'One for Safe Keeping', 'What Goes Without Saying', 'The Tale of Bricks', 'A Wedding Cake' and 'Wind'. The first thing one notices in these poems is the change of style: rather than incessant echoes of Richard Howard, suddenly we hear the voice of Jeffery Donaldson. The brilliant wit and formal grace remain, accompanied now by strong feeling and an unleashed imagination no longer tied to the stake of biographical research. Rather than labouring wilfully to melt down and forge the diary entries or letters of some historical figure into dramatic monologues, the poet is free to transform his own imaginative experience into lyric poems.

What does the real Jeffery Donaldson sound like? Listen to the voice in the following passage from 'Above the River', another astonishingly beautiful pastoral poem, this one in the direct line of Wordsworth and Frost. As it happens, we've heard this voice before: it turns out that it sounds very much like the Donaldson we encountered in the descriptive passages I quoted above from 'A Floating Garden at Giverny', which helps to explain why that poem is so much better than most of Donaldson's other monologues. Here is the passage, chosen more or less at random:

A soft muck in the fields, and a small lake

always come of the rain that falls and clears,
falls and clears endlessly, gorging the streams
and running like silk over the filled cisterns.

This is beautiful. But why? The puns and italics are gone; the self-consciousness has disappeared. What remains is, first of all, an expertly woven piece of syntax. Listen, for example, to the rhythmic amplification of 'falls and clears,/falls and clears endlessly'. And notice the way the comma after 'fields' in the first line turns the phrase 'always come of the rain' into an adjectival phrase modifying 'lake', so that 'come' becomes intensely subjunctive rather than flatly declarative, as it would have been without the comma; and this also turns the entire sentence into a fragment, which suits the placid mood of the scene. Now, listen to the intricate sound-chains of Keatsian assonance and consonance: 'like/silk/filled'; 'soft/fields/falls/ falls', and 'muck/lake/come/clears/clears'. And listen to the subtly sprung rhythm that Donaldson achieves through metrical overstressing: 'soft muck', 'small lake', 'like silk over', 'filled cisterns'. There is also the sensuous vividness of the monosyllables: the soft muck, the small lake, the rain that falls and clears, the streams, the silk, the cisterns. And finally, consider the deftly patterned lineation: the sentence spans two pairs of lines, and in each pair the first line contains a caesura and is enjambed, and the second line has no caesura and is end-stopped, producing a kind of prosodic parallelism of tension and release, tension and release. Keep in mind these are just four lines of a stunningly executed ninety-seven-line poem — perhaps, although I don't have room to make the case here, the finest pastoral poem in Canadian poetry (and these are not even the best lines in the poem — wait till you read the ending). What a pleasure to find oneself, as a reader, in the hands of a poet who so wonderfully knows what he is doing.

The poem of Donaldson's that best accounts for this felicitous turn from dramatic monologue to lyric proper, and which explicitly repudiates his earlier, more derivative manner, is the haunting 'Feddy Doe' from *Water-glass*. The poem's subject is the poet's childhood memory of being sent to bed by his father each night with a mysterious and magical phrase: 'Cooshay and feddy doe: Up the wooden stair / and to sleep.' This makes the poem a kind of mystery story about language, delicately woven into a displaced myth in which the child-poet, 'Orpheus the wrong way round', ascends a staircase to his bedroom — which, as both a second-story room and a chamber of dreams, he calls the 'underworld's upper sphere'. What he encounters there in the moonlight is remarkable:

> ... in the chair, propped like a tippler
> bunched up under his own weight, my father's
> oak-carved, antique marionette looked out.
>
> Cuttings of sun-browned curtain for a suit
> patched with neat squares of a checkered dish-cloth.
> One leg was off. All up in arms with string.
>
> Its face was painted like a tart's, red cheeks,
> red lips, hysteric smile, and oak-hard stare
> that returned the blank appearances in kind
>
> of whatever it saw there in the dark.

What we are dealing with here, to borrow a critical term from Donaldson's teacher Northrop Frye, is a demonic version of the myth of Orpheus, the ur-poet of Greek mythology: this 'Orpheus the wrong way round' finds, when he gets to his bedroom 'underworld', not the shade of his dead Eurydice, but a simulacrum, a disconcerting, even frightening puppet belonging to his father. It seems to me the father's antique marionette stands precisely for all the one-dimensional historical speakers in most of Donaldson's dramatic monologues, the ones who all seem to sound like Richard Howard, Donaldson's poetic father, throwing his voice like a campy ventriloquist. If I'm right, it would make this poem a crucial act of self-overcoming on Donaldson's part, a repudiation of his dramatic method in his earlier work.

But with what does he propose to replace that method? The answer lies in the solution to the mystery about language in the poem, the meaning of the father's strange bedtime salutation. In response to those magic words, the boy repeats 'Cooshay and feddy doe',

> feeling that often, with no stronger spell
> to ward off chimeras I knew were there,
> a home-made incantation worked as well.
> And chimed 'up the wooden stair and to sleep....'
> For that was what they meant, the cryptic sounds,
> my father said. Two ways to put the same thing.

The main 'chimera' which must be warded off with this magic spell is clearly the marionette, the boy-poet's demonic Eurydice. However, it turns out the father is mistranslating as well as mangling the incantation, which suggests it can't be a very effective protection. Only in the epiphany that closes the poem is the mystery finally solved:

> The magic part was French Canadian,
> that much I knew ...
> ...
> By the time I heard 'coucher' in first-year
> French, I was only just learning to lie
> down among half truths, and wanted the rest.
>
> But *feddy doe?* ... how would I get from there
> to *wooden steps* in French? I didn't know.
> And then one night, a movie on TV,
>
> a woman sees her daughter off to bed,
> reads to her from a book until she sleeps,
> kisses her brow good night. 'Fais des beaux rêves',
> she whispers in her ear. And I saw a child,
> with closed eyes, long gone for a sweeter dream,
> lost in translation on the wooden stair.

The incantation does *not* mean 'go up the wooden stairs' to encounter the nightmarish 'oak-hard stare' of the marionette; it means, on the contrary, 'go to bed and have sweet dreams', or, literally, 'make beautiful dreams'.* The mystery's solution is thus the positive complement to the negative lesson taught by the encounter with the marionette; when the magic words are finally understood by the poet as a grown man, the displaced myth of Orpheus is transformed thereby from its demonic into its authentic version. The exquisite pun on 'translation' as transfiguration in the final line makes the point perfectly: in the demonic version of the nightly episode, the boy is merely lost in translation, that is to say, misguided by a mistranslation. In the authentic version, he is rapt, translated by the imagination. All of this makes for a profound act of self-instruction by the poet: his advice to himself is to eschew ventriloquism, the black magic of necromancy, for the transfiguring 'beautiful dreams' of the visionary imagination, what he calls in his essay on Merrill the 'infinitely expansive interior spaces of myth and metaphor', the white magic of lyric poetry.

There is, by the way, even more to the phrase 'lost in translation' in the last line; it is also an allusion, which is another of this scholarly poet's favourite spells. 'Lost in Translation' is the title of a much-anthologized poem by James Merrill, which is dedicated and addressed to none other than Richard Howard, who is, among other things, a celebrated translator from the French. Merrill's poem is also about childhood, and involves marionettes, mysteries, a translation from French, and a woman saying goodnight to a child in another language; indeed, 'Feddy Doe' as a whole strikes me as a brilliantly executed response to Merrill's poem. The allusion in the final line reads, therefore, like a valediction to Richard Howard, and a transfer of poetic allegiance not only from dramatic monologue to lyric but specifically from Howard to Merrill.

Indeed, one of the pleasures of reading a scholarly poet like Donaldson comes from discovering so often, as in 'Feddy Doe', that he is responding powerfully to someone else's poem. Take the aforementioned 'Bearings', from his first book, which strikes me as an agonistic revision of Elizabeth Bishop's poem 'The Map'. Donaldson is careful to drop clues for his reader to pick up whenever he does this sort of thing; he uses, for example, the

---

* There is a Québécois lullaby called 'Fais Dodo', roughly 'Go Beddy-Bye', which suggests Donaldson's correction may itself be a mistranslation — a delightful irony which only increases my pleasure in this poem.

word 'outsize' early in his poem — see the fifth line in the passage below —
a word referring here to angels but also echoing Bishop's memorable use of
it to describe birds in her poem 'The Bight'. Both poems — that is, 'The
Map' and 'Bearings' — describe maps that represent the east coast of
Canada. But whereas Bishop's map is modern, produced by a 'printer', Donaldson's map is ancient, and that difference is crucial. Here is the beginning
of Donaldson's poem:

> Four chubby angels, like grown cherubim,
> blow at their simple trumpets from the four
> corners of the page, a yellowing cloth
>
> aged some few hundred years, wrinkled and stained.
> Such outsize messengers are the only
> recognizable human furniture
>
> to be found on this chart of otherwise
> distant islands, faintly green blocks of land
> sketched within the margins of drawn water,
>
> numbers of ink-spill settlements upstream,
> and more than enough sea to get there by,
> from where we begin. And still further north,
>
> regions of the unobserved, with the odd
> guessed-at frontier ventured: the conveniently
> unknown used for titles and legends.

If you recall 'The Map', Donaldson's point of contention with Bishop will be
clear: she prefers, at least aesthetically, the geographer's perspective to the
historian's, insisting in her final line, 'More delicate than the historians' are
the map-makers' colors'. But Donaldson, in describing an ancient map,
implicitly objects that, because maps change over time, Bishop's distinction
is an illusion. Map-makers *are* historians.

This point is reinforced by the way Donaldson reveals what his map
represents. Whereas Bishop explicitly names Newfoundland and Labrador,
Donaldson never actually comes out and says he's describing a map of

Canada. But that the 'regions of the unobserved' in Donaldson's map must refer to what we now call Canada will be clear to anyone familiar with maps of the world 'a few hundred years' old. This is because in such maps it is always northern North America which is left largely blank; it is always the last 'odd/guessed-at frontier'. In other words, there is no way to escape Donaldson's equation of mapmakers and historians; our very recognition of what his map represents depends, itself, on historical contingency.

The main point of contention between the two poems, however, has to do with the speakers' attitudes toward their respective maps. In Bishop the observer is bemused and detached, able to fault the map-makers for a kind of sentimentality: 'the printer here experiencing the same excitement/as when emotion too far exceeds its cause'. Donaldson, in contrast, sympathizes with the explorers who made the ancient map, and ultimately identifies with them: notice the moment in line twelve above, where he speaks in the first-person plural of 'where we begin'. By the time the poem reaches its climax, the identification of speaker and explorers is complete:

It isn't anywhere that we know of
by heart, a landscape only dimly
reminiscent of where people might once

have got to, or neared, circling and recircling
till the track they followed forward was their own.
How they must have looked then by the green place,

beyond themselves, entrusting their giddy
presence to the bearings they jotted down,
recounting details that returned to them

of the ways taken, wanting as they did
to come back. Hard to believe, as it is,
that anyone then or even later

could have used this page, water stiffened,
to get anywhere, least of all that broad
unfinished landscape we navigate towards,

being, as we are, unable to point out,
put a finger on, the small print that legend
has it marks our setting forth: *you are here.*

Who is this 'we' that Donaldson is speaking for? It clearly includes, besides
the ancient explorers, the poet himself. It also means 'every person', the
reader included, or at least everyone who finds him or herself on a journey
in life, navigating toward the unknown. But in the context of the place the
map apparently represents, 'we' seems to me to mean especially 'we Canadians'. This reading is clinched in the final line, with its allusion to a famous
passage in Northrop Frye which argues that the question of identity for
Canadians isn't so much 'Who are we?' as 'Where is here?' The point Donaldson's poem makes so movingly at the end is that, as Canadians as well as
human beings, we don't know where we are. Donaldson is hardly the first
Canadian poet to use exploration as a trope for national identity, but he is
certainly among the most sophisticated and profound.

As a solution to this old dilemma of ours, Donaldson offers the ancient
explorers as models for emulation, since they were able to move 'beyond
themselves, entrusting their giddy/presence to the bearings they jotted
down'. Granted, he imagines the explorers 'circling and recircling/till the
track they followed forward was their own'; but this suggests not only that
they were getting lost, but also that they were somehow taking possession
of the path. In context it is clear that this taking possession is only hypothetical; the map represents 'a landscape only dimly/reminiscent of where people might once/have got to, or neared' by circling in this way. And yet the
suggestion is clearly that such jotting down of bearings, such circling-and-
recircling, constitutes the most promising method we have for making the
way forward our own, and thus for discovering where we are.

Donaldson's third collection, *Palilalia,* appearing nearly a decade after *Water-
glass,* feels like a transitional book, a movement into what is, for this poet,
new territory. The dramatic monologues are gone, replaced by several confessional narratives — a remarkable change for a poet who started out so
self-consciously anti-confessional. To be sure, these are confessional poems
as written by Jeffery Donaldson, all erudite allusion and skilfully turned
blank verse, and thus stylistically much closer to the autobiographical
poems of James Merrill than, say, Lowell, Berryman or Plath. Which is to say,

the transfer of loyalty from Howard to Merrill announced in 'Feddy Doe' is borne out in these poems. Still, there are some genuine acts of self-revelation here, the most interesting for the poetry being that the poet has Tourette's syndrome (and, moreover, that his son has a related condition involving repetition of one's own words, called palilalia; hence the title of the book).

The Tourette's revelation comes in the most important of these confessional poems, 'Museum', which is in many ways a kind of companion piece to 'Feddy Doe'. The poet is making another underworld journey, this time as an adult in an underground subway station in Toronto. But instead of the myth of Orpheus, now it is the sojourns of Aeneas in Elysium and Dante in Heaven that come to mind. In each of these epic episodes the hero encounters a father-figure who offers advice and reassurance for the task ahead; and this is the theme of Donaldson's poem. In *The Paradiso,* cantos XV–XVII, Dante meets the spirit of Cacciaguida, his great-great-grandfather, who urges him to be fearless in writing his poem, and to let his poetic mission be his guide. And in *The Aeneid,* book VI, Aeneas meets the shade of his father Anchises, who, besides encouraging Aeneas in his mission, makes a famous distinction between two gates of Sleep, the gate of horn through which true shades pass, and the gate of ivory which sends false dreams into the world above.

In Donaldson's poem, the father-figure whom the poet-hero meets is, delightfully, the spirit of Northrop Frye, the poet's one-time professor at the University of Toronto. Frye's 'conjured presence' emerges, like a Blakean Emanation, from the poet himself, that is, from 'The clapping heel, nasal-snort, the lurching nod,/the whooped-up screech and cluck' of his non-voluntary (if not exactly involuntary) Tourette's tic. (What 'brought it on', he explains, was the sight of a crowd of students 'pouring from Northrop Frye Hall' above, and down the escalators to the subway platform of Museum station where he is standing.) The device is so surprising, self-deprecating (that is, confessional), confidently articulated, and expressive of the poem's central theme (more on this below) that it persuades me to suspend my disbelief; it is, indeed, figuratively *true.*

Frye's advice to the poet takes up about half of this 188-line poem, so I refer you to the poem itself for the details, but it boils down to an admonition: he criticizes the poet, essentially, for being too wilful, too much in control of his language even in his first drafts, and as much as calls him an anal-retentive 'perfectionist' too afraid of his own 'vocal dirt'. 'You're a

Touretter,' he says in the key passage. 'Why not write like one?' The source of the poet's genuine conjuring power, he suggests, is primal, unconscious, like the ultimately irrepressible vocal tic that conjures Frye's spirit out of the poet himself. If 'Feddy Doe' is, as I've argued, a repudiation of the poet's inner necromancer as a mere ventriloquist, 'Museum' seeks to assimilate that necromancy and turn it into something authentic, namely, a divination of wisdom from the gods; the poet, Frye is saying, should be, not a ventriloquist, but a medium. This is a poem that thinks seriously about what it means to be a poet; and in reading it I'm convinced again that Donaldson's gift for self-overcoming is one of the things that gives him his unmistakable authority. While it is true, as the spirit of Frye says, that he still has 'a way to go', one gets the sense, following his development from book to book, of an excellent poet striving mightily to turn himself into a great one.

Such advice as Frye gives is, to be sure, easier to give than take, and Donaldson isn't always able to follow it in the poems in this book. In 'Museum' he speaks of his

> bygone
> paternal mentors, fathers in whom I planted
> the seeds of long-nursed dependencies
>
> for the tall harvest that never came

and I wonder sometimes in reading *Palilalia* if the dependence on Merrill isn't as much of a burden for this poet as his former dependence on Howard. Some of the confessional narratives feel too willed, notably 'Gloucester's Dover' and 'Enter, Puck', both of which yoke personal material to Shakespearean, Boston Pizza to *King Lear,* shinny to *A Midsummer Night's Dream,* producing an effect that is, I'm afraid, elegant but bathetic. Some of the poems — for example, 'Ode on a Henry Moore' and 'Life Guard and Four Echoes' — for all their prodigious wit, are ultimately overwhelmed by their literary echoes, especially in their last lines. As in the Shakespeare poems, the difficulty is that the subject matter — a childhood act of immaturity, a life guard on a beach — is not in tune with the sublime echoes of Keats, Rilke, Dante and Eliot in the poems' language. This sort of thing is exquisite in, say, the mock-epics of Pope, where bathos is the whole point, but Donaldson is not writing mock-epics.

Except for 'Museum', the best poems in *Palilalia* aren't the autobiographical narratives, but rather a couple of erotic lyrics made out of conceits ('Spoken For' and 'Cashew') and several excellent poems about death: 'Hereafter I', 'Hereafter II', 'Home Body' and 'While We Grow Tired, Like Swimmers'. In 'Home Body', for example, the echoes of Robert Frost are finely calibrated to the poem's death-wish mood and tone, in a way that, as I say, eludes the less successful echo-poems in the book.

The finest thing in *Palilalia*, a poem as good as anything Donaldson has written, is an astonishing elegiac meditation on memory and loss called 'Where We Are Now'. The title recalls the final words of 'Bearings' — '*you are here*' — and in fact it is a kind of companion piece to that poem, the theme now being, not place, but time. I call it a meditation, and it is, but it would be more precise to say 'speculation', since the entire poem poses a pair of fascinating hypothetical questions and thinks them through, one at a time. The first question is this: 'What would it be like if we saw everything/in front of us now as a distant memory...?' His answer is that everything would be full of blanks, so that a childhood walk home from school, for instance, would already be suffused with a sense of loss even as it was happening:

> and the sidewalk you moved along seemed somehow
> not there at all and you felt a heartache
> at not seeing it any better than you could,
>
> so that the time between two dim images
> of your foot falling on the sidewalk
> and of your hand on the door of the house
>
> where Mother must have been waiting
> for you was a blank even then,
> not filled out with the trees, sky, and people
>
> you imagine you've forgotten.

The sense that the poet may be speaking of his own childhood memory here, or rather his difficulty recalling it, is unmistakable; but the framing of this little episode in the detached and hypothetical tone of philosophical

speculation lets the moment of feeling, that 'heartache', ambush us all the
more effectively — more effectively, I think, than in the straight narratives
of most of Donaldson's other autobiographical poems in this book.

The contrary speculation that follows seems to promise a much happier outcome than the first; and yet look how devastatingly Donaldson
turns it inside out in the poem's last line:

> Imagine ... that the hour at hand
> is not really at hand at all, that now
> isn't now but thirty years from now,
>
> and that before you are the concrete details
> of perfect memory, the present moment
> before you — with the cup there and the table
>
> and the light — in all its immediacy
> is what you have at last called to mind
> after years of practice and concentration.
>
> You could just open your eyes, and say, look,
> that cup I broke years ago, here it is,
> whole again, and that table I never liked,
>
> so palpable to the touch, and heavens,
> those iris-widening shadows I hardly
> ever glanced at in the curtained light
>
> are summoned here in my living memory,
> and look how well I do it, and how free
> it turns out I was to give it all away.

There are very few images here: just the cup, the table, the 'iris-widening
shadows' and the 'curtained light'. It's mostly abstract philosophical speculation, apparently, and yet I find it powerfully moving. What is going on
here? Certainly the direct address to the reader turns up the emotional temperature. But in fact Donaldson is doing something astonishing: imagining
experience from the perspective of eternity, from a god's point of view, so to

speak. (His characteristic pun in the interjection 'heavens' is a kind of verbal wink and nod in that direction.) What makes this so moving is the tragic recognition that such a perspective from outside of time is forbidden to us, imprisoned as we are in time. This recognition comes in the last line or so — 'how free/it turns out I was to give it all away' — and after reading it we recall that of course we have no choice in the matter; the speaker gives himself an ironic pat on the back for having so generously given it all away, knowing that ultimately that is all we are free to do with it. But the tragedy of this recognition is tempered because the poem itself gives us access, through the imagination, to that godlike perspective of eternity. What is this if not a poem written, through the medium of the poet, by the gods?

This meditative or philosophical mode in Donaldson's poetry is not entirely new; there is something of the kind in 'Bearings', and 'Above the River', for example, although they are not nearly so abstract as this. And yet to me this mode, and not the autobiographical narrative of the confessional poems, feels like the genuinely new and exciting direction in Donaldson's poetry; it is in fact the mode of several of the excellent poems in *Palilalia* that I have already mentioned, including 'Hereafter I', 'Hereafter II', and 'While We Grow Tired, Like Swimmers'. It does remind me a little of Wallace Stevens, or certain poems by John Ashbery or John Koethe. And yet it is really Donaldson's own thing, unburdened by over-dependence on paternal mentors: the blossoming of a mature and middle-period style.

☆

Marlene Cookshaw:

What to Pack

The story of Marlene Cookshaw's poetic career — five books of poems so far over the course of about twenty years — is a tragicomedy, like a Jacobean play in which two loosely related plots play out in alternating scenes, one plot headed for a happy ending, the other for disaster. On the happy side, there is the story of her developing command of the autobiographical lyric, from mawkish beginnings to consummate maturity, which has resulted in about thirty excellent poems over the course of her career. On the unhappy side, we have her attempts in other modes, including prose poems, third-person narrative verse, and most recently a sequence of largely impersonal lyrics on the subject of time, each of which, I'm sorry to report, has come to grief. It is understandable that a poet of Cookshaw's generation, born in the early fifties, would feel the pull of the anti-confessional impulse, a sense that she ought to be writing something beyond, or at least besides, personal narrative poems in the tradition of Robert Lowell's *Life Studies* (1959). But the truth is that, with a very few exceptions, only Cookshaw's best personal lyrics are worth keeping.

What's more, it must be admitted that Cookshaw's first two books, *Personal Luggage* (1984) and *The Whole Elephant* (1989), their autobiographical lyrics notwithstanding, are almost uniformly bad. The first third of the former is a series of prose poems, or at any rate brief prose pieces, which read like unintentional parodies of Alain Robbe-Grillet and his *Nouveau Roman:* descriptions of mundane objects that linger excruciatingly over insignificant details (two paragraphs devoted to describing a *cheque*), and brief, anti-climactic narratives involving hollow characters about whom we are told almost nothing of interest. The prose is an unrelenting series of short, flat declarative sentences. And when Cookshaw tries her hand at authorial commentary, her diction grows clotted with abstractions: 'More adept at response than at direction, she gives immediate reply to a moment that has been endlessly constructed. She reacts, in context, to the only performable note.' Any hint of human emotion or rhetorical competence in these pieces has been severely repressed.

The lyrics in the rest of *Personal Luggage* are, as the title suggests, brief personal narratives. Unfortunately they are not much better than the prose. One encounters poem after poem of dull sentences arranged in slack free verse, with hardly a figure of speech, rhetorical pattern, or expression of feeling among them; it leaves one gasping for poetic oxygen. There are two or three flashes of feeling in these poems, and even of lyrical promise, as in this stanza from 'Resolutions':

> *The air filled with cottonwood*
> *and lightning The slow click*
> *of dog's nails on the hall floor*
> *The streets breaking snow into flame*

The parallelism of the syntax here, the clear images, the metaphor in the last line (however awkwardly expressed), and the surprising enjambment of '*cottonwood / and lightning*', make this the most competent and interesting stanza in the entire book, a fact the poet seems to have recognized by placing it in italics. But there are no completely successful poems.

The Whole Elephant (1989), Cookshaw's second book, leaves a similar impression. It contains a tedious and incoherent narrative poem in thirteen parts entitled *In the Swim*, which, like the prose pieces in the earlier book, consists of disjointed narrative episodes involving a small group of lightly sketched and not very interesting characters. And there are thirty-two personal lyrics, mostly bad. Here is the last stanza of 'Cupboards', in which the speaker is talking about her feelings for her two lovers, both of whom she is leaving behind:

> This is not animal leaning, but desire for flight
> when muscle has shrunk and skin no longer shelters
> This is the I loving each of them whole, wanting
> to enter the seventh or eighth level of consciousness
> without war, abolition of the body, division
> of soul, or the need for net and gun

There is some syntactical energy here in the parallel syntax and apposite clauses, and in this sense the poems in *The Whole Elephant* are an advance over the poems in the first book. But why use an abstract and pretentious, not to mention silly, expression like 'the seventh or eighth level of consciousness' to express intensity of feeling when she could use a metaphor instead? Cookshaw is still struggling for technical competence in these poems, struggling to develop a repertoire of rhetorical and prosodic skills, to write interesting and helpful titles, and endings that don't fall flat. There's no shame in this; every poet must undergo an apprenticeship, though why any editor would think this apprentice work ought to be published in a book is beyond me.

There are, however, one or two promising poems, or parts of poems, in *The Whole Elephant*. 'The Sudden Drop in Temperature', for example, is about a frightening conversation between the poet and her mother over the telephone. The mother is ill, and the daughter's fear seems to be that she might develop Alzheimer's disease. This is the final stanza:

> Give my love
> To ———— , she says, with a terrifying
> gap before the name, me in Victoria
> on the easy side of winter, breath
> gone suddenly blue in my throat

Here we have, at last, a real human emotion, and, moreover, it is expressed powerfully in a palpable, lovely metaphor in the last line.

This is just the sort of pleasure to be found in abundance in *Double Somersaults* (1999), Cookshaw's first mature book of poems. What a relief to discover the new rhetorical confidence and formal control, and, moreover, the new open-heartedness and spiritual power of the best poems in this book. Of the forty lyrics in the collection, seventeen are very good indeed. They include 'Jan Garbarek's Saxophone', 'Cheating Death', 'Open and Close', 'Playing Fair', 'Holes in the Snow' (one of the finest poems ever written about Montreal), 'House', 'Grandfather Harrows the Garden With Horses', 'I Make Noise With My Mouth', 'Praise', 'Grays Harbor County', 'Blue Mexican Glass', 'Whoever's Responsible', 'Gli uccelli', 'What Is Promised', 'White Noise', 'Maybe the Body After All' and the second part of 'Everything Necessary'. These poems are so good I want to quote from them all, but one or two examples will have to do. Watch what happens in these lines from

'Open and Close'. The poet has just met her neighbour on an evening walk:

> Fine night, he says,
> breathless, and I say yes,
> and the frogs agree, and we all
> perform astonishing
> feats of levitation in the wavy light
>
> and then are set down neatly
> in our separate worlds.

The metaphor ('levitation' standing not only for the optical illusion, but also the emotional and spiritual experience of communion with the evening which the poet and her neighbour share momentarily and out of the blue) is surprising, beautiful, and in context, vivid; and moreover it is enacted beautifully in the verse, especially in the enjambment across the stanza break, so that the levitation, our imagining of it, is suspended between the stanzas. I can't read these lines without a physical sensation of delight. Or consider these opening lines of 'Playing Fair':

> Next, Michael and I walk the road to the Centre
> between new-mown fields to buy whiskey for us
>
> and greens for the ducks. Coffee and éclairs
> at the picnic table beside the gingko — ancient,
>
> long-lived — among other details make me weep.
> I go into the grocery for lettuce but can't
>
> get past the first line of a questionnaire:
> Do you think you need a new Centre?

Notice how each sentence leads up to something surprising; the surprises come over us subtly at first ('greens for the ducks'), then more dramatically and emotionally ('details make me weep'), until finally we're knocked out by that serious pun on 'Centre'. The lightness of touch here, combined with the poem's emotional and spiritual seriousness (for we soon learn the poet does think she needs a new Centre, and in fact is desperate for one), is moving, and very fine.

Cookshaw's next book, *Shameless* (2002), continues the achievement of the earlier, breakthrough collection, although not with the same rate of success. Of its thirty-five mostly personal lyrics, just nine meet the high standards of the best poems in *Double Somersaults*. These include 'The tiny silver luck of minnows', 'Genesis Again', 'Bruise', 'The Thumbprint of the Picker', 'Letter to a Husband Who's Moved Out', 'Chatelaine', 'When the Light Changed' and 'The Field'. Here is 'Elbow on Knee', one of my favourites:

Before all voyages by car, on the eve
of my sister's wedding, Good Fridays also,

my father prays with his family.
By the footstool of my mother's chair

he plucks his trouser crease
between fingers that know best machines,

and know them intimately, the way their souls
can be eased with gravity and grease,

and drops to one knee, seizing
the gaze of his daughters, who

can neither look nor look away. He drops
to one knee, his left, gives up

the trappings of this world.
His right hand cups his forehead.

I don't know what I am to do. My mother
has swept the hall and scrubbed the sink. Suitcases

are lined up by the car. If this
is Friday, it will be long, and what's ahead

unknowable. If my sister's getting married,
the fifty covered buttons of her gown are

perfect. Elbow on knee, that is how he prays,
drawing all light in the room

to the palm of his hand. When
he lowers his head, night falls.

This is well done. Notice the way Cookshaw begins with nonchalant allusions to three great though displaced archetypes or myths: the journey, the crucifixion, the wedding. The poem describes in present tense what could be happening on any one of these three domestic occasions, and we also soon gather that this is all happening in the poet's memory; the effect is to begin to lift the poem out of time, until by the end of it, with the magical or godlike father 'drawing all light in the room/to the palm of his hand', we're in a kind of poetic eternity. There's hardly a metaphor *per se* in the whole poem, and the diction barely strays from the ordinary, and yet by the end the whole thing resonates with myth: the death of Christ ('If this is Friday, it will be long, and what's ahead/unknowable'), the marriage of Jerusalem and the Lamb ('If my sister's getting married/the covered buttons on her gown are/perfect'), and God the creator dividing the darkness from the light ('drawing all light in the room/to the palm of his hand. When/he lowers his head, night falls'). Of course, it's just the poet's father praying by her mother's footstool, but Cookshaw's powers of suggestion here are marvellous. Her ability to turn autobiography into vision here, as in that moment of levitation in 'Open and Close', feels like a major development of her art.

Her most recent book, *Lunar Drift* (2005), is clearly intended to be a new departure. The first fifteen poems in the collection make up *Time's Arrow*, a series of lyrics mostly about human efforts to measure time with clocks and calendars. The poems are, for the most part, impersonal, and make use of some interesting historical material. Thus we learn about how the ancient Egyptians used the Nile as a kind of calendar, how Charlemagne received a gift of the Great Waterclock from Sultan Harun al-Rashid, Fifth Caliph of the Abbasid, and so forth. A few of the poems bring some personal experiences into play, though not usually very successfully;

one is left with the impression that all this would have been wonderful material for an erudite personal essay, but unfortunately it all seems much too willed for lyric poetry. I don't feel the kind of spiritual openness, the sense of there being something serious at stake for the poet in most of the *Time's Arrow* poems that I do in Cookshaw's strongest lyrics. The poet may be diagnosing the problem herself in one of the best poems in the book, entitled 'Farewell', which is included among the twenty-three other lyrics in the collection:

> I don't dream much of flying anymore. The technique
> that hurled me over hydro wires …
>
> …
>
> … proves less effective with the years.
>
> …
>
> …
>
> The gesture's more controlled,
> more willed, and deeply pleasing for that,
>
> though I regret it's not as high.

More willed indeed; but while the *Time's Arrow* poems may be 'deeply pleasing' to the writer, they aren't to the reader, at least not this reader. It's not that they are incompetent, or badly written; it's just that for the most part I don't sense the poet's emotional or spiritual investment, and so they leave me cold.

I am grateful, however, for the best of the other lyrics in *Lunar Drift*, since these are, I am pleased to say, among Cookshaw's most powerful poems to date. They include, besides the marvellous 'Farewell', the poems 'Redbreast', 'Brava', and 'The Hour'. I also like several other poems here a great deal; namely 'Blue-Eyed Grass,' 'Porch,' 'Le Cheval Blanc,' and 'The Dream of the River'. Let me close by quoting one of these poems in its entirety, an introspective lyric that, it turns out, expresses precisely what it is I find lacking in the *Time's Arrow* poems. The poem is called 'Brava':

> And if I give up, what
> then? Give up, I mean,

the shell of who
I think myself to be. The still

life.
    Ah, little one, wanting
to negotiate a scenic route, the right

to drive, wanting to know
what to pack:
        Nothing.

The barest sliver of yearning
goes forward, remakes you.

Nothing to do but look lovingly
at the upturned self,

kiss that uncomprehending
face goodbye.

This strikes me as recommending, and taking, the true path for Cookshaw's work, one of introspection, the dialogue of self and soul. The wisdom of this poem makes it the poet's most profound self-critique. The *Time's Arrow* poems, in my estimation, take the 'scenic route', and, insofar as they are willed, assert 'the right to drive'. Instead of packing the history of time, would they had packed nothing — as in this fine and haunting little poem.

☆

Karen Solie's Triple Vision

After a promising if uneven start, Karen Solie has been steadily turning herself, over the course of three collections, into a more and more wide-ranging and sophisticated poet, one who continually experiments with subjects, modes, rhetoric and diction. She is the author of satires, pastorals, elegies, philosophical poems, dramatic monologues, character studies, found poems, love poems, travel poems, and poems of sympathy for animals and other people. And yet much of her best work falls into, or combines, three dominant and complementary modes that, taken together, amount to a strongly ethical (and traditional) triple vision of the world, namely: sardonic satire of contemporary life; a balancing pastoral vision, or at any rate a clear-eyed respect for nature domesticated or wild; and, more recently, sympathy for other human beings, especially, as she affectionately calls them, 'losers' and 'unfortunates'. She uses diction of the kind that Wordsworth aspired to, writing poems, as he put it, 'in the real language of men', poems that eschew the corruptions of artificial poetic diction, that try out instead 'how the language of conversation in the middle and lower classes of society may be adapted to the purposes of poetic pleasure'. Her up-to-date idioms have earned her a reputation as a poetic hipster, and yet in her best work she often engages authoritatively with the poetry of the past.

The finest dozen poems in her first book, *Short Haul Engine* (2001), though considerably outnumbered by weaker ones, are, nevertheless, the work of a mature and confident poet. They include 'Thief', a wry fantasy about being a criminal; 'Dear Heart', a witty apostrophe to the poet's cardiac muscle; 'Real Life', a lovely epiphanic anti-epiphany poem that manages to have it both ways; a couple of fully imagined character studies called 'Roger the Shrubber' and 'The Only Living Half Boy'; and an exuberant dramatic monologue entitled 'A Treatise on the Evils of Modern Homeopathic Medicines'. (The other good ones are 'Sick', 'Ill Wind', 'Waking Up in Surgery', 'Alert Bay, Labour Day' and 'Java Shop, Fort McLeod'.)

Among these better poems is 'Sturgeon', a good confessional lyric (in the Catholic sense) about catching a fish. If you read this poem aloud you'll hear a subtle but clearly audible undercurrent of Old English verse, since the lines are well-stocked with alliterative pairs and triplets: 'River Runt', 'simple spoon', 'kin to caviar', 'ground glass' and so on. It's enough to remind one of *Beowulf,* which makes it an excellent choice of style for this fish-tale about a 'prehistoric' and monstrous creature with scales like rusty 'armour'. Here is the poem:

Jackfish and walleye circle like clouds as he strains
the silt floor of his pool, a lost lure in his lip,
Five of Diamonds, River Runt, Lazy Ike,
or a simple spoon, feeding
a slow disease of rust through his body's quiet armour.
Kin to caviar, he's an oily mudfish. Inedible.
Indelible. Ancient grunt of sea
in a warm prairie river, prehistory a third eye in his head.
He rests, and time passes as water and sand
through the long throat of him, in a hiss, as thoughts
of food. We take our guilts
to his valley and dump them in,
give him quicksilver to corrode his fins, weed killer,
gas oil mix, wrap him in poison arms.
Our bottom-feeder,
sin-eater.

On an afternoon mean as a hook we hauled him
up to his nightmare of us and laughed
at his ugliness, soft sucker mouth opening,
closing on air that must have felt like ground glass,
left him to die with disdain
for what we could not consume.
And when he began to heave and thrash over yards of rock
to the water's edge and, unbelievably, in,
we couldn't hold him though we were teenaged
and bigger than everything. Could not contain
the old current he had for a mind, its pull,
and his body a muscle called river, called spawn.

The 'lost lure' in the sturgeon's lip tips us off that the poem is a response to Elizabeth Bishop's widely anthologized poem 'The Fish', which is likewise about catching a fish that returns to the water, still alive, at the end of the poem. Both fish are old warriors: in Bishop's poem the fish has medals and weapons, in Solie's, armour. And both poems rely on biblical tropes, Bishop's from the Old Testament and Solie's from the New: Bishop alludes to the rainbow of Genesis — symbol of God's mercy in ending the flood and promising never to send another — precisely at the climactic moment when the speaker decides to throw the fish back into the water: 'everything / was rainbow, rainbow, rainbow! / And I let the fish go'. The 'victory' Bishop speaks of as 'fill[ing] up / the little rented boat' is two-fold; it refers both to her victory in catching the fish (and having mercy on it), and to the fish's victory in surviving. In Solie's poem, the sturgeon is Christ-like, a 'sin-eater' to whom people take their 'guilts', a 'prehistoric' fish (the fish being an ancient symbol of Christ) which, like Jesus, is mocked and left to die, only to return to the river miraculously to eat our sins again. And yet, in Solie's poem the victory is singular: it belongs to the fish alone; the one guilt he doesn't eat is the guilt of the teenagers (including the poet) who tried to kill him. Solie's fish is, moreover, also a kind of pagan river-god, with an 'old current' for a 'mind', 'his body a muscle called river'. This slippage from Christ to river god is a key to the poem; ultimately, the fish is more a symbol of the resilience of nature than anything else; the last word in the poem, 'spawn', refers not to resurrection or transcendence, but sexual rebirth.

Solie's command of literary tradition here is expansive and sure, and indeed allusiveness is one of the poem's chief strengths. I can't say I've ever heard this poet praised for her allusiveness; Carmine Starnino, her best critic to date, even goes so far as to suggest her motto could be 'screw precedent'. But I beg to differ; in fact, it turns out that allusiveness — or, to be more precise, an impulse to respond to particular poems from the past by alluding to and then revising them — is a recurring element in Solie's best work.

Her poem 'Roger the Shrubber', for example, also from *Short Haul Engine,* is evidently a sympathetic but distinctive response to Andrew Marvell's anti-pastoral lyric 'Damon the Mower'. Here is the poem:

> How contemptible, the lawns.
> These ridiculous plots, selfish little beds,
> the alarming stupidity of pansies staring

like nasty children dressed for church.
Hadn't he counseled, precisely, against this plum?
Shards of kitschy yard ornaments
are blood clots to the brain of his mower.

Disinclined to college, he told his parents
that out *there,* he can *really* think,
gestured vaguely toward a cool chlorophyll evening,
lilac-tinted air. And has done well,
owns the truck. How long has it been?
Years.
His knees are shot.

Mornings, now, before the heat and flies
he thinks of napalm in his Spray-Pac,
of laying the lot of it to gravel and shale,
shutting the mouth of the earth
once and for all.

Slugs foul his shoes.
Ants mine for his anklebones.
Russian Olives are profane with wasps.
He's had more thorns in his head than Christ.

Christ. He can't sleep.
Has been dreaming of graveyards,
How fir roots break through casket walls
To bear bones away on a creaking arboreal flood.
Of his wife's smooth young limbs
thickening, scabbing, twisting around him.
Of the baby in his pine crib,
face covered with leaves.

Let me take a moment to admire this poem's structure, a masterful sleight-of-hand. The first stanza is a feint; Roger's deftly dramatized annoyance here apparently concerns only his clients and their 'contemptible' lawns, their 'selfish' flowerbeds and 'kitschy lawn ornaments'; Roger comes across as a landscape artist who despises his customers' bad taste. By the third stanza, however, it's clear that his true antagonist is earthly nature itself. The flashback in the second stanza shows that he feels betrayed by nature; his initial desire to take up his calling springs from a romantic vision of a 'cool chlorophyll evening' and 'lilac-tinted air', but now, after some years on the job, '[h]is knees are shot', the insects and thorns are relentless, and by the final stanza the trees are invading his nightmares like a murderous 'arboreal flood'. Each stanza efficiently develops a new, essential and, in retrospect, inevitable stage in Roger's case history, and yet by means of her initial feint, Solie manages to make each of these stages feel surprising.

Both 'Damon the Mower' and 'Roger the Shrubber' are, as I say, antipastorals. Damon, as a mower, is a self-conscious rival of the shepherds who boasts, 'though in wool more poor than they,/Yet am I richer far in hay.' And given the pastoral imagery associated with Jesus (the Good Shepherd, the Lamb of God), this rivalry makes Damon, whose name sounds a lot like 'demon', a kind of displaced anti-Christ, a sort of Grim Reaper who carries a scythe for 'Depopulating all the ground'. As Marvell puts it in his poem's closing line, 'Death thou art a Mower too.' All this should help us see that the references to Christ in Solie's poem ('He's had more thorns in his head than Christ') are ironic, since, like Damon, Roger is also a kind of Grim Reaper, with his Spray-Pac full of (imaginary) napalm, and his desire to 'lay … the lot of it to gravel and shale,/shutting the mouth of the earth/once and for all.' If anything, Roger is even more demonic than Damon, both in motivation and intent. Whereas Damon's desire to mow down the grass springs from his despair at finding his love for Julia unrequited (as Damon puts it in a companion poem called 'The Mower's Song', 'she/What I do to the grass, does to my thoughts and me'), Roger the Shrubber's more radical desire to wipe out all vegetation forever springs from a kind of madness, a paranoid terror at nature's resiliency. The impulse to destroy nature, Solie is suggesting, springs ultimately from our fear of nature, which, as her final stanza indicates, is ultimately a fear of death. This strikes me as a brilliant psychological insight, one that helps explain our difficulty as a species in restraining our destructive impulse with regard to natural things. This makes Solie's poem political in a rare way; instead of merely taking a side, it contributes a genuine insight.

As with many first books, however, the best poems in *Short Haul Engine* are, alas, not representative of the volume as a whole. Solie's main weakness in her early work is a limited rhetorical range; she relies too much on certain stylistic clichés of contemporary poetry, including sentence fragments, the address to the self as 'you', and the present tense narrative. There is nothing inherently wrong with any of these techniques in themselves, but their overuse is tiresome. Some forty poems in her first book strike me as apprentice work: poem after poem about trysts and road-trips, guns and whisky, beer parlours and cheap motels, most of them suffering from rhetorical monotony, a lack of syntactical energy, and an overall shaky grasp of technique. Several seem to concern a variety of characters, but it's often hard to tell: the voice hardly changes, the settings blur together, the characters appear as vague pronouns: 'he', 'she', 'you' and 'I'. And many suffer, moreover, from a certain tedious self-absorption and sentimentality, notwithstanding the poems' hardboiled ironic poses. Here's a representative example which, while it avoids some of the pitfalls I've been describing, still isn't a fully realized poem:

Anniversary

It was the summer some rank fever weed
sunk her bitch hooks in, sowed my skin
to itch and ooze, that we shared a bed
for the first time. It's not so bad,
you said, looking for a clean place
to put your hands while I stuck to the sheets
and stunk up the room with creams
and salves. You didn't cringe,
(though in those days my back was often turned)
took your showers at the usual time, rose,
a bank of muscled cloud above
my poisoned field, and blew cool
across the mess. I said, eyes shining
with antihistamines, that you were potent
as a rare bird sighting, twenty on the sidewalk,
straight flush. It was only falling
into sleep that your body twitched away
from mine, a little more each time
I'd scratch, and I knew then we were made

for each other, that you lie as well as me,
my faithful drug, my perfect match.

This poem has its virtues, including clear images and a certain rhythmic tautness deriving from all those metrically overstressed monosyllables: 'some rank fever weed/sunk her bitch hooks in.' But signs of artistic immaturity are everywhere. For one thing, the poet seems not entirely in control of the syntax. Consider the sentence, 'I said, eyes shining/with antihistamines, that you were potent/as a rare bird sighting, twenty on the sidewalk,/straight flush.' I'm guessing she means 'potent as sighting a rare bird, finding a twenty on the sidewalk, drawing a straight flush'; but without some such syntactical parallelism what the sentence actually says is he's potent as sighting twenty rare birds on the sidewalk, adding that these twenty birds are a (five-card) straight flush. The central metaphors in the poem ('a bank of muscled cloud above/my poisoned field') strike me as grandiose in this context, suggesting as they do sky god and earth goddess. Moreover, do antihistamines really make your eyes shine? Not, alas, in my experience; Solie seems to be saying something that's not true here for the sake of the lyrical effect. And finally, the poem climaxes with a couple of ragworn romantic clichés: 'we were made for each other,' 'my perfect match'. Solie's critics have often described her poems in this mode as 'tough' and 'unsentimental', and you can see why; 'Anniversary' is a love poem in which the speaker describes herself as afflicted with an unpleasant rash; she calls the weed she caught it from a 'bitch', and her lover a 'drug' and a 'straight flush', and adds that what makes the two lovers perfect for each other is that they are both liars. Hard-boiled stuff, surely. But on another level, the level of the imagination, isn't the poem saying the lover is a sky god and the speaker an earth goddess, and thus they're a 'perfect match', they're 'made for each other'? On the surface the poem is tough. Below the surface it's soft as feathers. In short, the *film noir* diction is a pose.

Moreover, *Short Haul Engine* is overloaded with epigraphs, fourteen in all and sometimes more than one per poem. (One epigraph is a dictionary definition of 'homeopathy'.) And there are even a couple of gaffes in usage that ought to have been caught by her editor: the poet writes 'hung himself' when she means 'hanged himself,' and 'Ice lays low' when she means it lies low. But the main problem is the book's preponderance of weak poems.

* * *

What a pleasure and relief it is then to turn to *Modern and Normal* (2005), Solie's second collection, and find a much better book. This volume expands her generic and rhetorical range considerably, and includes many more successful poems: out of fifty-two, some two dozen are very good, and a few others come close. She does offer up some more hard-boiled romances, I'm afraid, though fortunately their technique is better now. And a few of her love poems even manage, in the best tradition of love poetry, to turn her subject into conceits, and are consequently much more promising and interesting. These include 'Love Song of the Unreliable Narrator', 'Emergency Response', and 'Larking'. Another good one is 'Sleeping with Wittgenstein'; the key difference between it and Solie's earlier poems on this theme, like 'Anniversary', is that the lover is for once fully imagined, not just an anonymous cipher. That he is, as the title indicates, imaginary, or metaphorical, seems to have a lot to do with the poem's success. As for the weaker poems in this line, it is heartening to find that Solie at least provides an incisive self-critique in the closing lines of one of them, a poem called 'Your Premiums Will Never Increase':

> Sure, here was the trouble
> all along. Some things don't turn out for the best,
> and are not even interesting. Forget them.

Amen to that; not interesting, that is, unless transformed successfully by the imagination, as in the handful of love poems I've named above. My heart sinks, however, when I read the lines that follow:

> Forget them. Because
> this is about you, and what happens next.

No, no, I splutter, it's not about *you!* In fact, the problem with much mediocre confessional poetry is precisely this kind of solipsism; it thinks that what matters is the poet, when what really matters is the poem.

Fortunately, in some of the best poems in the book, we can hear Solie's *noir*ish posing maturing into a sardonic and satirical vision of contemporary life that reminds me of Michael Hofmann, a contemporary English poet of roughly the same generation. (Hofmann was born in 1957, Solie in 1966.) For comparison, here's a stanza by Solie, from a marvellous poem called 'Chance':

> Theory grins like a rat and won't flip. Gives up only that nothing
> is forbidden: time backpedalling toward the great divide
> and air haywiring out of the room
> altogether, weird as a cat. Whatever.

And here's a stanza by Hofmann, from 'Summer', a poem in his collection *Approximately Nowhere* (1999):

> The London plane tree by my window
> hangs its green leatherette sleeves, exhausted by a hard May.
> My varsity jacket. The sky between leaves is the brightest
>   thing in nature,
> Virginia Woolf told the inquiring Rupert Brooke. Whatever.

The similarity in these poet's attitudes is crystallized by that final 'Whatever' in each case: what they both dismiss, or seem to dismiss, is something they've read, whether postmodern theory or High Modernist aesthetics. Each prefers his or her own lived experience, which is the real strength of the confessional mode; it is what gives such poetry its vividness and emotional intensity. The danger is that the experience can be too narrow, or its treatment too narcissistic; the subject of the one homage poem in *Short Haul Engine* is Anne Sexton — in my opinion rather too solipsistic a figure to serve as a good model for a young confessional poet — and I suspect Sexton's influence may have had something to do with the weaknesses of Solie's first book. However, in her second collection, Solie seems to be in the process of transferring her allegiance from Sexton to Hofmann, whose larger satirical mode owes much, in turn, to the example of Robert Lowell.

The triumph of this satirical mode in *Modern and Normal* can be seen in poems like 'Mirror', 'Montana', 'English Bay' — and, especially, 'Cardio Room, Young Women's Christian Association', which I quote here in full:

> You won't know me. Any resemblance
> to the woman I was is purely
> agricultural. That fluff. A pink annual

given to low-born intemperate acts
unbecoming a modern person. No more.
I'm tough. Nothing
could eat me. No profligate billy
with a hacking cough, or that old goat
and his yen for plagues, floods, and burning
fun places to the ground. Not you,
either. There was a time
I rolled like dough, plumped up
to be thumped down with artless yeasty
chemistry. Dumpling. Honeybun.
I sickened some. But evolved
in a flash, like the living flak
of a nuclear mistake. In space-age fabrics
I've moved more iron than a red
blood cell, climbing and climbing
the new world's dumbest tower. I'm on
to this. Alongside the rest
I sweat it out with the smug one-party
affability of a sport utility
vehicle. Deceptively little cargo space.
Even covered in mud I look great.

This is very good satire. One of the things that makes it good is that it's so sympathetic to the fantasy of self-transformation that it skewers. Consider the multiple layers of anxiety it expresses. First, region and class: the speaker is trying to throw off her former identity as an 'agricultural', 'intemperate', and 'low-born' person and become someone who is 'modern', that is, urban and middle-class, 'modern and normal' in the words of the book's title. Second, gender: she resents being condescended to as a 'dumpling' and 'honeybun' by 'profligate billy[s]' and 'old goat[s]' alike, but now that she's gotten tough she will suffer this humiliation no longer. The third anxiety is sexual; in her past love affairs, she's been 'plumped up/to be thumped down with artless yeasty/chemistry', but now, presumably because of her increased sexual prowess, 'Nothing/could eat me.' And finally, there's her religious anxiety: she's beyond, or longs to be beyond, the reach of God, that censorious 'old goat/with his yen for plagues, floods, and burning/fun places to the ground.' Who among us moderns hasn't had some or all of these same desires? We're on her side. And yet Solie's metaphors knock the Stairmaster out from under us. The speaker's on fire, but she's 'a nuclear mistake'. Far from being an individual, she finds herself a mere 'red/blood cell' '[a]longside the rest', a member of a 'smug one-party' state of strivers. Instead of climbing a stairway to heaven, she's 'climbing and climbing/the new world's dumbest tower.' And her body is a mere 'sport utility/vehicle'; that is, not only a machine whose main purpose is merely to 'look great', but, to read her puns, a vehicle of utilitarianism imagined as a sport — or, to unpack this a little, she's just a consumer in the world of transformational advertising, the smug one-party system of capitalism. She has entered an empty, even nihilistic world, and this suggests in retrospect a more ironic way of reading the sentence 'Nothing/could eat me': Nothingness could eat her, indeed. In an age so ripe for satire as ours, I have sometimes wondered why satire is not a more prominent mode in modern poetry, and the answer seems to be that our poets are so busy dramatizing themselves and their own transformations of identity that they too often lack the self-irony necessary to satirize their own desires. But this poem does it brilliantly.

Solie's word 'agricultural' in the third line suggests an alternative to the urban world the poem satirizes — and this brings me to the other significant development in *Modern and Normal*: an expanded engagement with humanized nature, a fuller pastoral counterweight to the poet's developing satirical vision of contemporary life. The best poems of this type here are 'Parallax', 'Pastoral', 'Thrasher', 'Thanksgiving', 'Under the Sun' and 'Lines Composed a Few Miles Above Duncairn Dam'. Here is the latter:

The reservoir is fed by Swift Current Creek. It's small,
a half mile by six, and has the itch going for it. Snail flukes
can't feed on people but they try. The fishing's good.
It's stocked.

On the north side, squatters' cabins and planted
shade trees. Further up is the dump. Burn pit, fish guts,
trash. Recall the neighbours. You can't just do
whatever you want. There are certain kinds
of boating. Gull Lake's close. We all drive.

On the south side are bluffs, and cows meant
for beef. There are dens in the few wild groves. Muskrats
like thin old men who've made machine shops
in their living rooms. Coyotes too. It's not a great idea
to keep chickens.

There's a rumour. A pipeline leak below the lakebed
and natural gas bubbles the size of apricots popping
at the surface. This may or may not be true,
as usual.

Simmie, adjacent, was a town once. The little plank church
makes a good photograph. Someone's junk is in it.

The store, next to the beverage room, sells smokes
and low-end booze, rat traps, potato wedges, shampoo,
Raid, ice cream, cribbage boards, Crazy Glue,
buffalo wings, rubber gloves, line and lures,
etc. Leeches can be purchased from the pop machine
outside, a half-dozen for $1.25. A sweet life:
Coke, Seven-up, water, bait. You could walk from the lake
but no one does.

To follow a sightline over the fields is a long, long
look. Wind has a good time there. Your eye
will tear over and close.

I write this on a plane, two days before
the 100th anniversary of flight, 37,000 feet above
Lake Ontario. Above the cloud above Lake Ontario.

The master-text of this poem is clearly Wordsworth's great Romantic lyric, 'Lines Composed a Few Miles Above Tintern Abbey, on Revisiting the Banks of the Wye During a Tour July 13, 1798'. Besides the allusion in her title, Solie has sown her lines with references to Wordsworth's poem: her squatters' cabins and shade trees recall Wordsworth's cottages and copses, for instance. Swift Current Creek suggests Wordsworth's River Wye. And the picturesque little plank church, defunct and full of 'someone's junk', recalls Wordsworth's ruined Tintern Abbey. Both empty churches, moreover, suggest a loss of Christian faith. Wordsworth's faith has been replaced by Nature worship, Solie's by nothing, apparently; that is, until we come to her declaration that 'Wind has a good time there'. The wind is an ancient symbol of the divine, and in this context Solie's personified wind recalls momentarily the divine wind in that quintessential Saskatchewan novel *Who Has Seen the Wind,* not to mention the displaced wind of the English Romantic imagination. Which helps explain why, in response to this wind, 'Your eye / will tear over and close'.

The main parallel between the two poems has to do with the attitude of both poets toward the pastoral landscape they describe. (Wordsworth uses the word 'pastoral' twice; and strictly speaking in Solie's case the proper word would be 'bucolic', given the grazing 'cows meant for beef'.) Wordsworth is concerned with what he owes to his memory of the place — in short, pleasure, serenity, vision, and acts of kindness — and Solie likewise recognizes what she owes to her home place, although she is far less explicit; indeed, our understanding of this depends largely on our seeing the parallels with Wordsworth's poem. The key echo here is the word 'sweet': Wordsworth says the landscape gives him 'sensations sweet', and Solie describes the 'sweet life' of her home place. And just as Wordsworth says that 'in lonely rooms, and mid the din / Of towns and cities' he returns in memory to the Wye for spiritual 'restoration', so Solie returns in memory to this bucolic reservoir of sweet life while flying in an airplane above cloudy Lake Ontario.

But Solie's poem feels far more desolate than Wordsworth's. For one thing, Wordsworth has his beloved sister with him, but Solie is alone; in her memory she speaks of 'we', but in the present, 'I'. Moreover, in 'Tintern Abbey' the speaker is actually standing in the pastoral landscape, whereas in Solie's she is far away, not only thousands of miles to the east, but, in a brilliant pun on a preposition, miles above in an airplane: the very difference between 'above' in Wordsworth's sense ('A Few Miles Above Tintern Abbey') and 'above' in Solie's serves to emphasize how far away she is from her bucolic world. This is made clear throughout the poem, as well, for whereas in 'Tintern Abbey' nature is wholly good, trustworthy and unharmed, in Solie's poem it is both mildly threatening (with its coyotes, itch and hungry snail flukes) and possibly threatened (with its dump and rumoured gas leak).

Solie achieves still another effect of distance by mentioning that she is writing two days before the hundredth anniversary of flight; literally, it is one hundred years since the Wright brothers, but figuratively — that is, psychologically — it feels like a hundred years since the speaker's flight from Saskatchewan. Still, she is present in her bucolic landscape in memory and imagination; this is made obvious by the vividness of the poem's description of the place, and in another serious pun: Solie 'write[s] this on a plane', but in her imagination she is still back in Saskatchewan, 'on a plain', as it were, and her poem is the incontrovertible evidence of that.

This brings me to what is probably Solie's finest poem to date, another Saskatchewan nature poem called 'Thrasher'. It takes its place not so much in the pastoral tradition (though there is an element of the georgic in it, the poetry of farming) as in the newer tradition of the thing-poem, that is, the kind of careful study of a single object or animal familiar to us from the work of Rilke, Francis Ponge, D. H. Lawrence, Marianne Moore and, closer to home, Eric Ormsby. As for style, it's the language of Ormsby, with its virtuosic sound effects, that seems closest to Solie's method here:

Yellow-legs ekes lower at nightfall to a stick nest
brambled in the shade-kill, doing for himself, deft

as a badger in a hammock. Mornings, toeing wracked heights
of the cottonwood, he flaps his brown flag above alkaline

slough beds, over plowlands attesting
to the back and forth of work, their brown degrees

scriven by road allowance cut at right angles through shriven
weeds, fenceposts bracketing brown rut lines slantwise

in relief. In relief at the topmost, he mimics domestic, migrant,
spaniel, spring peepers, quacks, urks, and gurgles akin

to a four-stroke in heavy water. He's slightly

off. None respond. His own call is the vinyl scratch
between tracks, a splice point. He was hatched

that way, ferruginous, a wet transistor
clacking from the egg in which he had lain curled

as an ear with an itch inside. He carries on
like AM radio. Like a prison rodeo. Recounts loser

baseball teams, jerry-riggers, part-timers, those paid in scrip,
anyone who has come out of retirement once

too often. He is playbacks, do-overs, repeats, repeats
the world's clamorous list, makes it his, replete,

and fledges from persistence what he is.

There's so much to love about this poem: the continually surprising images in their rhythmically apposite clauses, the subtle and complex sound effects, the relaxed but effective prosody, the beautifully folded syntax of the final line. The sound effects are especially strong: like its precursor 'Sturgeon', from Solie's first book, this poem echoes Old English verse, although this time the echoes inhere not only in alliterative pairs, but also in the liberal use of assonance, consonance, internal rhymes and off-rhymes, and metrical overstressing, all of which makes the poem a delicious pleasure to read aloud. (It isn't hard to hear Hopkins's 'Windhover' hovering in the background, though Solie's diction is very different.) It's so well done, in fact, that it makes me wonder why Solie doesn't write with this much aural intensity more often.

In the traditional thing-poem, the object is often transformed by means of tropes into something else, but here the metaphors proliferate wonderfully: the bird is a badger, a flag, a spaniel, spring peepers, a duck, an outboard motor, a scratchy vinyl record, a transistor radio, and so on, and every one of these metaphors is perfectly apt. Moreover, the poem engages with a great tradition of lyrics about birds, in which the bird, because it both sings and soars, is usually an emblem of the poet. ('Bethou me,' says Shelley to the skylark.) In other words, the unstated but evident conceit in 'Thrasher' is that the poet identifies with this bird, with his sympathy for losers, his persistence, and his promiscuous skill in mimicking other singers both domestic and migrant, though always 'slightly off'. For this reason the poem is also a marvellous *ars poetica*, and, paradoxically, more revealing of this poet as poet than any of Solie's more obviously autobiographical lyrics. Speaking of mimicking other singers: it's not just the sound-effects and the thing-poem mode which apparently derive from Ormsby here. 'Thrasher' also reads in particular like a response to Ormsby's poem 'Grackle', from his second collection, *Coastlines* (1992):

> He has an acrid cackle,
> a cacophony of slick and klaxon cries,
> with tinsel whispers like a breathy flute.
> His repertoire seems meant to flatter
> us by mimicry....

Both birds mimic human beings, and are described doing so in delightfully onomatopoeic language. But whereas Ormsby's bird mimics us in order to 'flatter/us' and 'exonerate our ... faults' (with, moreover, an ulterior motive: greedy hunger), Solie's thrasher mimics us out of sympathy, a kind of fellow-feeling for 'loser baseball teams' and 'jerry-riggers', a sympathy that will become more pronounced in Solie's next book.

One other new and welcome development in *Modern and Normal* is Solie's experimentation with diction and rhetoric in a series of found poems. The best of these are 'Found: One Easy Lesson', 'Found: Problems (A Meditation)', 'Found: Elementary Calculus', and 'Found: Publications in Natural History'. The rhetorical resources she discovers in these poems give her, in turn, new rhetorical possibilities for still more successful poems that make use of the language of specialized discourses, notably 'Bomb Threat Checklist' and 'Self-Portrait in a Series of Professional Evaluations', as well as a couple of philosophical poems that make use of specialized mathematical language, including the above-mentioned 'Chance', and 'Cipher Stroke', a remarkable sequence on the subject of nothingness. I should add that *Modern and Normal* also includes a remarkable visionary poem called 'Meeting Walter Benjamin', a couple of fine poems with questionable endings, namely 'Determinism' and 'The Bench', and a mostly very strong sequence called 'The Apartments' which, unfortunately, has a few weak sections that would have been better left on the cutting room floor.

The best poems in Solie's third and most recent collection, *Pigeon* (2009), provide more evidence of her ever-expanding range. They include travel poems ('Erie' and 'Medicine Hat Calgary One-Way'), pastorals and georgics ('Postscript', 'Geranium' and 'Bone Creek'), a vivid love poem called 'Casa Mendoza', an oblique and moving elegy entitled 'Migration', a sardonic satire on a high-school reunion ('The Girls'), and, surprisingly for this poet, a remarkable religious poem: 'An Acolyte Reads *The Cloud of Unknowing*'. Here is the latter:

Aspiring, not to emptiness, but to continually empty
one's self as a stream pours into a larger body
what it receives from the watershed — how midway
it carves a bed in this life, a clarity of purpose —
never ends. Simone Weil starves herself to death
again and again in London while the great mystery
appears to me as through a pinhole camera: reduced,
inverted, harmless. It's hard to concentrate, living
between Fire Station 426 and the Catholic hospital,
though the man shouting on the steps of the drop-in centre
appears, as much as anyone could, to be heroically
wrestling himself free from reality, his pain the soul's pain
in knowing it exists. I have dissolved
like an aspirin in water watching a bee walk into
the foyer of a trumpet flower, in the momentary
solace of what has nothing to do with me, brief
harmony of particulars in their separate orbits,
before returning to my name, to memory's warehouse
and fleet of specialized vehicles, the heart's
repetitive stress fractures, faulty logic, its stupid
porchlight. If virtue is love ordered and controlled,
its wild enemy has made a home in me. And if
desire injures the spirit, I am afflicted. Rehearsing
philosophy's different temperaments — sanguine, contrary,
nervous, alien — one finds a great deal to fear.
A lake-effect snowstorm bypasses the ski hills,
knocks the power out of some innocent milltown.
The world chooses for us what we can't, or won't.

What makes this interesting as a religious poem is that it is both epiphanic and agonistic, that is, it is concerned with both momentary spiritual fulfilment and spiritual struggle. The agonistic elements of the poem are full of allusions to religious poems, from Dante's *Inferno* ('how midway it carves a bed in this life') to John Donne's late sonnet beginning 'Batter my heart, three person'd God' ('its wild enemy has made a home in me'). I am particularly taken with the dark humour in this part of the poem: the four temperaments of ancient physiology (sanguine, choleric, phlegmatic, melancholic) become four modern analogues ('sanguine, contrary,/nervous, alien') and this knowledge produces not the consolation of philosophy but 'a great deal to fear'. The humour comes in the series of little surprises as one reads, the darkness in the import of what is being said.

The speaker says that 'Aspiring ... never ends', and yet she sounds more resigned to her spiritual affliction than she is filled with any fervent zeal for religious transformation. Nevertheless, she does have a religious experience in this poem. The epiphany comes in the middle, and is described, beautifully and convincingly, in past tense:

> I have dissolved
> like an aspirin in water watching a bee walk into
> the foyer of a trumpet flower, in the momentary
> solace of what has nothing to do with me, brief
> harmony of particulars in their separate orbits....

The bee and the flower are natural, and for that reason they recall Solie's pastorals; but they also allude to Dante's vision of heaven in the *Paradiso* as both a beehive and a flower, with the added touch that Solie's flower is not a rose as in Dante but a trumpet flower, which recalls the last trumpet of the Book of Revelation. The significance of this epiphany comes in the next clause, where the speaker calls the experience 'the momentary solace of what has nothing to do with me'. This is the exact opposite of the impulse that drives the self-dramatizing confessional poet, of the kind who says to herself, 'this is about you, and what happens next'. The poet's selfhood 'dissolve[s]/ like an aspirin in water' precisely at the moment of greatest spiritual intensity.

An ethical counterpart to this poem may be found in a memorable travelogue called 'Medicine Hat Calgary One-Way', also from *Pigeon*. The

poem succeeds better than any of Solie's earlier prairie-*noir* road-trip poems
by turning the journey into a kind of light and loose allegory of human life.
Here is the poem:

The bus is a wreck, and passengers
respect that, a mild unease aboard
this have-not province
with its per-capita demographic representation
of unfortunates, poor-earners, procrastinators,
the criminal element, hammering away
at the dullest stretch of highway
on earth. Local industrial calamities,
unmistakable turquoise PVC of the deadly prairie
waterslide, tractor-trailers, poorly tied
private loads, all of it
ill-used and ugly in early spring,
though bright hawks balance on warming
updrafts, and a young sun tosses its jewelry across
tabletops of Ducks Unlimited wetlands
fed by a late snow. Your lives are neither
before nor behind you. In the limitless
present of schedule 0063, you embrace
secret multitudes. Suffield, Brooks, Gleichen,
Bassano, Strathmore, taking on
packages, grey water of smoke
breaks, in eyeshot now of the Purcell Range
and into subdivisions named, it seems,
out of malice, grief, or confusion, and perfunctorily
treed. Walk-in closets and walk-
out basements march forth in staggered
plans. Oldies stations. Man-made
lakes. Strip malls and big box stores whose
faces regard with solemn appreciation
the shifting congress of late-model vehicles
that attends them. Skyline
sunk in a brown fog. The zoo. *Dow Chemical
Corp. is devoted to fostering community*

leadership. Downtown deserted as the coda
to biological disaster. Then
the purgatorial boredom
of the Greyhound depot. Beige food, beer
in cans, between a Toyota
dealership and nowhere you'd want
to walk. As you leave with your bags,
hire a taxi for the airport, is it not possible
to look with love upon your fellow travellers?
Theirs is the infinite patience born of reliance
on mass transit. They wear
the arrows of their circumstance
like Saint Sebastian. Night's mountain passes,
hallucinatory tundra, its aches,
dark thoughts, anticipations
belong to them, queuing at the steel door
to the brutal asphyxiant garage. You've been
often in this company, together
resembling survivors of an apartment fire, or,
despite the odd hidden flask, children, carrying pillows
before you, a destination to live up to
in the only way you can afford.

The Hofmannesque satirical wit is here ('subdivisions named, it seems, / out
of malice, grief, or confusion'), and so is Solie's pastoral vision ('bright hawks
balance on warming / updrafts, and a young sun tosses its jewelry
across / tabletops of Ducks Unlimited wetlands / fed by a late snow'). ('Pastoral' isn't quite the right word, though, is it; we need a new word for the
poetry of wildlife conservation.) But a third, ethical dimension — human
sympathy — comes in when the speaker asks, in what feels like a breakthrough for this poet, 'is it not possible / to look with love upon your fellow
travellers?' This is the Christian ethical imperative posed as a rhetorical
question, and it reminds me of a similar impulse of sympathy for 'unfortunates, poor earners, procrastinators, / the criminal element' that one finds
in the poetry of James Wright and Philip Levine. There's a related allusion to
Walt Whitman's open-heartedness — 'In the limitless / present of schedule
0063, you embrace / secret multitudes' — and indeed, despite its short lines,

the poem's main rhetorical method of wonderfully surprising disjunctive lists also reminds me of Whitman. The significance of this poem in Solie's development is that it returns to the scene of the weaker poems in her first book, the low-life road-trip world of the prairie, but replaces the hardboiled diction and self-dramatizing rhetoric of those early poems with a mature mixture of the sardonic, the pastoral, and the sympathetic that does justice to the people and the place.

As so often in Solie's best work, this poem too appears to be a revisionary response to an earlier poem. This time it's Daryl Hine's 1962 poem about crossing the plains by bus, entitled 'Plain Fare'. The key allusion occurs in Solie's last line ('in the only way you can afford'), which echoes Hine's ending ('The way that I could not afford to go'). Once we recognize the allusion, it soon becomes clear that Solie's revision is total and exact: for whereas Hine hardly notices the landscape and fairly dismisses the other passengers, preferring to spend the journey reading a novel instead, Solie's poem is, as I've shown, precisely about observing the world outside her window, and empathizing with her fellow travellers.

Of the thirty-nine poems in Pigeon, besides the nine very good ones I've mentioned, another seven are fine except for some small but serious flaw, often in the final line, as in 'The Cleaners', 'Parasitology', 'Archive', 'Wager', 'Prayers for the Sick' and 'Meditation on Seaforth'. The lines in question are brow-furrowing disappointments, coming as they do at the ends of such otherwise excellent poems. The problems include the usual suspects in dud endings: flatness ('still wearing our hospital wristbands'), vagueness ('what has been rediscovered' and 'the character of the new day emerges'), and clichés ('his one chance on this earth' and, worse, 'a singer/whose songs have inspired generations/and who is a national treasure'). In 'Archive', which is both a very interesting prose poem and a kind of mystery story, Solie introduces a red-herring (or is this who done it? who knows?) at the end; some readers may find this cleverly 'open-ended', but it leaves me feeling tricked. And in one poem, 'The Ex-Lovers', there's another single false phrase, though this time not in the last line: one sentence describing the ex-lovers — 'they have mathematical/implications' — strikes me as vague to the point of meaninglessness; what doesn't have mathematical implications? Here's hoping Solie revisits these poems in the future, since a few brief but strong revisions would nearly double the count of excellent poems in the book. (I would be remiss, however, if I didn't acknowledge that *Pigeon* also contains one truly bad poem, a long sequence called 'Norway' which amounts to a disjointed mess.)

It is a pleasure, despite such caveats, to follow Solie's development from book to book, to observe her increasing technical command, her spiritual self-overcoming. What I long for is to see her incorporate the high technical virtuosity she achieves in 'Thrasher' and perhaps a few other poems more fully into the main stream of her development, in much the same way that she brings the other tributaries of her work together (satire, pastoral, human sympathy, and the impulse to respond to others' poems) in 'Medicine Hat Calgary One-Way'. Her development has been dangerous from the beginning; each of her three books has been received with tremendous enthusiasm in the small pond of Canadian poetry, and in such an environment it can be very difficult for a poet to recognize her shortcomings and overcome them. That Solie is managing to do so anyway bodes well for her, and especially for us.

Eric Ormsby:

Sympathetic Magic and the Chameleon Poet

Eric Ormsby had an epic apprenticeship. He began writing poetry in the summer of 1958, when he was seventeen years old, but didn't publish a single poem until twenty-seven years later, when two of his lyrics finally debuted in the New York journal *Chelsea*. He was almost fifty by the time his first book appeared. And as you might expect, this long struggle in obscurity left its mark on his work. His first collection, *Bavarian Shrine and other poems* (1990), is palpably the work of a middle-aged man; the poems suggest that Ormsby saw himself by then as a kind of posthumous poet, a Lazarus resurrected after an imaginative death. *Bavarian Shrine* is also one of the finest poetic debuts ever published in Canada.

Remarkably, Ormsby didn't begin submitting his poems to journals until a year or so before that first appearance in *Chelsea* in 1985. He must have known he wasn't ready to publish before then. In any case, the available evidence suggests the poetry he wrote in his twenties and perhaps even his thirties was not very good. In an illuminating interview with Carmine Starnino published in 2002, he explains, 'in my twenties ... I lacked the discipline and the restraint necessary for creating a fully finished poem. I wrote wildly.' And sure enough, though it is unclear when he wrote them, the handful of 'Uncollected Poems: 1958–2006' which appear in Ormsby's most recent summation, *Time's Covenant: Selected Poems* (2006), are, frankly, embarrassing. It would have been much better to leave them in the drawer, though a few do contain hints of much finer things to come.

If you're wondering what Ormsby was doing for all those years, I assure you he was no idle apprentice. After a Southern Gothic childhood in Florida (which he has described memorably in a brief memoir called 'The Place of Shakespeare in a House of Pain'), Ormsby set about acquiring an extraordinary education and, in particular, investing his talent for languages. He learned French as a teenager, majored in ancient Greek and Latin at Columbia University, and graduated from the University of Pennsylvania in

Oriental Studies — Arabic and Turkish — in 1971. That date would have made him about thirty when he earned his B.A., which suggests a sojourn in the wilderness, or at any rate a biographical lacuna in his early twenties about which Ormsby has publicly said and written almost nothing. Three graduate degrees followed: a master's in library science from Rutgers, and an M.A. and Ph.D. in Near Eastern studies from Princeton, where he specialized in medieval theology and philosophy and studied classical Arabic and Persian, both language and literature. During this period he worked as bibliographer and later curator of the Near East Collections at the Princeton University Library. He also studied Semitic philology and Islamic theology and philosophy at Tübingen University in Germany, and learned Italian, Spanish and German in order to read the poetry of those great traditions. In his interview with Starnino he says that these studies gave him, among other things, 'the odd sensation at times that English was rather an impoverished language and, quite definitely, that too much contemporary poetry in English was paltry and anorexic.'

The nature of Ormsby's imaginative 'death' we may only guess, based on a few hints in this same interview: he speaks of a 'failed marriage', of ceasing at some point to practice as a Catholic — Ormsby had converted to Catholicism many years earlier — and of the sudden death in 1982 of a very good friend of his, a fellow poet who had got him started writing poetry. The precise timing of Ormsby's crisis is a subject for his biographers, but it seems likely that it occurred sometime in the mid-1980s when the poet was in his forties, and that it had both spiritual and emotional implications.

In any case, what most concerns us as readers of his poetry is what Ormsby calls the 'reluctant ... resurrection' that followed. He says the turning point came when, sometime in the mid-to-late 1980s, he wrote a sequence of six poems on the subject of the resurrected Lazarus, a sequence he 'immediately recognized as good'. These remarkable poems adopt the character of Lazarus as an alter-ego or mask, not unlike the Crazy Jane lyrics of the late Yeats, or the Mr. Cogito poems of Zbigniew Herbert.

There was, however, unless I'm mistaken, a still earlier breakthrough poem, one which prepared the imaginative field not only for Lazarus's rather startling appearance, but for much of Ormsby's poetry since. I'm referring to one of those two debut poems Ormsby published in Chelsea in

1985, and the only one of these to make the cut for his first book. The poem, entitled 'Fetish', seems to be a direct response to the spiritual and emotional crisis of which I speak:

After we came home from the Exhibition,
I felt drawn to make a figure out of wood.
I took a bulgy anonymous chunk, with bark
Attached and gummy tears near the frequent knots.
First I hacked and chopped; and anger
Somehow welled up, impelled my hands.
But the rough bristling form emerged:

Its hands were fingerless fists,
Its feet were lopped blocks.
Gently I gouged its bellybutton out and then
The face took its terrible shape —
That knobby lumb of grieving watchfulness.
I suggested breasts and nipples
With red pegs. But then, as though instructed,
I modeled a fierce priapic flare,
Instinct with secret seed, double as snail-sex.

But the mouth's awe
Oppressed me — that torn place that prayed ...
Upstairs I heard dinner and the gameshows begin.
Beyond the basement windows, rain prepared.
I had before me such a crooked god
Huge in the spotted bulb. So I took nails,
The shiny wide-head wood-nails from a keg,
And drove them skreaking home. Each spike
Increased its light, each hammer blow spilled
Adoration on the hunching thing, and I
— I knelt down before it while my lips burned.

My fetish swelled against its blinking nails,
Assumed a crabbed magnificence: *My pain had form.*
Its chopped mouth mirrored darkness: cascades

Of mirrors reflected an infinitude of dark,
Night within multiple night.

And then it spoke:
With upheld beggar's stumps *Bend down*, it said,

Bend down

And cherish me!

The poem is unmistakably inaugural and vocational, like Whitman's 'Out of the Cradle Endlessly Rocking' — a little origin myth about becoming a maker, a poet with burning lips. And the writing is self-assured, vivid, and powerful: notice, to take one small but typical example, how Ormsby musters assonance and consonance in describing the two clumsy feet, in a stumbling spondee, as 'lopped blocks'; the words, which sound alike but not identical, sound out the imperfect mutual resemblance of the feet.

There are hidden depths here, too. Consider the memorable description of the statue's face as a 'knobby lumb'. 'Lumb' is a neologism; it seems to be a portmanteau of 'limb' and 'numb', which makes some sense here; the wooden face is a kind of numb limb. But a little door opens in the poem as soon as we recognize that 'lumb', for all its Old English complexion, is in fact borrowed from Latin, and means literally 'loin'. The face is a knobby loin, a kind of phallus that, along with the rest of the figure, 'swell[s] against its blinking nails'. This image of a facial loin recalls that passage in Rilke's 'Archaic Torso of Apollo' in which 'a smile run[s] through the placid hips and thighs' of the god's statue 'to that dark center where procreation flared'. In Rilke's poem the loin has a face; in Ormsby's the face is a loin. The allusion is nailed down by Ormsby's 'fierce priapic flare' a few lines later, and again in the fetish's 'increas[ing] … light', which as you may recall is a central motif in Rilke's sonnet. In short, 'Fetish' reveals itself as a revisionary response to Rilke's famous vocational poem about a statue of a god: in both poems the god enters the statue and makes commands, but whereas in Rilke's poem the god speaks to a relatively passive 'you', a mere observer, in Ormsby the god addresses its own maker. The poem, perhaps Ormsby's first fully successful lyric, is thus brilliantly allusive. A poet who can do this sort of thing clearly knows what he's doing.

Consider, as well, how the speaker in 'Fetish' models that priapic flare 'as though instructed'. The phrase is uncanny. Ormsby provides a crucial gloss when he tells Starnino about his starting to write poetry at age seventeen: 'I could hear, if I listened with the utmost attention, a strange sort of talking in my head that had nothing to do with my speaking voice and which demanded an almost trance-like attention on my part. I can even remember the July day and the room where I was standing when I first became aware of it. I recognized then that this was my "daemon" in the Socratic sense. So from the beginning writing entailed the utmost attention followed by a struggle to transcribe that innermost voice. By "transcribe" I mean finding a style in which to reproduce that interior summons literally. It took me years.' 'Fetish', it seems to me, is precisely about finding that style at long last. It's about giving the poet's daemon objective form.

'*My pain had form*': this is the revelation that shocked the wild, undisciplined poet into maturity. For '[f]orm', Ormsby tells Starnino, 'is all that we have.... Form is what allows an experience to be so objectified that another can enter it as you yourself did.' Ormsby is speaking primarily of prosody here, but the point applies equally well to the feat of psychological projection, or, to put it another way, sympathetic magic that is performed by the speaker of 'Fetish', both in making the statue and in making the poem. The fetish, which with its nails resembles a voodoo doll, is a kind of Blakean emanation or Frankenstein's creature; it is the poet's agonized and hermaphroditic spirit or daemon torn out of him and made into a work of art. The speaker's pain is both erotic, with its erect nipples and 'fierce priapic flare', and religious, with its 'mouth's awe .../— that torn place that prayed'. As a god it is a mirroring god, one who mirrors, and what it mirrors back to its maker is the maker's own spiritual and emotional darkness, 'night within night'. It has a 'grieving watchfulness', that is, a watchfulness that springs from grief. And it tells the speaker to bend down before it not to worship but to 'cherish', not to idolize but to love. The poem is inaugural not least because these themes — psychological projection (or sympathetic magic), watchfulness, suffering, cherishing, mirroring, the transcendent and the erotic — get played out again and again in Ormsby's poetry, as I will show, in fascinating combinations.

Ormsby was born in 1941, twenty-four years after Robert Lowell, nine years after Sylvia Plath, and the belatedness of his breakthrough as a poet may well have had to do in part with a struggle to find a successful way to avoid the solipsism of the confessional mode these poets and others had made dominant. He wanted to write with his daemon, not his ego, and this must have been difficult to do as a young poet in the heyday of confessionalism. One successful alternative he found is the mythical alter ego of his post-crisis Lazarus poems. Here, for example, is 'Lazarus in Skins':

After his long recovery, Lazarus
Began wearing lizard-skin boots.
He sported cravats of rich kid
And black lustrous jackets of young calf.
He couldn't endure the cling
Of fabric, the insinuations of silk.
Even textiles woven of moth-soft cloth
Aggravated his dreams.

Not suffering, he said, but hope
Had made him hysterical and vain.
Now he desired the sinuous
Space of other skins, those fresh
Folds of amplitude, the beautiful
Blueness of snakes' eyes, cloud
Lenses, when they shed their last skin.

It's not as though the poet is nowhere to be found here; Lazarus is clearly Ormsby's stand-in, and indeed, adopting a mythical alter ego is a familiar technique for expanding the significance of autobiographical material. Think of Plath's 'Lady Lazarus', for instance. But where Plath's poem is decidedly self-dramatizing and self-absorbed ('Dying/Is an art, like everything else./I do it exceptionally well'), Ormsby's poem is about overcoming self-absorption through self-criticism: 'Not suffering, he said, but hope/Had made him hysterical and vain.' He is finished with the vanity of the ego; now he wants to be something else. But even the human mask of Lazarus is not different enough; his resurrected alter ego wants to put on 'the sinuous/Space of other skins', that is, animal skins and not manufactured fabrics. To paraphrase T. S. Eliot, Ormsby at this point doesn't want to express his personality; he wants to escape from it. His impulse here strongly recalls

Keats's argument in his letters — an argument much admired by Eliot — against the Wordsworthian 'egotistical sublime', and in favour of an alternative conception of the 'poetical character' as one lacking an identity of its own, that is, the Shakespearean type, the 'chameleon poet' who is continually 'filling some other Body'. As Keats puts it, 'if a sparrow come before my window, I take part in its existence and pick about the gravel.' In a review, Ormsby approvingly calls this idea of the chameleon poet 'utterly at odds with poetry as it is practised nowadays in America', and adds that it is 'still so radical that it leaves all our "experimental" and "celebrity" poet-performers looking staid and dull.' Like Keats, Ormsby has called Shakespeare his 'ultimate model in English', and Shakespeare's unrivalled capacity to imagine his way into his characters is clearly one of the qualities he admires most.

But Ormsby's Lazarus wants to inhabit the skins of animals, not people. This proved prophetic for Ormsby's early books of poetry, which are full of lyrics about flora and fauna: starfish, lichens, moths, wood fungus, bee balm, spiders and so on. These poems, he says, were originally inspired by Rilke's thing-poems, although Marianne Moore and Francis Ponge also come to mind, along with certain poems of D.H. Lawrence and Paul Claudel. He might as well be describing himself when he calls Moore, in a review of her letters, 'a shape-shifter, protean in plasticity, a sort of ageless and sexless, almost shamanistic being who through the alembic of language could become now a pangolin, now a wood-weasel, now an ostrich that "digesteth harde yron".' Like Moore, Ormsby in this mode is a chameleon poet *par excellence*.

Let's look at one of Ormsby's thing-poems, a blank-verse sonnet called 'Skunk Cabbage,' from *Bavarian Shrine*:

The skunk cabbage with its smug and opulent smell
Opens in plump magnificence near the edge
Of garbage-strewn canals, or you see its shape
Arise near the wet roots of the marsh.
How vigilant it looks with its glossy leaves
Parted to disclose its bruised insides,
That troubled purple of its blossom!

It always seemed so squat, dumpy and rank,

A noxious efflorescence of the swamp,
Until I got down low and looked at it.

Now I search out its blunt totemic shape
And bow when I see its outer stalks
Drawn aside, like the frilly curtains of the ark,
For the foul magenta of its gorgeous heart.

This may remind some readers of Al Purdy's 'Trees at the Arctic Circle'; both poems are palinodes in which the speaker recants his former attitude of disdain for an uncharismatic plant. But where Purdy belabours the point in hectoring and self-dramatizing verse ('To take away the dignity/of any living thing/.../is to make life itself trivial/and yourself the Pontifex Maximus/of nullity'), Ormsby devotes himself instead to atoning for his prior disdain by looking carefully at the skunk cabbage and describing it vividly.

Indeed, the poem is explicitly about the rewards of careful and even humble perception, of getting 'down low' to look at something often overlooked, and this valuing of careful observation is a delightful element in Ormsby's thing-poems. The emphasis seems attributable to the influence of Moore especially, with her ferocious exactitude of perception and description. Ormsby tells Starnino that his 'original and governing impulse was to look at a thing, to look at it absolutely, and then try to say something about its essential nature, whether a pickerel weed or a sea shell or a grackle or my mother's face. For a long time, and certainly during the writing of my first two books, and even perhaps my third, I believed that description alone, if done accurately, could stand by itself.' Indeed, this is the conventional wisdom about Ormsby's thing-poems, that they are mere descriptions. As one reviewer puts it, 'For the past twenty years, Ormsby has been writing poems that are ... keenly observed and delicately adorned ends-in-themselves.'

But as far as I'm concerned (notwithstanding the poet's own commentary, which in any case he contradicts elsewhere) this is a serious misunderstanding of what he is doing in these poems. Ormsby's gaze has the intensity of, not the field naturalist, but the fetishist, in the erotic sense of one who gazes obsessively at an isolated thing. (He has also written several poems about parts of the human body). It is a gaze which tends to turn things, by means of tropes, into objects of erotic and transcendental desire, not unlike the way D.H. Lawrence's poems in this mode do in *Birds, Beasts and Flowers.* (Think of his erotic fig-tree, for example, and his god-like snake.) The wooden god in 'Fetish', and the skunk cabbage in the poem of that name, both become under Ormsby's gaze hermaphroditic sexual objects. The skunk cabbage is a kind of phallus (with its 'blunt totemic shape') which, like a Georgia O'Keeffe painting, also resembles a vulva (its 'outer stalks/Drawn aside, like the frilly curtains of the ark'). Moreover, as these same passages demonstrate, the poet turns the skunk cabbage — precisely at the sonnet's *volta* — simultaneously into a totem pole and a temple of the covenantal ark: into, in other words, a vessel of divinity. Another example: the poem 'Conch-Shell' similarly describes an erotic conch whose 'flaring lip' '[d]isplay[s] a pinkish, petal-like interior', and then proceeds to transform it into a 'trumpet of solemn festivals', a 'Palace ... of glory' which houses a 'seraphic' animal. In short, erotic and religious tropes abound in these poems; nearly everything this poet looks at intensely becomes, in his own phrase, both 'lewd and holy', like the erotic figure of Christ in the Bavarian shrine of his first book's title poem. If this is 'description alone', I'll turn in my reading glasses and take up drinking.

Ormsby acknowledges, as I say, that he was 'in part inspired by Rilke and his ... "thing-poems"', but he goes on to claim that he himself 'went far beyond this, in the end, to an obsessive intensity'. But Rilke's thing-poems are precisely about looking at things with obsessive intensity, such that the things observed become transformed in the imagination through metaphor: a Spanish dancer becomes a flame, one's reflection in a cat's eye becomes a fly encased in amber. 'Build your house in transformation', Rilke advises; and this is just what Ormsby is doing in these poems.

Ormsby's real difference from Rilke has to do, not with intensity of observation, but with his allegiance to the idea of correspondence. For Rilke, the purpose of observing a thing this intensely is to absorb it into the imagination, to take it into one's inner life; he aspires to a Blakean state of consciousness in which 'All Things Exist in the Human Imagination'. In other words, Rilke's impulse is Romantic and modern. But Ormsby thinks about things rather differently; as he tells Starnino, 'I believe quite strongly in what Baudelaire called "correspondences", the conviction that things are not only what they appear to be in themselves but that they correspond to something else, either from within the mind or within another realm. This has always governed my poems about plants or animals.' To spell this out a

little: Ormsby believes there are natural or at any rate pre-existing correspondences among things, between things and another realm, between the
human mind and things, and in particular between words and things, and
among words; for him the purpose of observing a thing intensely seems to
be to uncover those correspondences, and thus a sense of unity in the
world. This is a much older vision, closely related to the Renaissance and
Hermetic notion of the human being as a microcosm of the universe. If we
may describe Rilke's impulse as post-Kantian or 'Protestant' in its emphasis
on the individual imagination, then Ormsby's impulse is 'Catholic' or esoteric in its emphasis on cosmic unity. When it comes to his language, moreover, Ormsby seeks what he calls a 'sacramental' quality of 'words vibrating
over many octaves and possessing transformative power,' like a priest tran-
substantiating the communion wine into the blood of Christ, a shaman
transforming herself into a pangolin, or a poet turning a block of wood into
a god, or a conch into a palace of glory.

We're not just talking about tropes here, although metaphor is obviously fundamental to this process. Ormsby's method also has much to do
with aural correspondence among words, the auditory resemblance of
words to one another achieved primarily through the repetition of vowel
and consonant sounds. Listen again to the opening of 'Skunk Cabbage':
'The skunk cabbage with its smug and opulent smell / Opens in plump magnificence near the edge ...'; already, in the first two lines, we have a passage
that is positively Keatsian in its repetition of sounds — consonance, assonance, alliteration, even an internal off-rhyme in 'cabbage / edge' — and the
effect of all this quite literal sympathetic vibration (besides the aesthetic
pleasure it gives, which is considerable) is to suggest very strongly not only
that these words belong together but also, by a kind of magical extension,
that they therefore truly correspond to the things they describe. The same
principle operates throughout the poem. If we read the poem aloud, the
repetition of sounds helps to persuade us of the imaginative transformation
of the skunk cabbage into the Ark of the Covenant. (It helps, for instance,
that the words 'skunk' and 'ark' sound alike.)

And there is still another kind of correspondence which is important in
these poems. You will recall that the wooden god in 'Fetish' is a kind of psychological projection of the poet's daemon, and there is a definite sense in
which the objects in Ormsby's thing-poems tend to become, like the animal that lives in the conch-shell in the poem of that name, '[e]mblem[s] of

the self'. On some level they are all projections of the poet or his daemon. As Ormsby explains to Starnino — and this is one of those places where he contradicts his claim that his thing-poems constitute 'description alone' — 'A colleague who read my first collection said that I should really stop writing about "weeds and grasses" and tackle something important like "the failure of my marriage". What he didn't realize is that I had tackled that very topic but had expressed it at a remove through a series of very intense verse meditations on ... plants or animals.' This helps explain why Ormsby's objects are so often embodiments of pain and breakdown. The skunk cabbage reveals its 'bruised insides'; a garter snake in an eponymous poem 'slips along a stone/... like the ardent progress of a tear'. Even the conch is described as 'docked and husked .../ like tongues/torn from mouths'. When you start looking for these agonized passages you find them everywhere, like the erotic and religious tropes I have described above. Indeed, the poems in *Bavarian Shrine and other poems* are so laced with images of suffering and decay they sometimes recall the poetry of Gottfried Benn, the German Expressionist, with the crucial difference that Ormsby's images are also images of beauty, 'peacock[s] of decay', to quote again from the book's title poem, a phrase which in context describes the decomposing statue of the crucified Christ. Indeed, the suffering things in these poems often demand or inspire an attitude of adoration, a kind of religious cherishing and praise; in looking at the skunk cabbage, remember, the poet notices its 'bruised insides', the 'troubled purple' of its flower, and responds with reverence: 'I bow when I see its outer stalks/Drawn aside, like the frilly curtains of the ark.' Ormsby's thing-poems tend to praise and lament at the same time, although he is most interested in praise; they are in this sense both odes and elegies, and this is another thing they have in common with the poetry of Rilke.

Bavarian Shrine and other poems, as edited for its appearance in *Time's Covenant*, is nearly a perfect book, and even in its original form it is, as I say, certainly one of the finest first books ever published in Canada. Besides containing twenty-seven very good poems, an extraordinary success rate, the whole thing works as a carefully arranged sequence, which repeats themes and topoi with variations, along with several key words ('lichen', 'slag', 'lopped', 'moths', 'corrosion' and 'cherish', among others). That phrase in the book's title, '*and other poems*', which suggests a miscellany, is misleading; like the decaying Bavarian shrine in the title poem, the whole book is a kind of shrine to decadence, which sees the erotic and the divine in every image of beautiful suffering and decay. In that sense, Ormsby's book is a kind of late Romantic answer to, or revision of, George Herbert's great book-length sequence of religious poems entitled *The Temple*. *Bavarian Shrine* is one of Ormsby's finest achievements as a poet, and an indispensable book for readers of fine contemporary poetry.

Not quite everything in the book is good, however. Several of the weaker poems from the original book have been wisely removed in *Time's Covenant*, but the poet might happily have suppressed or revised three more, namely 'Statues and Mannequins', 'December' and 'Craneworld'. In the latter poem, otherwise very good, Ormsby lapses momentarily into preciousness; to wit: 'Thatchiness, a prickledom of aromatic/Nestnesses'. 'December' is sketchy and undeveloped. And in 'Statues and Mannequins', a much more grievous case, he repeatedly falls into the vice Ezra Pound warns fledgling poets against in his essay 'A Retrospect', that is, the use of phrases in the pattern, 'the [image] of [abstraction]', or, to quote from Ormsby's poem, 'the sepals of nobility', 'the lacquered isinglass of hurt', 'the drowsy verdigris of disenchantment', 'the open hands of triumph', 'the plazas of remembrance', 'the ornamental fountains of decay'. As Pound admonishes, 'Don't use such an expression as "dim lands *of peace*". It dulls the image. It mixes an abstraction with the concrete. It comes from the writer's not realizing that the natural object is always the *adequate* symbol' (the italics are Pound's). Fortunately, this is exactly the lesson nearly all the other poems in the book embody so very well.

Given what I've been saying about Ormsby's allegiance to the Keatsian notion of the poetical character as lacking an identity of its own, it comes as a surprise to turn to Ormsby's second book, *Coastlines* (1992), and find him engaging full-on with the Wordsworthian autobiographical tradition in a series of poems about his childhood in Florida. (There are, however, several thing-poems here as well, which would not have been out of place in *Bavarian Shrine*.) It is as if an autobiographical impulse which had been suppressed or sublimated in the earlier collection needed to be let out for a run. The book is uneven in quality: of the two dozen poems from it that appear in *Time's Covenant,* a dozen or so are very good, the rest indifferent or worse; but a dozen very good poems is nothing to sneeze at.

Ormsby cultivates a certain Stevensian looseness of prosody in his first book, but here he is stricter in his metre and uses rhyme more often, with, unfortunately, occasional lapses of felicity, as in the modified *ottava rima* poem 'Florida Bay'. Like many poets still polishing their formal craft, Ormsby is much better in this book when he is colloquial, as in 'Cellar' ('This is where we keep them: toy trucks/With busted wheels, the broken stuff/We can't get rid of, our old books,/The splintered chair, the fractured tabouret'), than he is when he reaches for sublimity, as in, say, 'Savannahs' ('There were no wings unequal to my heart then') and 'Mullein' ('Sentinel the emptiness seraphically', and — here's that Poundian no-no again — 'yellow flowers of astonishment').

Among the new thing-poems, the best are 'Grackle', 'Live-oak, with Bromeliads', 'Cellar', 'Garter Snake' and 'Of Paradise as a Garden'. Of the autobiographical poems, the stand-outs are 'Adages of a Grandmother', 'My First Beach', 'Fragrances', 'Childhood House', 'Railway Stanzas', 'Getting Ready for the Night' and 'Halifax'. These latter poems successfully avoid the sentimental nostalgia of the weaker autobiographical lyrics like 'Remembrance' and 'Savannahs', sometimes by focusing on catalogues of concrete things, as in 'My First Beach' and 'Fragrances', sometimes by explicitly rejecting nostalgia, as in 'Childhood House' and 'Adages of a Grandmother'. 'Halifax' really belongs in a middle category, as a thing-poem about a city which becomes, delightfully, an unsentimental metaphor for remembered childhood.

Another dialectic synthesis of thing-poem with autobiography occurs in one of the very strongest poems in the book, 'The Public Gardens', a poem of almost British disenchantment, reminiscent of Auden and Larkin, a powerfully moral and expertly formal poem that nevertheless questions moral order and aesthetic form. Although, as I say, it combines elements of both modes, it feels like a development beyond or rather through the thing-poems and autobiographical poems of what now, with this poem, suddenly feels like Ormsby's early period. It is apparently set in Halifax's Public Gardens, 'a place of order/Despite its delicate wilderness disarray'. Being in this place reminds the poet of having seen, three years earlier, a swan penned there in the park, 'not the virile, ominous/Swan of Yeats, the gliding cynosure/of all imagination', but rather one 'muddy and obese'. Here we have a thing-poem about a swan, embedded in an autobiographical poem of memory; but the memory is anything but nostalgic, and the swan is not a beautiful 'peacock of decay', but an ugly image of squalor that 'unnerve[s]' the poet. The swan is presented, moreover, not in fetishistic isolation, but in a social context in which 'police/Cars by the black gates wetly reconnoitred/Where hunched unshaven men smoked and loitered'. All this is presented in a style of vivid and clear-eyed realism, although on another level this is all clearly happening in a displaced and fallen Garden of Eden, whose gates are guarded not by the Archangel Michael but by the police, and where the swan of the human imagination is caged in a chicken-wire enclosure: 'Only a close-docked wing/Remained of all that majesty.'

Into this expertly established milieu Ormsby introduces a shocking image of pain, one that makes the fetishized suffering of his earlier poems appear mild by comparison:

> The swan brought back to mind a horrible
> Thing I'd seen there once, a hungry seagull
> Perched upon a half-dead mallard's back
> And eating its raked and squirming flesh alive.

This is not merely another case of 'my pain had form'; the duck is not primarily an emblem of the self. On the contrary, to his horror, the speaker finds himself identifying with the killer:

> I remembered how, some weeks before,
> I'd eaten roast duck with a rich plum sauce.
> Here was the flesh itself, with crass
> Thrashings agonizing, while the quick gull tore
> Slivers of slitted skin and dabbled its bill again
> In flinching meat.

It is true that later in the poem the poet says the duck 'suffered so like me' — though he quickly adds 'Or you' — but even this momentary identification with the suffering bird causes him to feel, not pity (and thus by extension self-pity) but, disconcertingly, a terrible loathing for the bird. When I say this feels like a development beyond or through Ormsby's earlier poems, I don't mean an aesthetic advance, I mean a psychological or perhaps moral advance in the poet's struggle against solipsism. An imaginative world in which nearly everything is an emblem of the self or its daemon is much less egotistical than the world of the confessional mode, but it is not exactly free from narcissism either, especially when those emblems tend to become objects of erotic and spiritual desire. In 'The Public Gardens', however, the suffering of the mallard signifies the suffering not primarily of the self but of others:

> Pain estranges,
> Cordons the sufferer and disarranges
> Pity in its strict perimeters:
> I thought of people I'd known, sufferers
> So perimetered by pain that only love
> Could touch them still — sometimes not even love.

This passage reminds me of Keats's letters again, but this time it's Keats's 'chamber of maiden thought' that comes to mind, that stage in one's intellectual and moral development which begins as an intoxicating world of 'pleasant wonders', but gradually darkens to the point of 'sharpening one's vision into the heart and nature of Man — of convincing ones nerves that the World is full of Misery and Heartbreak, Pain, Sickness and oppression'. Keats adds that Wordsworth had reached this stage when he wrote 'Tintern Abbey' — 'it seems to me that his genius is explorative of those dark passages,' he says — and this is a major caveat in Keats's critique of the 'egotistical sublime'. Wordsworth's vision of human suffering is a vision that Keats shares, particularly in the odes; and Shakespeare, especially in the tragedies, is its master.

What a pleasure then to find that 'The Public Gardens' musters some of the moral force of Shakespeare's tragic soliloquies toward the end of the poem as the speaker agonizes over what he has seen — not to mention what he's done, because in the meantime he has killed the duck to put it out of its misery:

> The horror in my mouth was almost prayer,
> The stumbled syllables of those in despair,
> And yet, so poetical, so apposite!
> Does order merely gauze the infinite
> Wince of the debrided skin? And was pity
> Conferral of extinction or the first stone of the city

Founded in love?
That day, I saw the fountains with their casual
Music of refusal
Splash beyond while in its pen the great
Mud-spattered swan beaked its black gate.

Notice the serious and revealing pun on 'pen' in the penultimate line: part of what makes this a bleak vision is that it ends with the fallen swan of the imagination, 'in its pen', helplessly trying to escape its imprisonment; in other words, the futile action is a despairing metaphor for the poet's effort in the poem. It is true that the Christian vision of 'the city/Founded in love' is offered as a possibility in these lines, but the poet has no faith in it here, only the barest implied hope. The poem itself, however, not least because it has the strength to admit its own doubt, is a triumph of hard-won art.

Ormsby may not have realized for a while that he had crossed the imaginative Rubicon with this poem, because he returns with still more thing-poems in his next collection, *For a Modest God: New and Selected Poems* (1997), with very uneven results. Four of the new thing-poems are very good, namely 'Anhinga', 'Turtle's Skull', 'Hand-Painted China' and 'Spider Silk', for which we may be grateful, but the rest of the new poems in this mode feel forced and tonally artificial, as if the poet knows he is repeating himself, willing the poems into existence; in the weaker poems, as he puts it himself in 'The Ant Lion', 'everything takes place mechanically/Despite the shrieked beseeching of your will'. The poet's usual luscious sound effects and interesting diction are here in full force, but the rhetoric flags, the syntax feels awkward. In 'What It Is Like to Be a Bat', three sentences in a row begin with the inert pattern 'There are the [adjective] [noun]', and the energy drains out of the poem as a result. In 'An Oak Skinned by Lightning', we can hear the poet getting bored with his standard *modus operandi* of turning things into emblems of divine suffering; instead of transforming the oak tree with metaphor, he just comes out with it, eschewing all subtlety:

The oak was Christlike as the lightning stripped
Its seamless raiment off and the rain whipped
It while it shook, a suffering being....

'Christlike', 'suffering being': the poet is resorting to shorthand here. It's hard even to see the images because everything is happening at once, 'as' and 'while' everything else is happening. To take another example, listen to how forced and arch is this opening of 'Flamingos':

My quarrel with your quorum, Monsignor
Flamingo, is that you scant the rubicund
In favour of a fatal petal
Tint.

The sound effects and Stevensian diction here would be, as usual, a pleasure, but wait a minute: in what sense is a complaint about the flamingo's colour a 'quarrel with [its] quorum'? And anyway, to pick a fight with a bird over the colour of its feathers is ridiculous. I could go on, but suffice it to say that Ormsby is spinning his wheels in most of the new thing-poems in this book.

Besides the four fine exceptions I have mentioned, there are six other new poems in *For a Modest God* that are very good. 'Quark Fog', is an exuberant little creation myth of a poem about language. 'Hate' is a terrific sonnet that shows what this poet can do when he applies himself to the social dimension of human feeling. The same is true of 'Mutanabbi Remembers His Father', which successfully adopts the mask of the great tenth-century Classical Arabic poet Abu Tayib al-Mutanabbi; the latter poem is also notable as the first successful instance in which Ormsby brings his scholarly training and interests explicitly to bear on his own poetry, a development that would pay large dividends in his next book. There are also three very strong poems that are nominally about family members: 'The Gossip of the Fire' is a marvellously displaced version of the Orpheus myth in which the poet's grandfather charms the animals by telling stories; 'Blood' is a very fine poem in couplets addressed to the poet's adopted sons; and 'The Suitors of My Grandmother's Youth' imagines its way memorably into the lives of young people in an earlier generation.

I must say it's a relief to enter the human social world in these poems; in retrospect, Ormsby's less successful thing-poems in this collection feel not only rhetorically wilful but claustrophobic in their continued narrow focus on animals and plants. In his interview with Starnino, Ormsby says that 'Writers who have garnered too much attention tend to fall easily into dishonesty; they pander to the taste that rewarded them by repeating *ad nauseam* whatever style or tone or mannerism first made them celebrated,' and my sense is that this was starting to happen to Ormsby in this period with regard to his thing-poems. Not that he was wildly celebrated, but he had received some complimentary reviews and an Ingram Merrill Foundation Prize, and had appeared in the *Norton Anthology of Poetry;* this must have been a little heady to a poet who just a few years earlier had gone twenty-seven years without publishing a poem. What I admire is that it took so little time for Ormsby to pull himself out of it, to try something new, and especially that the results were often so successful. As he jokes with Starnino, 'I have begun to work my laborious way upward along the evolutionary chain from lichens and wood fungus to camels, vultures, baboons, and finally humans!' Consider, for instance, 'The Suitors of My Grandmother's Youth', which I quote in full:

At dusk on Sabbath afternoons the slow-
Voiced suitors came, with awkward hat brims in
Their field-burred hands. They tipped themselves
On the very brinks of the Sunday chairs.
Their napes were fiery under their collar starch.
The knees of their blue serge suits looked rubbed and smooth.

Fireflies would be winking then, across the lawns.
Under the hedge, like small and sleepy stars
Witnessed through mist, they glittered and went out.
And everywhere, lilac would spire in June
Its chaste and promissory fragrance. Her
Sisters broke off sprays and clasped them
With half-ironic passion to their throats.
The boys were mute, traded long-suffering
Conspiratorial looks. On speechless
Strolls their beaux would hand to them
Desperate fistfuls of wild violets.
All their futures still appeared
Benign with promise, all their loves
Still hovered before the transactions of the blood.

This is masterful. You can see how Ormsby is adapting his earlier methods to a new type of subject: the fireflies and lilacs are still emblems of the human, but now they stand for his characters, not himself. This gives him a new detachment, and lets a new sense of humour and dramatic irony into the poem; notice for instance how he turns his old subject of suffering into the boys' 'long-suffering / Conspiratorial looks', and, more darkly, notice the dramatic irony he gets out of the little word 'still' in the last sentence: we know, if the boys and girls do not, what will happen to their futures 'Benign with promise' after 'the transactions of the blood'.

As I hinted above, Ormsby's next book of poems, *Araby* (2001), draws extensively on his scholarship in Islamic studies, and in reading it, it is helpful to know something about his scholarly career and interests. In the eighties, while his apprenticeship as a poet was mercifully coming to an end, Ormsby launched a career as an academic librarian and a scholar of medieval Islamic and Jewish thought. He held the posts of director of libraries at the Catholic University of America in Washington, D.C., in the mid-eighties, and, after moving to Canada in 1986, director of libraries and associate professor in McGill University's Institute of Islamic Studies in Montreal, a post he held for ten years. Besides articles and reviews on various aspects of medieval Islamic theology and mysticism, he published three scholarly books in this period: *Moses Maimonides and His Time, Theodicy in Islamic Thought,* and, with co-author Rudolf Mach, *Handlist of Arabic Manuscripts (New Series) in the Princeton University Library.* Ormsby was later promoted to professor and director of the Institute of Islamic Studies at McGill, a position he held for another decade. He is currently professor and chief librarian at the Library of the Institute of Ismaili Studies in London, UK. His most recent scholarly book is *Ghazali: The Revival of Islam,* a profile of Abu Hamid al-Ghazali, an eleventh-century Islamic theologian and Sufi mystic who, like Ormsby, underwent a kind of mid-life spiritual death and resurrection.

All this scholarly experience, together with extensive travel in the Arab world, Ormsby poured into the writing of *Araby*. It seems certain that no one else could have written this book. What's more, it is a masterpiece, an astonishing and nearly perfect sequence of poems. (Just two of its thirty-eight lyrics strike me as lapses, namely 'Mrs. Jaham' and 'A Duet with the Wolf', and that is an extraordinary batting average; the former poem is uncharacteristically flat, prosaic and undeveloped, and the latter, with its singing wolf who 'keens' things like '*I who whelped my thousands am now Time's eunuch, / castrato of vicissitude*', is just silly, but everything else in the book is superb.) The book's subject would be unlikely if Ormsby weren't the scholar he is: the lives, deaths and afterlives of two modern Arab characters, a semi-nomadic Sufi poet named Jaham, known as the Father of Clouds, and his friend, an Islamic fundamentalist auto mechanic named Bald Adham. (That the book was published the same year as 9/11 is almost too weirdly good to be true; it is, among other things, a profound act of cultural empathy that deserves to long survive the current round of strife between the West and some in the Islamic world.) The book is simultaneously a collection of discrete lyrics and a unified poetic sequence, and in this way not unlike an Elizabethan sonnet sequence; there is not much of a plot, so it would be misleading to call it a verse novel, but the characters are fully developed, and change over time, and feel more real than many real people, if only because Ormsby helps us enter so fully into their inner lives. Ormsby is at his most Shakespearean in this book, all but disappearing into his characters the way he nearly disappears into animals and plants in his best thing-poems. His technique is as rich as ever, and if anything, even more supple in its handling of the mostly iambic, mostly pentameter verse. And Ormsby's range here is a delight: his subjects include sex, baboons, hashish, theology, cars, jinn, poetry, vultures, childhood, insomnia, death and more. The tones range from the high lyrical to the hilarious, from the vituperative to the erotic, and the poems are spoken sometimes by Jaham, sometimes by Adham, sometimes by a knowing narrator, and once, in a parody of the end of the Book of Job, by Allah. In short, *Araby* is a richly human book; its motto could be that of Terence: 'I consider nothing human alien to me.'

How to choose examples from this embarrassment of riches? Here's a poem that illustrates well the advantages that Ormsby's relatively new concern with human characters confers on the poems, at the same time that it clearly harkens back to his earlier thing-poems. The poem is called 'The Junkyard Vision of Jaham':

> In paradise the smell of engine oil
> Will undercut the roses. The carburetors
> Of Eden will distract the seraphim,
> Those jukebox lutanists in phosphate trees.
> The vaporous hush of essences

At the pinging pump will cauterize
The contusions of love, and the houris all
Will bask on velveteen and naugahyde
Bucket seats in a Russian Leather breeze.

The camshafts of heaven will outlive the axle trees.
The music of the manifolds will gown the clouds.
I see the black-seamed fingertips of the mechanics
On the copper-coloured keys of their accordions
And hear the ditties of the pit-stops pool.
The music of paradise will be shirt-sleeved and cool
And brandish red bandannas of rough flannel.
The integrity of metals will marmorealize
Fleeting affections yet be various.
Amber oils will coronate chrome impulses
And be steadfast at last.

                    The dark order
Of the mechanisms of heaven will be intricate
And unending, bedewed with rich grease
And yet, withal, imbued by the love
Of couplings and black
Gaskets, the grit of the known
Lingeringly delivered back to innocence.

On one level this is another masterful Ormsbian thing-poem: exuberant
and aurally delicious language, vividly describing a place full of decaying
things imagined as both erotic and divine. The speaker here is not Ormsby,
however, but his character Jaham, and this enriches the poem considerably.
The lyric is placed near the end of the sequence, after the death of Bald
Adham, whose erotic passion for the cars he works on has been well established early in the book. Given this context, it is clear that 'The Junkyard
Vision of Jaham' is an elegy; Jaham is mourning his dead friend and envi-
sioning the paradise he has departed to, a mechanic's paradise full of beautiful car parts. There is something very amusing about those houris basking
on 'velveteen and naugahyde/Bucket seats in a Russian Leather breeze',
and yet we know Jaham is truly anguished over his friend's death; I find this

new tonal mixture of the humorous and the broken-hearted both moving and true. At the same time, the poem is also an embodiment of Jaham's aesthetic as a poet, and as such it expresses the essence of his character, which may be summed up in his own epitaph that concludes the final poem in the book: 'I love everything that perishes, / Everything that perishes entrances me.' This is recognizably Ormsby's (Rilkean) aesthetic, too, and yet Jaham is not reducible to a mouthpiece of the poet any more than Prospero is reducible to a mouthpiece of Shakespeare; they are both fully drawn characters in themselves.

To demonstrate this last point, let's take a look at another poem from *Araby*, this one spoken in third-person by a narrator about what can only be called Jaham's daemon. The poem is called 'The Caliph of Confusion':

> There is a tiny speck in Jaham's eye
> where the Caliph of Confusion rents a room.
> The Caliph is insane and loves costume.
> One day a nuncio, the next an Albanian spy.
> He is no principle. He is an imp.
> He enacts the spasm in the woof of time
> but stands for nothing at all beyond a crimp
> in comprehension, that small, sublime
> stammer we enunciate when sense breaks down
> and the smug palate and the thuggish tongue
> baffle their delphic and lubricious truths
> to stuttered stillness.
>   When he was young
> Jaham's eye was a perfectly pure, nut-brown
> orb without a single speck and his strong
> throat sang with all the certified youths
> of his tribe. The Caliph was his Iblis
> — a nip of darkness in the skin of the light,
> the sly flea that itches the lobes of peace —
> and he taught him how to navigate the night.

Both Ormsby's daemon and that of his character Jaham 'love costume', it's true. But whereas Ormsby's daemon speaks, Jaham's stammers. While Ormsby's is a mirroring god of grieving watchfulness, Jaham's is an Iblis (that is, a devil), an insane Caliph of Confusion. Ormsby's daemon sees divine and erotic emblems everywhere, and describes them; Jaham's 'baffles' the mouth's 'delphic and lubricious truths/to stuttered stillness'. The cultural differences between Ormsby and Jaham have much to do with these differences between their daemons, not to mention the very different metaphors Ormsby uses to describe them, and it is a credit to Ormsby's imagination and scholarship that he takes these differences fully into account. In his career-long and heroic struggle against solipsism, the poet in this book emerges victorious.

Ormsby's most recent full-length and independent collection is *Daybreak at the Straits* (2004), another transitional book which is chiefly admirable for the energy with which it strives again to break into new territory, to avoid the self-satisfied repetition Ormsby so dislikes in other poets. It is a wild, reckless book, one that tries to do all kinds of new things, and consequently it is highly uneven. In fact, the poems are often quite bad, as in the *Six Sonnets on Sex and Death,* which read, for all their strict formality, like exercises in writing with the unconscious, as though the poet had let the rhymes lead him on, and declined to revise much afterwards. It's full of nauseating and wince-inducing passages like, 'They sent a dancer with red razor shoes/to trot the cha-cha on his lollipop', and 'A melancholy baby in a pram/barfed a gout of frothy, fragrant scum./A dachshund lapped it while a falling star ...' and so on. You get the idea. Throw in some godawful rhymes — '[He] ... learned to wind the gauze/of hypochondria around his median;/learned banks of exile quite Ovidian' — and it's enough to make you wonder what Ormsby and his editor were thinking.

Still, the book contains seven or eight superb poems. A lot of the poems in the book are, as I say, wildly imaginative — in this sense it may be a kind of throwback to Ormsby's undisciplined apprenticeship — but the best ones are also sufficiently under control that the results are marvellous. They include 'What the Snow Was Not', 'Another Thing', 'Childhood Pieties', 'Vacuum Pantoum', 'The Gorgon in the Urn', 'A Dachshund in Bohemia' and 'Microcosm'. 'Another Thing' is a wonderful sonnet about the poet's daemon, with its 'chameleon eye'. And two of my favourites are responses to famous poems by two of Ormsby's poetic predecessors. 'What the Snow Was Not', for instance, is a marvellous response to Wallace Stevens' famous anthology-piece 'The Snow Man':

The snow was not liver-spotted like a gambler's
Hands. It did not reflect
Violet abrasions at the hubs of wheels
Or the well-glossed ankles of policemen.

The snow did not mimic flamingo rookeries
Or bone-stark branches where the spoonbills nest.
It had no single tint when it negated gold.
The snow was not duplicitous like arc

Lamps at sunrise that encairn the curbs
In lavender melodics. Snow did not web
The hands of women with their sudden hair
Electric-trellised in a blue downdraft.

The snow did not consume the eager mouths
Of children. It did not inhabit the skimming owl's
Concavity of surveillance and it did not flock
In grackle-shadows near the eaves of courts.

When you endow the snow with what it's not —
Mere shivering crystals blown by January
Over the squares in frosty negatives —
The snow becomes a god and nothing's lord.

Ormsby's technique of imaginative negation here — vividly imagining in exuberant language what is denied existence by the grammar of the sentences — is itself apparently borrowed from Stevens's poem 'The Disillusionment of Ten O'Clock' ('People are not going / To dream of baboons and periwinkles'), and so in a sense Ormsby's poem uses the pro-imagination Stevens of that poem against the more austere, realist Stevens of 'The Snow Man'; and as every good student of rhetoric knows, there is no more effective technique of refutation than turning an opponent's words against him. (No real victory in this case, however, since Stevens was nothing if not of two minds on this question.) It is more interesting to read this poem as a gloss on Ormsby's own poem 'Fetish'; both are about the making of a god, but by now Ormsby just about identifies that god with the imagination itself. Or to be more precise, he is saying that 'when you endow' something 'with what it's not,' that thing 'becomes a god and nothing's lord', that is, both a lord of nothingness and a lord over nothingness. The real antagonist here is the earlier Ormsby who saw himself as tied to description à la Marianne Moore, although I hope I have persuaded you that, really, he was always a poet of metaphor and transformation. This poem, coming as it does early in the book, serves as a kind of poet's licence for the imaginative licentiousness of the poems to follow, with, as I say, mixed results. In itself, however, the poem is a triumph.

Another poem in this book I especially admire, entitled 'Microcosm,' is a vivid commentary on Baudelaire's sonnet 'Correspondences,' and thus it spells out one of Ormsby's core convictions as a poet more fully than we have seen before:

> The proboscis of the drab grey flea
> Is mirrored in the majesty
> Of the elephant's articulated trunk. There's a sea
> In the bed-mite's dim orbicular eye.
> Pinnacles crinkle when the mountain-winged, shy
> Moth wakes up and stretches for the night.
> Katydids enact the richly patterned light
> Of galaxies in their chirped and frangible notes.
> The smallest beings harbor a universe
> Of telescoped similitudes. Even those Rocky Mountain goats
> Mimic Alpha Centauri in rectangular irises
> Of cinnabar-splotched gold. Inert viruses
> Replicate the static of red-shifted, still chthonic
> Cosmoi. Terse
> As the listened brilliance of the pulsar's bloom
> The violaceous mildew in the corner room
> Proliferates in Mendelian exuberance.
> There are double stars in the eyes of cyclonic
> Spuds shoveled and spaded up. The dance
> Of Shiva is a cobble-soled affair —
> Hobnails and flapping slippers on the disreputable stair.
> Yggdrasils
> Germinate on Wal-Mart windowsills.

Where Baudelaire speaks of a 'forest of symbols', and seems to have believed, at least sometimes, in a kind of mystical unity of all things,

Ormsby prefers to rely primarily on the language of science (the adjective 'Mendelian' refers to the laws of genetic inheritance articulated by the father of genetics, Gregor Mendel). By the end of the poem, however, with its Siva and Yggdrasil, the language of religion and myth returns, and the title recalls the Renaissance or Hermetic idea of correspondence between small things and large, man and the universe, microcosm and macrocosm. And in the end, Ormsby's poem is a much clearer explication of the notion of magical correspondences even than Baudelaire's famous sonnet.

It is very interesting to compare 'Microcosm' with 'What the Snow Was Not', because on one level they contradict each other. In the latter poem, the emphasis is on the creative power of the imagination over 'nothing', which puts the poem in the Romantic and modernist tradition. But in 'Microcosm', the poet asserts that it is the nature of reality to be full of correspondences; the cosmic dance of the god Siva is not created by the imagination but is already present, even in humble 'Hobnails and flapping slippers on the disreputable stair'. Despite their disagreement on doctrine, however, both poems are persuasive as poems, not least because they deploy their sounds so expertly as to make us believe that these words belong together and correspond with their objects and ideas. Consider how in 'Microcosm', for example, the four-letter words and overstressed monosyllables of 'drab grey flea' seem to represent that small brief bug by the very abruptness and monotony of their sounds, and how the repeated consonants and multisyllabic words in the phrase 'elephant's articulated trunk' seem to represent the length and continuity of that animal's 'proboscis'. Similarly, in 'What the Snow Was Not', listen to the difference between the phrase 'the skimming owl's / Concavity of surveillance', and the phrase 'flock / In grackle-shadows': the first sounds smooth because of its liquid v's and l's, and because of the vowels at the edges of its words which, musically speaking, slur together 'the skimming owl'. The second passage, by repeating certain vowels and consonants, sounds harsh and clacking like a flock of grackles. Ormsby's deepest conviction as a poet, in other words, concerns not so much metaphysical as linguistic correspondence; it is, in short, Pope's doctrine that 'The sound must seem an echo to the sense.' And in poetry, aesthetically speaking, this is the kind of correspondence that really matters.

At the end of *Time's Covenant,* Ormsby offers a preview of a work in progress that he calls his 'Big Book', a long and ambitious sequence of poems also to be called *Time's Covenant*, based on his family history, and in particular its association with a semi-mythical nineteenth-century Utopian community, Covenant, Tennessee. Based on the selection he offers, I must say I have mixed feelings about these poems. Ormsby seems to have two main models for his project, and as far as I'm concerned, one is much better chosen than the other.

The weaker choice is *The Canterbury Tales*, from which Ormsby borrows, among other things, the formal device of a large cast of characters. It also inspires his 'Prologue' which, like Chaucer's 'General Prologue' is written in heroic couplets. Unfortunately, unlike Chaucer's prefatory poem, which establishes a shared social context for the *Tales* that follow, Ormsby's 'Prologue' seeks to establish a merely personal and sentimental motivation for his research into the past, and I'm afraid the effect is like listening to one of those genealogy enthusiasts who are always trying to get you interested in their hobby. The poem takes 115 lines to narrate the speaker's arrival at the restored historical site of Covenant, complete with some heavy-handed allusions to Chaucer's poem:

> In Covenant, at the Tabard as I lay,
> a century later, on Commemoration Day,
> I witnessed pilgrims one by one file by
> and could not wipe the wonder from my eye.

This is just bad writing, and not only because the echoes of Chaucer are so insistent. (Must the inn really be called 'the Tabard'?) The last line, in this context, is sentimental; I'm not persuaded that it's really so misty-eyed and wonderful to see a bunch of historical tourists converging on a place that the poet himself calls a 'Disneyfied/simulacrum' of the past. The essential problem with this Prologue is that Ormsby hasn't decided whether he is enchanted by the place ('The central stair/lent majesty to the reception room') or disenchanted ('a Disneyfied/simulacrum of a Southern Fried/ synoptic gospel of what never was'). The latter tone strikes me as true here, the former false.

With one or two exceptions among the selection of new poems on offer here, the 'character' poems that derive superficially from Chaucerian influence aren't much better than the Prologue. Ormsby does not usually describe his characters interacting with each other vividly in the third person as in Chaucer's 'General Prologue', nor does he have them tell stories, as in the *Tales* proper. Sometimes they soliloquize, as in Edgar Lee Masters' *Spoon River Anthology*, but the Chaucerian machinery here seems beside the point, especially since Ormsby's characters are mostly historical, and not, as in *The Canterbury Tales*, contemporaries of the narrator. Moreover, at least among the poems of this type included here, there are few connections among the poems to lend them much contextual significance beyond their own rather wooden and sentimental navel-gazing. The exceptions are 'Two Private Prayers of the Reverend Blacklock', which has some lyric fire in it, and 'The Crossing', which draws a moving and fully imagined picture of the poet's grandmother as a child. I should add that the selection ends with two poems, 'Time's Covenant (2006)' and 'Coda', both, oddly, on the subject of 9/11; neither strikes me as a particularly good poem in itself, and their relevance to the poetic sequence they apparently conclude is, to say the least, mysterious.

Much more accomplished, and promising, are two poems apparently influenced by *Anabasis*, that great poem about the founding of a civilization by the French modernist poet Saint-John Perse, namely, 'The Founding of Covenant' and 'The Landscape of Covenant'. What these poems have in common with *Anabasis* is a sense of collective enterprise, the almost mythic founding of a civilization by a communal 'we'. Thus, in a passage from 'The Founding of Covenant', the speaker says:

> What had been formless before took form as soon
> As the Master leaned upon his spade
> And struck the sudden rock. And we
> Couldn't remember how the place had looked
> Before it became a *place*.
> Out of that almost laughable small stroke
> The imminence of order stood revealed.

The echoes of the first chapter of Genesis here are light but unmistakable, and the collective speaker makes the grandeur of the allusion entirely appropriate. This new ambition to speak for a community is the next step in Ormsby's long struggle against solipsism, a step even Shakespeare didn't quite take (except, perhaps, in some of the history plays), constrained as he was by the conventions of the stage. It is a sign of Ormsby's mature, if elsewhere inconsistent, mastery as a poet that the poem, for all its ambition, is convincing.

Ormsby achieves an even more powerful sense of dignity in the companion poem, called 'The Landscape of Covenant'. Here is a selection:

> The God who dwells within has visited
> And bides among us here. The God whose voice is in
> The small, soft air has touched us with benediction.
> He does not ask for sacrifices, for
> Holocausts of bullocks on a brazen altar. He
> Is insistent in His silences. A stillness as of
> Adamant emanates from Him. He pours His calm
> Upon the grasses that toss in the gale,
> In the bitter snowflakes that glitter above our tombs
> On the hill. His calm is in the ice
> That clasps the double promise of His brooks
> And binds us to Him all the winter long.

This is gorgeous, especially in context. Its stateliness derives in part from the blank verse, in part from the beautifully modulated syntactical parallelism, which strongly recalls the Old Testament. But again it is the collective voice that is new here; in this case, what the voice says doesn't precisely correspond with what we know of Ormsby's own world-view, and this makes it all the more impressive as an act of dramatic imagination. Ormsby seems to be writing *Time's Covenant* with the spirit of Perse on one shoulder and a pseudo-Chaucer on the other. In that contest I hope fervently the former spirit wins.

Ormsby's influence on younger Canadian poets has already been notable and salutary. To cite just one small but particularly striking instance, his example seems unmistakable in helping Karen Solie, who began as a largely confessional poet, to write her poem 'Thrasher', an unforgettable thing-poem about a bird which is clearly an 'emblem of the self', written in aurally rich language that continually echoes its sense: 'In relief at the topmost, he mimics domestic, migrant,/spaniel, spring-peepers, quacks, urks, and gurgles akin/to a four-stroke in heavy water'. I'm willing to bet Ormsby is precisely the 'migrant' Solie herself is 'mimic[king]' here to such effect. And she's not the only one to learn from Ormsby. Certain poems of Carmine Starnino come to mind, and Sue Sinclair, among others.

The other invaluable thing Ormsby brings to Canadian poetry (besides his own best indispensable poems) is a truly cosmopolitan sensibility. I'm referring here primarily to his polyglot literary education and scholarship and the effect these have on his poetry; but there is also a sense in which he is a kind of post-national poet, a Keatsian poetical character without a single national identity of his own. When asked about this by Starnino he replied that he has a 'dual identity, or dual self-confusion'; like Clark Blaise, he is both American and Canadian, and yet neither. To make matters even more complex, he now lives in the United Kingdom and, moreover, he says that at times he has felt so steeped in French poetry that 'I fancied myself a French poet condemned to write in English.' In a literary culture in which poets are usually anthologized and studied according to national categories, Ormsby is not easily classified, and that has its advantages and disadvantages, both for him and for his readers. The disadvantages have to do with reception; everyone's knee-jerk provincialism shies away from investing too much in a poet who doesn't fit easily into one's own national literary history, at least until he or she reaches a certain threshold of international fame that is very difficult to achieve. The advantages, however, have to do with the poetry itself; a poet free from national constraints, the expectations of readers in a particular national tradition, has greater access to the larger international tradition of poetry. In his interview with Starnino, Ormsby complains that 'American poets ... have a strong notion of what an American "voice" should be,' adding that this '"notion of 'voice" has imposed itself to the point of eccentricity. In the best American poets the search for a voice is inseparable from a rather lavish pleasure in their own identities.' As he sees it, the prevailing expectations in American poetry, in other words, are antithetical to the Keatsian view of the poetical character that has been central to Ormsby's own development as a poet. 'English Canadian poets,' on the other hand, Ormsby argues, 'have access to the larger poetic tradition that Americans do not,' though he wonders why, on the whole, they 'don't take advantage of the fact.' This access, he suggests, springs from the very lack so far of a recognizable Canadian identity to our poetry. If Ormsby's influence can help us see this lack, which we have been terribly anxious about, it seems, from time immemorial, as a tremendous opportunity, well: he will have done our literary culture even more of a service than his superb poetry already has.

PART II

Critical Mess

Ideology has been the serpent in the garden of literature and literary criticism for a very long time. In Canada it has been there, unfortunately, from the beginning, whether the dogma in question has been imperialism, nationalism, or any of the various newer isms in our current Medusa's hairdo of poststructuralist theories. What a relief, then, to find a Canadian critic who sees himself as rejecting ideology and standing up instead for aesthetic value.

'I read literature unashamedly for pleasure,' writes W.J. Keith in the preface to the revised and expanded edition of his two-volume critical survey, *Canadian Literature in English*, '[and] this book is a report on what has pleased me.' I must say my reader's heart started to beat a little faster when I read this sentence. And there's more. Keith quotes Neil Bissoondath approvingly as insisting that 'writers have one function, and that is to tell a good story', and adds that this 'is the conviction upon which the present book is based'. Such an avowal is very promising indeed. And listen to these ringing words from his 'Polemical Conclusion':

> The realm of literature needs to be won back from the sociological, the ideological, and the politically approved, and restored to the human spirit of delight, originality, imagination, and, above all, the love of what can be achieved through verbal sensitivity and dexterity. There is no inherent reason why Canadian writing, prose or verse, should not take a major part in this endeavour.

So rare is such a liberated attitude among Canadian academics (Keith is Professor Emeritus, University of Toronto) that one can't help but feel some excitement in reading this. Imagine a critical survey of Canadian literature informed by principles like these! It seems almost too good to be true.

Those familiar with Keith's career will not find his attitude surprising.

Born and raised in England, Keith came to Canada in 1958, when Northrop Frye was the dominant literary critic not only in this country but the entire English-speaking world. Keith's own 'independent stance', to borrow the title of one of his best-known books, was independent particularly in relation to Frye and his famous student Margaret Atwood, whose thematic study of Canadian literature, *Survival* (1970), dominated the study of Canadian literature for many years. This independence of Keith's has always consisted of two principles. First, against Frye's powerful argument in *Anatomy of Criticism* (1957) that literary criticism is a subject in its own right, and not a mere parasite on the body of literature, Keith objected, in *An Independent Stance* (1991) and elsewhere, that 'Literary commentators like myself are middle-men, and should be prepared to admit the fact.' Second, and most importantly, whereas Frye usually avoided evaluative criticism (with the notable exception of his incisive omnibus surveys of Canadian poetry in the 1950s), Keith consistently urged the importance of evaluative and formalist approaches, of close reading, and of paying attention to style and artistic value, and put his principles into practice in such books as *A Sense of Style: Studies in the Art of Fiction in English-Speaking Canada* (1989). While the tradition of evaluative criticism was alive if not always well in much of the Western world throughout this period, it is important to remember that Keith's position and practice were decidedly in the minority in this country; hence his importance as a model and inspiration for sympathetic younger critics.

But I'm afraid Keith's survey of Canadian literature, which I am concerned with here, is a major disappointment. The main problem is that, in practice, it contradicts its own professed aesthetic convictions. It is true that, unlike W.H. New's comprehensive and nearly unreadable sociology textbook entitled *A History of Canadian Literature,* Keith at least evaluates the writers he discusses. That is, he lets us know if he finds a writer good or bad, and says why. Moreover, the book ends with a useful fifty-page annotated bibliography, which is well worth having. These are virtues which, given the absence of any serious competition, still make Keith's book the best current critical survey of Canadian literature in English.

However, as one reads him it gradually becomes clear that Keith is basing his critical method here not on aesthetic value, but on some other principle altogether: in fact, a political ideology. The nature of this ideology is made explicit in the 'Polemical Conclusion', which gets off to a bad start; it begins with some quoted doggerel by Dennis Lee from his poem 'When I Went Up to Rosedale', which Keith calls, I'm afraid, 'superb':

The dream of tory origins
Is full of lies and blanks,
Though what remains when it is gone,
To prove that we're not Yanks?

As poetry, as verse even — that is, aesthetically — the lines are inept; it is apparently the mere allusion to an idea that matters for Keith here. He describes this passage as a 'deeply serious quip', and 'an excellent instance of the continuity of Canadian tradition'. Why? Because it 'demonstrates [Lee's] debt to and independence of the thought of George Grant', who happens to be one of Keith's intellectual heroes.

How my heart sinks when, leaving all aesthetic discussion aside, Keith then launches into an argument for a nationalist literary ideology, an argument I find terribly depressing. Here it is in its essence: '[A] Canadian [may be defined as] one who has rejected the American Revolution and its implications,' he writes. Therefore, he argues, the Canadian literary tradition is 'essentially negative', meaning that 'Canadians have no alternative but to insist upon what they are not rather than what they are.' Moreover, and here is where Keith makes his basic critical principle clear, 'A healthy and vigorous Canadian literature is therefore of immense importance because it helps to clarify and so to maintain the distinction [between Canadians and Americans]. If literature holds a mirror up to our Canadian nature, it plays a significant role in proving "that we're not Yanks".'

I'm sorry to report that the whole book is undermined by this ideological underpinning; Keith's professed aestheticism, it turns out, is really the shield-bearer of his nationalism. His aesthetic values disappear as soon as he sees a connection between one Canadian writer and another, however bad, because the connection serves to reinforce a 'continuity of Canadian tradition' whose purpose is to prove Canadians are not Americans. Why he thinks Canadians have 'no alternative' but to go on endlessly proving to themselves that they are not Americans, like little Sisyphuses in some nationalist hell, is a mystery to me, but my point here is not really about his Tory brand of nationalism per se. (For what it's worth, I prefer Northrop Frye's liberal notion that the country we owe loyalty to is the Canada we have failed to create, but that's an argument for another day.) What I object to is the idea that Canadian literature as a whole has, or ought to have, any ideological purpose whatsoever. Keith's claim a few pages later in the same chapter that 'literature needs to be won back from the sociological, the ideological, and the politically approved, and restored to the human spirit of delight' is, to say the least, contradicted by his larger argument. That he doesn't seem to realize this is astonishing.

The implications of Keith's ideological obsession are especially disastrous when it comes to his understanding of Canadian literary tradition, which is the subject of his book. His survey, he explains in his original preface,

> lays its emphasis firmly on cultural tradition, the way in which literature in Canada began as a continuation of what was being produced in Great Britain, had to define itself against the American tradition as it developed in the United States, and eventually evolved as a distinctive literature related to but independent of both parent and neighbor.

Notice the Tory-nationalist assumption here: that Canadian tradition 'define[d] itself against' American tradition. We wouldn't be surprised, would we, if a critic who holds such an opinion were to ignore the possibility that a given Canadian writer has engaged admiringly with American writers in her work. Moreover — and this is the basic problem — Keith is acknowledging just three national traditions here, rather than the international traditions of the novel or poetry or drama per se; that is, he is acknowledging only national and not aesthetic traditions. And it's the aesthetic traditions that really matter.

Now, it is true that Keith acknowledges elsewhere in his book that 'it would be a mistake … to assume that the outside influences upon Canadian writing are confined to literature in English.' Hear, hear. But the instances he mentions of influences from other countries are all dependent upon either geography (Canada as a northern nation, for instance, and therefore influenced by Scandinavian literature) or ethnicity (through the writing of immigrants). He never acknowledges anything like an aesthetic tradition of fiction per se, or a tradition of lyric poetry or drama apart from national traditions.

Never, that is, except for one brief passage that at least begins to recognize some of the problems with his approach. Keith admits that 'much Canadian criticism is weakened if not vitiated by a constricted, even parochial outlook.' I couldn't have said it better myself. Still, he insists that

> there is no reason to believe that the perspective of the larger context renders that of the smaller in any way invalid. Shakespeare, Racine, Goethe, Tolstoy belong properly to the whole world, yet they are in essence English, French, German and Russian respectively, and are best understood within the setting of their own national literatures. A critical history of Canadian literature ... [is] proper and desirable as long as it is not regarded as the sole context for those considered within it.

But this is the heart of the problem. It may be true that, from the standpoint of, say, New Historicism or cultural studies, Shakespeare and Racine may best be understood within the setting of English and French culture, respectively. But from the standpoint of drama, that is, the aesthetic standpoint, which is what Keith insists is his standpoint, it is simply not true. Shakespeare learned how to write comedies, in the first instance, by reading Plautus. Racine's plays are based on ancient Greek myths, not to mention Aristotle's *Poetics*. To ignore such facts blinds us to these writers' fundamental aesthetic contexts. The larger context is always precisely the aesthetic one, even for writers from nations with great literary traditions like England and France.

This does not mean that writers are never influenced by writers from their own nations; of course they are. Nor does it mean that a critical survey of a national literature isn't desirable; of course it is. But it does mean that, if such a survey is to be genuinely based on aesthetic values (rather than, say, national themes, as in Atwood's *Survival*, or a nationalist 'continuity of Canadian tradition', as in Keith's book), then to do its job effectively and consistently it must continually remind us of that larger aesthetic context. Certainly this aesthetic context should never be distorted or suppressed for the sake of ideology, nationalist or otherwise.

But I'm afraid this is what happens when Keith gets down to the work of surveying Canadian literature. He claims in his preface that 'it is the tradition established by the best that sets the standard', by which he means the tradition of the best writers, judged aesthetically. But in practice he has an ideological story he is determined to tell, based on his 'special concern with cultural continuity', and this renders aesthetic value secondary at best. He wrestles as many writers as he can into his narrative of a continuous Canadian tradition, and thus ends up discussing at length all kinds of writers he acknowledges to be mediocre or bad because he needs them for this narrative. Thus, for example, he devotes nearly two pages to excoriating John Richardson, author of the 'melodramatic but influential' novel *Wacousta*, at last calling him 'the classic example of the inability of fiction to attain literary excellence in the absence of intellectual depth and stylistic expertise.' Similarly, as a playwright, James Reaney 'has a superfluity of dramatic inventiveness but little tact; he is well-endowed with vitality but sadly lacking in self-discipline and self-criticism', although for Keith's purposes, and here is the giveaway, it is important to mention that Reaney wrote a play called *Wacousta!*, even though it is 'even more melodramatic than Richardson's original and includes some surprising and embarrassing lapses in dialogue.' Keith is not writing a 'report on what has pleased [him]' here, let alone describing a 'tradition established by the best'; he is describing a tradition established by national cultural influence, regardless of aesthetic value or significance. And I'm afraid he does this sort of thing all the time.

Keith's Tory nationalism also leads him to ignore or suppress central aesthetic influences that are incompatible with his story — especially American influences. Thus, for example, he ignores the crucial influence of the American poets Richard Howard and James Merrill on the poetry of Jeffery Donaldson, preferring to focus instead on an allusion to Yeats in the title of his first book. And while he makes much of the impact of Sinclair Ross, Frederick Philip Grove, and Hugh MacLennan on the novels of Margaret Laurence, he ignores the fundamental influence of William Faulkner's Yoknapatawpha novels on Laurence's decision to write a series of books set in the fictional town of Manawaka. No less a Canadian nationalist than Margaret Atwood has testified to the profound influence of Faulkner on her generation of Canadian novelists, but you'd never know it from Keith's book. It is hard to escape the conclusion that Keith suppresses such influences because, according to him, Canadian literature 'had to define itself against the American tradition'. The effect is to distort our literary history.

Keith's inclusion of so many bad writers in his survey wouldn't be such a problem, perhaps, if he didn't exclude so many good ones. But in fact he makes some flabbergasting omissions. In his preface to the new edition he dismisses Anne Carson, for example, the one Canadian poet who is widely read today by serious readers of poetry outside of Canada, as merely 'avant-garde' and therefore outside of the mainstream; for this reason, he says, he will leave her to look after herself. The irony is that, for all Keith's concern with tradition, he is here dismissing out of hand one of our most traditional writers. Granted, her traditions are those of ancient Greek literature, the Bible, the Romantic sublime, and twentieth-century European modernism, and not the tradition of, say, Dorothy Livesay and Miriam Waddington, and so she doesn't fit into Keith's nationalist narrative; but to dismiss her in the same breath as bpNichol, as he does, is just bizarre. One suspects he simply hasn't read much of her poetry. Of his decision to ignore her, Keith writes, 'if this is a damaging admission on my part, so be it.' So be it indeed.

Another example: while he devotes two admiring pages, in his section on non-fiction prose, to an appreciation of the philosopher George Grant, he fails to mention the one Canadian philosopher who is widely read by serious readers of philosophy (not to mention political science and many other subjects) outside of Canada, the profound and compulsively readable Charles Taylor. Again, ironically, Keith is ignoring the most traditional of philosophers, the one who, in his magisterial book *Sources of the Self*, essentially defines the self as being constituted by a great tradition of value-makers from Plato to Rilke. In this case Keith doesn't have the excuse of his nationalist agenda, since Taylor has acknowledged the influence of George Grant on his own thought. The omission is simply inexplicable. I should add that he ignores Bernard Lonergan, too, one of the most important philosopher-theologians of the twentieth century. One begins to suspect that international acclaim in itself is enough to disqualify a Canadian writer from appearing in Keith's book.

Simply to list some of the other good writers whose names do not appear is instructive: George Elliot Clarke, Karen Solie, Ken Babstock, Russell Smith, Tim Bowling, Stephanie Bolster, Daryl Hine, Douglas Glover, Guy Vanderhaeghe, Dionne Brand and Barbara Gowdy. And, by way of comparison, here is a list of some of the bad writers Keith does discuss: Mazo de la Roche, Oliver Goldsmith (the younger), Charles Heavysege, Charles Sangster, Fred Wah, Gilbert Parker and Ralph Connor. Keith himself tells us they're bad, and I agree with him. But the effect of all this attention to bad

writing at the expense of good is to give the impression that Canadian literature is much worse than it really is. Which is the last thing we need.

One more serious weakness: Keith usually quotes little in the way of
evidence from the writers he discusses; and when he does quote he often
chooses examples that are either not good evidence for his points, or that
reveal little about the writers in question. He makes a point of avoiding the
mumbo-jumbo of much recent literary theory, and I commend him for it;
but unfortunately he has no effective critical vocabulary of his own. Instead
he relies heavily on a few adjectives. His favourite is 'impressive', a word so
vague as to be nearly without content; he must use the word a hundred
times. 'The risk of occasionally blurring through imprecision is,' he writes,
'in my view, outweighed by the advantage of simplicity and straightfor-
wardness.' He is talking here about another matter altogether — using
modern names for places in Canada that were once called something else
— but I'm afraid he might as well have been talking about his critical
method in this book.

That said, when it comes to the writers Keith discusses, good or bad, I
do find myself agreeing with his judgments a lot of the time, however
unsupported they may be. His discussion of fiction is especially sure-footed
in its conclusions, and while he takes too many bad poets seriously (W. W. E.
Ross and Raymond Souster among others), he also defends several who are
not always treated justly by other critics. And this makes the book, on the
whole, fairly useful, if not always reliable, for readers looking for a basic ori-
entation in the field, particularly for writing published before 1984.

And indeed, this seems to have been the original purpose of the book.
In fact, many of its faults seem attributable in large part to its publication
history: it first appeared in 1985 as a volume in the Longman Literature in
English Series, whose mandate was 'to provide students of literature with a
critical introduction to the major genres in their historical contexts'. In
other words, it was originally an academic survey intended mainly for
undergraduate readers, which seems to have meant, among other things,
that Keith felt obligated to acknowledge certain writers regarded as influential in Canadian literary history, regardless of their aesthetic merits. Seen in
this context, it seems the basic problem with the current 'revised' version is
that Keith left his original arguments, designed to fulfill a (by now) obsolete
purpose, largely untouched. It would have been better if his editor had
pushed him, or if he had pushed himself, to reassess his twenty- or thirty-

year-old critical positions and bring himself fully up to date with regard to significant current developments and careers.

To try to compensate for this lack of fundamental revision, Keith ends the expanded edition of his book, as I've mentioned, with a new 'Polemical Conclusion' in which he addresses what he calls our 'current crisis'. 'This is no time to mince words,' he writes. 'Scholarly detachment and propriety may be admirable in certain circumstances, but, no longer recognizing the need to spare the blushes of my profession, I now feel the need to speak out.' What is the crisis? According to Keith, 'the body of educated and discriminating readers in Canada prepared to support its national literature ... has collapsed,' a claim which he confusingly describes as 'pessimistic' and 'melodramatic'. I agree that it is melodramatic. Nevertheless, although he offers no evidence for its existence, he takes the supposed crisis seriously enough to try to explain its causes. One by one he blames the rise of science in Western civilization — no, I'm not kidding — the higher education system in Canada, literary awards, cultural subsidies, multiculturalism, thematic criticism, and popular culture, including film, television, video games, sports, partying, discos, slang and the Internet. Why such things haven't caused the collapse of an educated readership in other countries is not a question Keith raises. In short, it's hard to take his polemic seriously.

Which is not to say there are no serious problems facing Canadian literature. There are. But they aren't social problems; they're literary problems. One of them is the stubborn, or perhaps unconscious, provincialism of too many of our writers and critics. The Czech novelist Milan Kundera, in his recent book on the novel, entitled *The Curtain,* defines provincialism as 'the inability (or the refusal) to see one's culture in the *large context*' (the italics are his). This, as I have been arguing, is precisely the problem with Keith's book. For all his fine words about the human spirit of delight, Keith is fundamentally more concerned with his nationalist ideology here than with aesthetic value, and, as Kundera puts it, '[i]ndifference to aesthetic value inevitably shifts the whole culture back into provincialism.' It is not a problem unique to Canada. All countries, large and small, suffer from it to some extent. But the '[s]mall nation', Kundera argues,

inculcates in its writer the conviction that he belongs to that place alone. To set his gaze beyond the boundary of his homeland, to join his colleagues in the supranational territory of art, is considered pretentious, disdainful of his own people. And since the small nations are often going through situations in which their survival is at stake, they readily manage to present their attitude as morally justified.

Doesn't he describe us all too well? *Survival. To prove that we're not Yanks.* Provincialism in the small nation, Kundera is saying, is so thoroughly bound up with nationalist political ideology that the two are almost the same thing. I would only add that our critics have a responsibility to fight this attitude with all the passion and imagination they can muster.

Book of Revelations

'Love poems wither,' writes George Elliott Clarke, 'in our bleak, stony,/ frigid, hostile, brutal Canuck anthologies.' The lines are from his poem 'Blue Elegies: IV'. Clarke might as well have been describing what happens to the hopes of the poor jaded readers of those anthologies, who keep going back for more punishment every time a new one appears. There are many people responsible for this: the too easy-going editors, the poets disdainful of their craft, the reviewers and blurb-writers who bury these books with praise. And yet we keep going back because we love poetry so much. We want the poems to be good so badly we are willing to have our hearts broken again, if we must; only let us read the poems and see for ourselves.

And so it is with some astonishment, and more than a little joy, that I have just finished reading *The New Canon: An Anthology of Canadian Poetry*. It is not a perfect book, certainly. No anthology is. (And there are just too many typos, all of the spell-checked variety: 'stars' becomes 'starts', for example, and 'thought' becomes 'though'.) And yet it is clearly the most competently edited, memorable, and useful anthology of Canadian poetry to be published in a very long time.

Before I get to the poets, let me say a few words about the intentions of the editor, Carmine Starnino. In spite of its misleading title, *The New Canon* is not meant to replace the hopelessly outdated *Oxford Anthology of Canadian Verse in English* as the official canon of Canadian poetry. Rather, this is a selection of just one generation of English-language Canadian poets, those born between 1955 and 1975. As Starnino explains in his forceful introduction, he means the word 'canon' primarily in its aesthetic sense, as 'tenet' or 'rule' or 'principle'. And the principle here is simple: Starnino was looking for 'the most aurally ambitious, lexically alert, and formally intelligent poems' he could find. He was looking for poets with an innovative command of craft and an individual style. That such an axiom could be considered controversial, even revolutionary — and Starnino devotes much of his twenty-two-page introduction to its vigorous defence — is already an indictment of the prevailing canons of taste in Canadian poetry. Starnino explicitly positions his book in opposition both, on one flank, to 'the ruling aesthetic since the 1970s — the soft-spoken, the flatly prosy, the paraphrasingly simple, the accessibly Canadian' and, on the other flank, to the avant-garde 'zoo of rampant esotericisms' whose 'embrace of — why not say it? — nonsense' leads to poetry that 'always looks like a random trawl through an information-processing textbook.' Starnino, who invokes military metaphors more than once, might as well have called his anthology *The New Cannon.* And three cheers for that.

As for the poets: there are fifty-one of them here, which is ambitious. What country in the history of the world has produced fifty memorable poets in a single generation? Alas, I find just fourteen of them to be completely convincing. But fourteen is extraordinary. For readers used to finding just two or three good poets in a 'Canuck anthology', fourteen is a cause for celebration. Another half dozen or so have at least one very good poem, and of the others, some are promising, some merely interesting, some spectacularly or elaborately bad, but relatively few are dull. This is a revelation.

And so is the fairly wide variety of international poetic traditions these poets are working in. The ignorant reader will glance at a few poems and want to dismiss this as a collection of largely 'formalist' poets, using the term as a label of abuse; I mean the sort of reader who thinks any poem that makes interesting use of the language's prosodic and rhetorical resources must be the product of a thoroughly colonized imagination. Nothing I can say here will change such a reader's mind. But for everyone else, let me say that these are poets who actually read poetry, including the best poetry written in other countries.

Of the fourteen, several will be familiar to many readers. George Elliott Clarke is represented by four splendid poems that, among other things, demonstrate his masterful absorption of Derek Walcott and the blues: see in particular, and respectively, 'Look Homeward, Exile' and 'King Bee Blues'. Stephanie Bolster is here, often giving the impression that her feelings have fought against great resistance on their way to being vividly expressed on the page, and they're all the more powerful for having done so; see her poem 'On the Steps of the Met', if you don't know it already. The prolific Tim Bowling makes an appearance, a craftier Al Purdy, and his 'Love Poem, My Back to the Fraser' is an unwithering answer to Clarke's criticism of Canadian love poetry, worthy to be read next to Clarke's own delicious

'Monologue for Selah Bringing Spring to Whylah Falls'. Karen Solie and Ken Babstock are represented, too, Solie with her impressive and moving control of diction and rhetoric, as in 'Sick' and 'Java Shop, Fort McLeod', and Babstock with his superb ear and prosodic sense, and his large generic range, from the movingly confessional 'Palindromic' to his delightful monologue for a convenience store entitled 'The 7-Eleven Formerly Known as Rx'.

But the purpose of an anthology is to lead readers to poets they have never read before, and so I want to pass quickly to the nine first-rate poets in *The New Canon* whom readers may be less likely to know.

Jeffrey Donaldson, who will be a familiar name to the *cognoscenti*, is among the most impressive of the *New Canon* poets, an heir to the formal grace and urbane metaphorical wit of a Daryl Hine or a James Merrill. I feel the authority of Donaldson's voice very strongly, as in the closing lines of his poem 'Bearings', about an ancient map which, one soon gathers, is a map of Canada:

> Hard to believe, as it is,
> that anyone then or even later
>
> could have used this page, water stiffened,
> to get anywhere, least of all that broad
> unfinished landscape we navigate towards,
>
> being, as we are, unable to point out,
> put a finger on, the small print that legend
> has it marks our setting forth: *you are here.*

[Note: the text reads 'settling forth' but it's a typo.]

When you read this passage in the context of its poem, which I urge you to do, you will find that the exquisite word-play here, the pun on 'legend' as story and as directory, for example, is in the service of a profoundly imagined trope for what journalists call our Canadian 'identity crisis'. But Donaldson's poem is no cliché; it is rather a moving and intellectually complex representation of our national experience.

Elise Partridge impresses me as a true Canadian heir of Elizabeth

Bishop and Amy Clampitt, as in her poems 'Ruin' and 'Plague', respectively. One of the most memorable poems in *The New Canon* is Partridge's 'Buying the Farm', in which she vividly resurrects a series of dead metaphors for dying: 'crossing over', 'it's the end of the line', 'buying the farm', and, in the fourth stanza:

It's *curtains* for us,
clasping hands behind the dusty, still-swaying swag —
at last these doublets can come off,
the swipes of rouge and sideburns, then we'll stroll
to greet the flashing city with our true faces.

This is just the kind of subtle off-hand charm that, in Bishop and Partridge too, often covers for a powerful displaced myth, in this case a kind of Gnostic marriage of 'All the world's a stage' with the Celestial City of *Pilgrim's Progress,* or the New Jerusalem of the Book of Revelation. The result, for this reader, is pure delight.

The thoroughly charming Richard Sanger is notable for his formal skill and his ability to mix the imagery of an imagined European past with that of a Canadian present, to delightfully witty effect, rhyming 'Lake Huron' with 'Lord Byron', for instance. Here is a representative stanza from his poem, 'Wish', in which the poet longs to *be* Lord Byron:

And the hum in my ears

Grows louder and louder:
Is it rush-hour Toronto,
The Turks storming Lepanto,
Or the winged god that stung
This ruddy, swollen sky?
I slap my shoulder. Blood.

The bewitching irony here is that the more ironic the poem gets, the more like Byron the poet becomes, though not the Romantic Byron of life and legend, which is what he wants, but the witty, satirical Byron of *Don Juan.* This and the other poems of Sanger's, who is also a playwright, have the well-timed quality of marvellous performances.

The poems of Sue Sinclair recall Rilke's *New Poems,* his 'thing-poems' as he called them, in their meditative focus on one small thing at a time: a red pepper, a green pepper, a pitcher, collar bones, shoes in a shop window. Like Rilke's, Sinclair's descriptions are richly metaphorical, and her chosen objects ultimately become tropes for aspects of our humanity. Consider the last stanza of 'Red Pepper', for instance, a poem in which the pepper is 'The size / of your heart':

It is almost painful
to touch, but you can't help
yourself. It's so familiar.
The dents. The twisted symmetry.
You can see how hard it has tried.

Sinclair's art is an art of transformation, of taking a closely-observed object into the imagination and changing it there, and she does this movingly.

Christopher Patton, who as I write this has yet to publish his first book, brings a Zen power of clear-seeing to his poems along with a formal style reminiscent of Marianne Moore's syllabic verse, as in the powerful lyric 'The Vine Maple', and 'Red Maple', which contains this beautifully controlled description of a new-born foal and the world it suddenly finds itself in:

Wobble-legs falls.
Gets up, different. Its red-green
flower: adders' tongues, flawed
trumpets, baby-
squalls of flower-birds:

the spring wind shakes
it through ten thousand forms,
forms falling through themselves like
a train-station
departure board's

rain of changes.

The pleasure of reading Patton's language is so great that it's easy at first to miss the subtle spirituality of what he is doing; that is, until he springs it on us, often at the end of a poem, often with a phrase that recalls the Zen masters, and then the spiritual significance of what we have been reading is suddenly clear.

Adam Sol, by contrast, shows the influence of John Ashbery, always seemingly coming out of left field with arresting lines, but still somehow managing to break one's heart by the end of the poem: 'Don't kill yourself, you asshole,' he writes, devastatingly, near the end of 'Life, McKenzie', in a line addressed to a friend. In 'Conciliatory Letter to Morgan', he gives up in exasperation in the middle of the poem, and writes, startlingly, 'Oh, trying to say what I feel / is like sculpting with live spiders.' And in 'Man Who Slept Between Blows of a Hammer,' he explains, 'It was a festival of denials: there was the No, / and the Nono, and the Please no.' Sol's inventiveness might be a curse, as it is in more than a few poems of Ashbery's, but he keeps it under control just enough so that his poems add up to more than merely a random series of brilliant lines.

Though perhaps best known for his fiction, Michael Crummey is also a moving, humane poet, among the most intimate with the human heart of all the *New Canon* poets, although this is a quality hard to demonstrate with selective quotation. He is also a poet of powerful similes, and sometimes of deliberately roughened formal verse à la Thomas Hardy. 'The Late Macbeth' begins with this stanza:

> His body divorced him slowly,
> like a flock of birds leaving
> a wire, one set of wings at a time —
> still in sight, but past retrieving.

And this is his description of what a sealing crew did when they were caught in a storm on the sea ice, in the poem 'Newfoundland Sealing Disaster':

> Hovelled in darkness two nights then,
>
> bent blindly to the sleet's raw work,
> bodies muffled close for shelter,
> stepping in circles like blinkered mules.
> The wind jerking like a halter.

Crummey is a poet working in the tradition of Hardy and Frost, keeping his diction simple and deploying his formal and rhetorical skills above all for the sake of the emotional, the ethical effect.

Anita Lahey is another *New Canon* poet who as I write this has yet to publish a book, though when she does it is certain the centrepiece will be her sequence *Cape Breton Relative,* which imagines its way into the world and the language of Cape Breton Island by following a seemingly autobiographical protagonist, referred to as 'you', on a visit to her extended family there. In the final 'chapter', final at least among the sections printed here, the island itself has become a mythic giant, a bit like Sylvia Plath's 'Colossus', except that here he seems to be a kind of lover:

> With him you belong
> any old place: faraway cliff-top
> blue in his eyes, grassy hollows
> warmed into his chest. You climb
>
> daily into that crevice
> below his jaw, survey the jagged,
> sculpted world.

I look forward to reading the entire sequence when it is published. And her other poems are just as remarkable.

And finally, there is Pino Coluccio, a formalist who masterfully deplo meter and rhyme to achieve witty and moving effects. Consider his po 'Imaginary Wife', quoted below in its entirety:

> This is my imaginary wife.
> It's lonely without someone in your life
> to talk to after work about your day
> and share your weekends with, or special dinners.
> But real wives marry only winners
> who net more than double my gross pay.
>
> And so I made one up. I bring her flowers,
> our Scrabble matches last for hours and hours —
> thank God I found somebody I could marry,

gorgeous, if, it's true, imaginary.
The highway of our love is paved in years.
And when I want her to, she disappears.

Readers will sense the influence of Philip Larkin on this poem: Larkin's self-deprecation, his misogyny, his wit, his formal control are all present. And yet the language, as in Coluccio's other poems, is North American. Here, for instance, is the opening stanza of 'Standards', with its brand names and local slang:

The bony babes in Gap who lazily
Stroll with Starbucks cups at U of T,
Photoshopped or bio-engineered,
See me dreamy-eyed and think I'm weird.

As with Larkin, it's the self-deprecation, and the wit, that keep the misogyny bearable in these poems, though no doubt more for some readers than for others.

There are some other poems in *The New Canon* that I like a great deal: Geoffrey Cook's 'Fisherman's Song', Steven Heighton's 'Constellations', John Degan's 'Neighbours Are Dangerous', Diana Brebner's 'Port', Barbara Nickel's sonnets, and an exuberant poem by Bruce Taylor entitled 'The Slough'. Other readers will have their own favourites, of course. But it seems to me that, of the poets selected here, these fourteen or twenty will be the ones to follow closely in coming years, although I hope some of the ones I have, anonymously, called 'interesting' and 'promising' will pay their interest and deliver on their promises. And I hope there are others of this generation we have not heard from yet, some poets in their twenties and thirties with first books on the way, some poets still to come out of nowhere in middle age, and perhaps even some glorious *isolato* who will greet us or our children some day from beyond the grave. But already, the sheer wealth of very good poets in *The New Canon* is a revelation.

Still Out in Left Field

Canadian poetry anthologies are so notoriously disappointing that it takes some sense of duty or at least masochism to bring oneself to try again whenever a new one appears. It is not that such books don't include good Canadian poets. The problem is that they are so poorly edited one is obliged to plough through pages and pages of mediocre and atrocious verse to find a small handful of names worth reading.

Still, I am not easily discouraged, and I approached *Open Field: 30 Contemporary Canadian Poets* with, if not faith, at least a certain amount of hope and charity.

I will get to the book's poets in a moment, but first I want to acknowledge the intentions of the editor, Sina Queyras. What distinguishes *Open Field* from most anthologies of Canadian poetry is that it was published in the U.S., and intended for American as well as Canadian readers. God knows such a publishing venture was long overdue. American readers of poetry seldom read Canadian poets, with the exception of Anne Carson. Certainly the poetry of Atwood, Ondaatje and Cohen is available in American bookstores, but it is read mainly by fans of their bestselling novels, or, in Cohen's case, music. Carson is the only Canadian poet you can be sure nearly every American who reads contemporary poetry has read, and if she were ever to edit an anthology of Canadian poetry for American readers (don't hold your breath), you can be sure it would get noticed. One thinks longingly of the impact that Czeslaw Milosz's anthology *Postwar Polish Poetry* had when it introduced that once largely unknown but now widely celebrated and very influential literature to English-speaking readers. Queyras has nothing like the international stature of Milosz or Carson, so she may be congratulated for having persuaded an American publisher to take on this project.

How successful is it? Of the thirty poets in *Open Field,* half a dozen or so are superb, and, it must be said, half a dozen is better than average for such an anthology. Unfortunately, the book is not nearly as good as it might have been; in fact, it amounts to a seriously missed opportunity that may not come again for some time.

The book begins with a friendly foreword by the American poet Molly Peacock, a kind of letter of introduction to American readers on behalf of the ingénue, Canadian poetry, which nevertheless manages to be both naive and gently condescending at the same time: naive about Canada, and condescending about its poetry. Peacock, who was living in Toronto when she composed her introduction, writes charmingly about her gradual realization that Canada is not an 'annex' of the United States, but in fact 'another country'. Her charm is that of the American liberal, mildly needling herself and her fellow Americans for their obliviousness to the rest of the world. She finds several things to admire about Canada: from reading the *Globe and Mail* and listening to CBC radio, she concludes that ordinary Canadians are 'literate, sharp, thoughtful, and educated'. She marvels at the Canada Council ('Was it possible that the Canadian government was actually interested in poetry?'). And she comes to realize by watching a Canadian election that the differences between Canada and the United States have deep historical roots. (Although when we find her apparently borrowing without acknowledgement Northrop Frye's little myth of the two countries, respectively, as the good and rebellious daughters of a common parent, one suspects her realization may actually have happened in the library.)

When she comes to the poetry, however, Peacock immediately sets about lowering her readers' expectations — '[A] Canadian poem may seem … interminable … you may find yourself wondering when these poets will get to their points' — and yet generously urging them to give it a chance anyway: 'Don't panic if each poem doesn't start with a bang.' She calls Canadian poetry 'young, vigorous, and varied', and ends by claiming, without a rag of evidence, that it 'holds the possibility of refreshing all poetry in English'. What she seems to find most attractive about it, however, isn't its aesthetic quality but its 'cultural ideas' of 'compromise, cooperation, and coexistence'. She imagines literary Canada as a kind of Garden of Eden, where the lion and lamb lie down together, 'Language poet [living side by side with] New Formalist'. When it comes to admiring any particular Canadian poetry *as poetry*, however, Peacock is silent. Be kind to your sweet young cousin, she seems to be telling her fellow Americans; she'll grow up some day, and then you'll be glad you did.

This does not bode well for the poems, assuredly. And Queyras's introduction, I'm afraid, nearly snuffs my hopes out altogether. In a rhetori-cal choice which could hardly be less calculated to seduce an American liter-ary audience, Queyras presents herself as a naïf, the earnest and innocent sister of Frye's myth, the perfect object of Peacock's worldly condescension: that is to say, she describes herself as an 'exuberan[t]' literary nationalist, 'wear[ing] her country like a badge of honor'. (Peacock refers to her as an 'intrepid proponent of Canadian poetry', going, one supposes, where even angels fear to tread.) Queyras reveals that her first step, before she began to consider which poets to include, was to think of a title for the book; she says she thought of *Open Field* not only because it refers to Canada's 'geographi-cal space', but because it alludes to 'open field composition', which 'evokes the powerful connection of west coast poets Fred Wah, George Bowering, Daphne Marlatt and others, to the American Black Mountain poets.' If you happen to believe, as I do, that the poets she mentions are, to put it mildly, not among the best in Canada, then your heart sinks. And since the Black Mountain school was generally far less admired in the United States than it was in Canada, no doubt many American readers will feel a similar trepida-tion at her words. Thereafter, Queyras goes on to repeat some well-worn critical bromides about how Canadian poets have especially complex and intense relationships with nature (eat your heart out, Virgil, Lucretius, Wordsworth, Clare, Frost, Lawrence ...). And that's about it. Queyras offers almost no explanation of her editorial intentions, her standards and criteria for selection, her limits of inclusion and exclusion. She mentions that she hopes the book will be used in classrooms (a wish no doubt shared by her publisher), and adds that if it leaves the reader 'a little disoriented', then 'that is a good thing'. If you read anthologies, as I do, precisely in order to get oriented, you're out of luck.

Given this blithe lack of critical self-awareness, or at least self-disclo-sure, on the editor's part, it comes as no surprise to find that while the book does include a handful of strong poets, her anthology is ultimately a mess, a hodge-podge. What does the editor mean by a 'contemporary' Canadian poet? It's hard to say. P.K. Page, who published a book this year [2007], is out; bpNichol, who died in the 1980s, is in. French language poets are excluded, except for Nicole Brossard. The poets are presented in alphabetical order, which obscures all generational differences. Moreover, there is no attempt to represent the span of any particular poet's career: all of the poems by Margaret Atwood, for example, are from her two most recent collections, whereas all of the selections from Anne Carson are from her first. It does seem to be true that most of the poems were originally published in book form more or less since the early 1980s, although publication dates are not included in the acknowledgements for every poet, so it's hard to be sure. The editor's most explicit statement about her intentions, however vague, is that she meant to include a 'blend of formal and innovative work'; although given that she also speaks of 'formal innovation', a much more meaningful expression, what she apparently means is a mix of 'traditional' and 'avant-garde'. After piecing these clues together, then, it seems that what we have is a collection of traditional and avant-garde poetry originally published in the last twenty or thirty years by (mostly) English-language Canadian poets who began publishing books in the 1960s or later. Why these limits and not others? Who knows? Whatever the answer, the main effect is to exclude many of our finest older poets who are still alive and publishing.

As for critical standards, there simply don't seem to have been any, and I'm not just talking about the editor's silence on the subject. The poets range from very good to mediocre to appallingly bad, with rather more of the latter two. The choice of poems for particular poets is sometimes perverse. And there are many egregious exclusions. Allow me to consider each of these elements in turn.

First, the very good, of which, as I say, there are about half a dozen. Serious readers of Canadian poetry will know most of them already, which makes this anthology of not much use to them. However, all but one, Anne Carson, will certainly be new to American readers. This is the book's one redeeming quality, and it is of course a significant one (although, unfortunately, there is no bibliography to help readers find books by the poets they want to pursue).

The Trinidadian-born poet Dionne Brand is represented by a substantial excerpt from her long poem *Every Chapter of the World,* a ferocious feminist Jeremiad, and a fierce waterfall of syntax and metaphor in the tradition of the great black charismatic preachers, the poetry of Robert Desnos and Allen Ginsberg, and ultimately the Old Testament prophets. Here is an especially harrowing example:

every chapter of the world describes a woman at her own

massacre, carvings of her belly, blood gouache blood
of her face, hacked in revolutions of the sun and kitchens,

gardens of her eyes, asphalt lakes, in telescopes and bureau
drawers, in paper classifieds, telephones, exalted memories,

declarations, a woman at her funeral arrangements, why
perhaps so much of literature enters her like entering

a coffin, so much props up a ragged corpse she thinks,
the dry thin whistle of its mouth, the dead clatter

of its ribs, the rain in its room all day, all night, all
evening, the women walking out of its skull one

by one by one ...

With the emotional temperature turned up so high it would be all too easy
for this to fly off its rhetorical rails, but Brand is always in control, always
carefully modulating her imagery and rhetoric to the purpose at hand.
Notice how, for example, in the passage above, she makes brilliant use of
rhetorical lists, each new image a surprise, new clauses sometimes beginning with a repeated word or phrase and sometimes not, as it suits the
rhythm. This is a masterful performance, and the result is moving indeed.

Karen Solie is also here, with seven well-made lyrics, including the
witty 'Cardio Room, Young Women's Christian Association' and the moving
'Meeting Walter Benjamin'. I am especially enamoured of her poem
'Thrasher', about the mimicking songbird of the same name whom Solie,
through her admiration, suggests is a kind of avatar of herself as a poet. Here
are the closing stanzas, which describe his multifarious calls:

... In relief at the topmost, he mimics domestic, migrant,
spaniel, spring peepers, quacks, urks, and gurgles akin

to a four-stroke in heavy water. He's slightly

off. None respond. His own call is the vinyl scratch

between tracks, a splice point. He was hatched

that way, ferruginous, a wet transistor
clacking from the egg in which he had lain curled

as an ear with an itch inside. He carries on
like AM radio. Like a prison rodeo. Recounts loser

baseball teams, jerry-riggers, part-timers, those paid in scrip,
anyone who has come out of retirement once

too often. He is playbacks, do-overs, repeats, repeats
the world's clamorous list, makes it his, replete,

and fledges from persistence what he is.

There's so much to love about this: the continually surprising images in their rhythmically apposite clauses, the subtle and complex assonance and consonance, the brilliant and fully imagined metaphors, the relaxed but effective prosody, the beautifully folded syntax of the final line. Reading this, I can't help but feel that Solie is one of our most striking younger poets.

It's a pleasure to find George Elliott Clarke here, as well, one hand in the blues tradition, the other in the great line of English poetry. My favourites among the poems of his included here are two love poems, the bluesy 'To Selah', and the delightfully open-hearted 'Monologue for Selah Bringing Spring to Whylah Falls'. Here are the final two verse paragraphs of the latter:

I'm scripting this lyric because I'm too shy
To blurt my passion for you, Selah!
My history is white wine from a charred log,
A white horse galloping in a meadow,
A dozen chicks quitting an egg carton tomb,
But also selfish, suicidal love.
I don't want that!
  Selah, I want to lie beside you

And hear you whisper this poem and giggle.
Selah, I thought this poem was finished!
Selah, I am bust right upside the head with love!

One would have to turn to the modern Spanish shepherd-poet Miguel Her-
nandez (whose selected poems in English is called *I Have Lots of Heart*) to find
quite this degree of unabashed emotional exuberance. Clarke achieves this
effect with a sophisticated weave of the high literary and the vernacular:
notice the final line above, at the same time a well-crafted alexandrine and,
of course, a charmingly effective deployment of African-American and
-Canadian idiom.

Ken Babstock makes an appearance with four poems, including his rue-
fully witty and moving confessional poem about a lonely and almost wasted
year, entitled 'Palindromic'. Consider these sardonic lines from near the end
of the poem:

> Stuff fell in the fall. No one took pictures.
> Or painted the scene on wood panel in oil, of the day
> none of my friends and I decided not to go halves
>
> on a driving trip through some of Vermont. I read Frost
> and stayed where I was.

And a little later:

> By November I was an art installation
> begging the question are empty days at the core
> of the question of begging the question.

This is very funny, but in the context of the rest of the poem, painfully so;
good comedians know that the best jokes come from painful experience.
When I say the poem is about an almost wasted year, I mean that Babstock
has redeemed it with his wit, his art. The same is true of his poem 'What We
Didn't Tell the Medic', about a terrible motorcycle accident. This is not all
Babstock is good at — indeed he is a poet of exceptional range — but this is
the quality that comes through most in the poems selected here.

I also enjoyed the poems of Todd Swift very much, most of them skilful and moving lyrics in the stoical English tradition of Auden and Larkin, as in 'Homage to Charlotte Rampling' and 'Ballad of the Solitary Diner'. But I'm especially attracted to his witty homage to Wallace Stevens, rather awkwardly titled 'The Influence of Anxiety at the Seaside With Tea', a kind of admiring and self-reflexive imitation of 'The Idea of Order at Key West'. Here are the closing lines, all meant to describe someone's experience of reading Stevens's *Harmonium:*

This was the first performance of the storm, the horn
Section was off. The rain pulled toads from its hat.

The world was brushed with cream like a scone.
Happiness was inherited and could not be taxed.
She swam Olympic strokes, and sang circular tracks.
The sea undressed, a Parisian girl, *oh la la, mais oui.*

How could one not be charmed by such a display of metaphorical inventiveness, particularly if one shares Swift's love for Wallace Stevens (and who doesn't)? Of all the best poets in *Open Field,* Swift is the one I was least familiar with, and I am grateful to Queyras for bringing him to my admiring attention.

The biggest surprise in the book concerns the poems of Dennis Lee, all from his 2003 volume called *Un.* I dislike Lee's earlier books, but several of the fifteen brief lyrics or sections included here are wonderful: they have the inventive diction and sprung rhythms of Hopkins or Paul Celan, albeit certainly without those poets' theological anguish. Indeed, sometimes they sound more like e.e. cummings. Here is one of my favourites:

gone
An earth ago, a
God ago, gone
easy:

a pang a lung a
lifeline, gone to
lore.

Sin with its
numberless, hell with its
long long count:

nightfears in
eden, gone eco gone
pico gone home.

I'm thoroughly charmed by this poem: by its big ideas and emotions con-
veyed in the simplest possible diction, its skilful free verse, its delightful
rhythms. Not all of his poems here are this convincing, but enough are that
I have started to change my mind about Dennis Lee.

Unfortunately, Lee's is the one case in which Queyras's habit of choosing poems from just one or two of a poet's books produces a happy result.
Usually the effect is strangely perverse. Take the case of Anne Carson, represented here entirely by selections from her first book, *Short Talks*, which are
certainly not among her best work. Carson at her best is one of the strongest
poets we have, not to mention our most internationally respected, and she
deserves to be treated accordingly in an anthology like this. The selections
here are interesting experiments, and some of them contain some memorable phrases, but none of them have anything like the power of later
poems like 'Isaiah' or 'The Glass Essay'.* One can only speculate that the
publisher considered it too expensive to purchase the reprint rights for her
later poems, and so made the decision to go with poems from a book published by Anansi rather than poems published by, say, Knopf. If so, shame on
the publisher. (Another example is George Elliott Clarke; all of his poems
are taken from *Whylah Falls*, whereas some of his strongest lyrics, like the
Blue Elegies, are to be found in later books.)

So much, then, for the best poets here. There are one or two other talents worth mentioning: I find the Newfoundland English of Mary Dalton's
poems to be a real pleasure, and look forward to following her develop-

---

* From the perspective of five years later — that is, since this essay was first published — I would have to say that very little of Carson's poetry since *Glass, Irony and
God* has the power of those poems, either, though she has done some fine things in
other genres, notably criticism and translation.

ment. I could say much the same thing about Joe Denham, whose poems about west coast commercial fishing, while slight, are promising.

There are a few other poems that I like very much, here, too, namely Don McKay's 'Sometimes a Voice (1)', and two loose translations in the tradition of translations by Ezra Pound and Robert Lowell: bpNichol's 'From Catullus Poem LI', and a selection from Erin Mouré's translation of Fernando Pessoa's 'Sheep's Vigil for a Fervent Person'. In each case, the poem in translation strikes me as far better than any of the other poems by Nichol or Mouré included here.

But if Queyras can take editorial credit for the good poets and poems I have mentioned so far, then she also deserves responsibility for the bad. And there are far too many of these here. I won't bore you by quoting every one. But consider some of the most egregious examples.

What lover of Rilke's *Duino Elegies* doesn't wince when he or she comes across the opening lines of George Bowering's bathetic travesty of that masterpiece, his *Kerrisdale Elegies:* 'If I did complain, who among my friends/ would hear?' It would be one thing if Bowering had produced a witty parody, a satire, the way Pope deflates Homer, Virgil, and Milton in *The Rape of the Lock,* or else given us an admiring and self-conscious homage to Rilke, as Todd Swift does in his poem on Wallace Stevens; but no, on the contrary, his poem has nothing to do with Rilke's poetry besides offering up some clumsy echoes of some of its phrases. Instead, it is full of clichés about romantic love that Rilke would have found appalling:

> You should know by now,
> the world waited
> to come alive at your step —
> could you handle that?
> Or did you think this was love,
> movie music
> Introducing a maiden you could rescue?
> Where were you going to keep her,
> and keep her
> from seeing those dreams you were already
> playing house with?
>
> When your heart hungers,

sing a song of six-
teen, remember your own maidenly love
and the girls that aroused it,

make them famous.

I find it difficult to believe any serious reader could be fooled by this. ('The world waited/to come alive at your step'? '[S]ing a song of six-/teen'?) And yet apparently Queyras is not the only one. Perhaps it's my fierce love of Rilke's poetry that makes this so infuriating, but isn't the fact that the author of these godawful lines was Canada's first poet laureate more than a little embarrassing?

Let us pass to another example: Christopher Dewdney, a poet so in love with vague and abstract diction, obfuscatory jargon, and dull syntax as to make one wonder whether the stuff is actually meant to be a parody of something. Consider the opening of his prose poem 'The Immaculate Perception':

Consciousness requires the immaculate 'separateness' of objects
of its attention. It is necessary that the boundaries of the 'object'
are clear, in order to fortify its identity, its distinction from the
matrix.

Identity is signification.

Perception, the actual neurochemical process of the nervous
system, is not as specific as the *ideal* of signified attention ascribed
to as 'consciousness'.

And so on. It reads like a badly written psychology textbook. As poetry I find it unbearable.

Or consider the opening of this poem by Fred Wah entitled 'Music at the Heart of Thinking 52':

tongue mist lip boat brown gull hill town bed
stone shadow crow tooth rain boat flood hammer star grill shadow skin hammer mouth town
mist hill rock brown bed bird tongue snow creek

You get the idea; the entire poem is like this, and it continues for seven more lines. Could anything possibly be more inert? Granted, this is an inter-esting exercise, but it's ultimately tedious and claustrophobic. In the world of this poem, all verbs and adverbs and all but one adjective have been amputated from the language.

I won't go on like this; it's too painful. Let me just say that too many of the poets in this anthology make the same kind of error: they adopt one technique, usually involving some arbitrary and severe rhetorical self-muti-lation, and beat it to death. For example, several poets reveal themselves here to be hopelessly addicted to the listless sentence fragment; these include Michael Ondaatje, Daphne Marlatt, Erin Mouré and Anne Simpson, the latter compounding the monotony by restricting herself for an entire interlocking seven-sonnet sequence to extremely short sentences and sen-tence fragments. Christian Bök, trying to be inventive, limits himself in Oulipo fashion to one vowel at a time, something another Canadian poet, Daryl Hine, did thirty or forty years ago in his poem 'Vowel Movements'. (Hine did it in metrical verse, however, whereas Bök resorts to prose.) In my opinion Hine comes out slightly the better of the two, but in neither case is the result anything but an elaborate parlour game, a fun but ultimately empty rhetorical exercise, and again, unbearably claustrophobic.

Why do these poets choose to hobble themselves in these ways? Per-haps they are tempted by what seems to be an easy way to appear singular and new. Perhaps, as in the case of the sentence fragment, they pick up the bad habit by emulating other poets because they think it sounds 'poetic'. Perhaps it has to do with a certain ad hoc or auto-didactic rhetorical train-ing, so that poets unaware of the vast range of possibilities (see the com-plete works of Shakespeare) become unhealthily enamoured of one or two techniques and simply won't let go. Who knows? But it needs to be said that this is not 'innovation', any more than it is innovation to step into a potato sack along with some other contestants and bounce up and down to a finish line. Great fun, yes; but it's ultimately a grotesque parody of human move-ment, and not serious or even interesting. Far better to discipline one's walking or running stride.

If I have been tough on these poets, and on Queyras for including them, it is only because there are so many better poets who deserve to be here instead. Even if she wanted to limit herself to younger ones, why not include such poets as Tim Bowling, Stephanie Bolster, Jeffrey Donaldson, Elise Partridge, Sue Sinclair, Richard Sanger, Christopher Patton, Adam Sol,

Michael Crummey, Anita Lahey or Pino Coluccio? They are, for all of their differences from one another, far more versatile and flexible in their use of rhetoric and prosody, among other things, than many of the poets included here. There are several strong middle-aged poets Queyras inexplicably ignores, as well: Eric Ormsby, Robert Allen, Robyn Sarah, among others. And why exclude Canada's finest older poets from the category of 'contemporary' if they are still very much alive and publishing? I have mentioned P.K. Page, whose absence here is scandalous, but it's just as mystifying not to find Margaret Avison, Don Coles, and Daryl Hine.* And finally, why include just one token French-language poet? Why not include the best translations available of the best contemporary French-language poets in Canada, and commission new translations if necessary? For the life of me, I have never understood why English-Canadian poetry anthologies since A.J.M. Smith's *Oxford Book of Canadian Verse* have marginalized French-Canadian poets in this way. It seems provincial to me, unsophisticated, and only impoverishes English language poetry in Canada.

So how is it possible that so many fine poets could be neglected and so many bad and mediocre ones innocently offered up for international inspection? The answer could lie simply in the choice of Queyras as editor. Or it could be that critics of Canadian poetry haven't been doing their jobs, or that not enough of them have been doing their jobs well enough or long enough to make much of a difference in the opinions of an editor like Queyras. My guess is that it's both. At any rate, what I know is this: just and clear-eyed critics of Canadian poetry have their job cut out for them. And we desperately need their services.

---

* Page, Avison and Hine have all died since this essay first appeared in 2007.

☆

Choosing the Best Canadian Poetry

Perhaps you have a copy of Margaret Atwood's *New Oxford Book of Canadian Verse in English* on your bookshelf. (Go ahead, blow the dust off it: ah, there it is.) This last real attempt to formulate a canon of English-language Canadian poetry for the common reader was published three decades ago, in 1982. It's true that a handful of classroom anthologies have appeared since then, but they're as full of howling gaps and bewildering misjudgments as a pre-Mercator map of *Nouvelle France*. A new reader waking up tomorrow morning in a hotel in the city of Canadian poetry will find herself not only without a concierge but without so much as a *Lonely Planet*, and will have to rely heavily on a rack of pamphlets advertising local attractions and tourist traps. It's an intolerable situation. A very few clear-eyed poet-critics are out there visiting the museums, sampling the new restaurants, and publishing their reviews, but we're still a long way from having any guidebook that is both comprehensive and reliable.

We have our excuses. It's hard to know what's happening overall, people say, because so many new poets and new books are published every year — though we have a mere market garden compared to the annual industrial farm crop in the United States. The truth is we need more good critics.

There's also a desperately needed revaluation of our older generations just getting under way, and this complicates things further. For every reputation that remains strong, P.K. Page's, for example, there are, or ought to be, half a dozen teetering on the brink: I'm thinking of George Bowering, Eli Mandel, bpNichol, Raymond Souster and Fred Wah, among others. And excitingly, there are a few excellent older poets, such as Daryl Hine and Richard Outram,* who are only now beginning to get the critical attention they deserve. There is no widespread agreement about all this; what looks obvious to me will probably be hotly disputed by others. In order to sort

---

* Hine, Outram, Page and Souster have all died since this essay first appeared in 2009.

this all out, what we need is a huge critical effort — excuses be damned — and a decisive debate.

Two generations of poets have come of age since Atwood's anthology appeared. In the older, middle-aged group are several poets who have achieved a pair of rare and beautiful things: technical mastery, and an authoritative engagement with international poetic traditions. Atwood more or less predicted that the first of these things would happen when she wrote in her introduction that 'There is a renewed interest among many of [the younger poets] in the intricacies of rhetoric, and an emphasis on the poem as consciously crafted.' Her comment ought to have prepared me for my gut-wrenching disappointment in reading the poetry of so much of Atwood's celebrated generation, too many of whose poets turned against rhetoric and conscious craft with a vengeance. What is astonishing to me now is who the supposed young virtuosos were that she was talking about: not Anne Carson, Eric Ormsby, Jeffery Donaldson, or George Elliott Clarke — masterful poets who would come along a decade later, often publishing their first books relatively late — but mostly middling talents or worse, like Susan Musgrave and Christopher Dewdney.

The younger generation, more or less in its twenties and thirties, is, I'm happy to report, full of excellent poets — many of whom you may not have heard of because they have yet to publish a first book, or have produced just one or two. The more prolific and better-known include Ken Babstock, Stephanie Bolster, Tim Bowling and Karen Solie, but there are plenty of others who are for the moment largely unknown, though no less gifted. What they all have in common is a deeply informed deployment of the whole magical repertoire of rhetoric and prosody, and a strong engagement with poetic traditions, including those of the best poets in other countries. Like certain poets of the older generation, Carson, Ormsby & Co., they have sloughed off at long last that inbred provinciality and bizarre disdain for the art of poetry that has crippled the work of so many Canadian poets in earlier generations, though, thank God, not all of them. It is a very exciting time to be a reader of poetry in Canada. But for this to be sustained and not wasted, what we need now, and urgently, is a clear-eyed, energetic and discerning critical response.

One of the most exciting of the new critical projects to take up this challenge is the inaugural anthology of a promised annual series of *The Best Canadian Poetry*, which will be guest-edited by a new poet every year. The series editor is the poet Molly Peacock, who is also poetry editor of the *Literary Review of Canada*. The guest editor of the first volume in the series (2008) is Stephanie Bolster, who, as an accomplished poet of the younger generation, was a superb choice. I do not agree with all her judgments, but I have the highest respect for her avowed principles of selection: 'good writing', 'depth and challenge', and 'an interesting, even strange, sensibility or imagination'.

There are, however, two conceptual flaws in the project, and the editors offer little or no explanation for them. Following certain rules she established in collaboration with Molly Peacock and the publisher Halli Villegas at Tightrope Books, Bolster chose one hundred poems, by one hundred different Canadian poets, published in Canadian journals in 2007, of which the top fifty poems have been printed in the anthology and the rest listed in a section at the back. But because the editors decided for some reason to choose no more than one poem per poet, no doubt some of the best poems by the very best poets were excluded from consideration, and that's a shame.

Moreover, since the selection was limited to poems published in Canadian journals, the best Canadian poems published in journals in other countries are not included either. As Bolster herself explains, few of Canada's established poets publish in Canadian literary journals much any more, for one reason or another, and so this decision limited her pool fairly drastically. Granted, much of this was out of the editors' hands, since some of these poets seem to have eschewed journal publication altogether in 2007. But why make the problem worse by ignoring foreign journals? The reduced pool explains the disappointing absence of Anne Carson, Don Coles, George Elliott Clarke, Eric Ormsby, Dionne Brand and several others whose poems many readers would have expected to see.

And all this helps explain why, of the fifty poems printed in the book, I find just sixteen first-rate, though another five come close; the latter are very good but could benefit from some further revision. The other twenty-nine range in quality from the talented to, I'm afraid, the truly bad.

So why do I find this anthology so exciting? Because I discovered so many fine new poets in its pages, no less than fifteen in all. Of my favourite sixteen poems, just five are by poets I knew: Ken Babstock, Tim Bowling, Jeffery Donaldson, A.F. Moritz and Todd Swift. The other twelve were new to me: Maleea Acker, John Wall Barger, Brian Bartlett, Yvonne Blomer, Heather

Cadsby, Anne Compton, Susan Elmslie, Iain Higgins, Amanda Lamarche, Craig Poile, Anna Swanson and J.R. Toriega. And of the five near-first-rate, just one was by a poet I knew, Carmine Starnino; the others, Jason Houroux, Michael Lista, Heather Sellers and David Seymour, were new to me as well. For these discoveries I am exceedingly grateful to Bolster for her industry and critical acumen.

I do have a suggestion, however, for future volumes in the series, which, if adopted, might do its part to help us build the critical effort we so desperately need. A critical judgment is only as good as it is persuasive; that is, it depends, or ought to depend, not on the inertia of tacit and passive agreement, of the sort that keeps anthologizing our dear bad poets, but on the force of the critical argument that can be made for it. Therefore I suggest that in future volumes the guest editor write a brief critical argument, say one page, on behalf of each chosen poem. If that means choosing fewer poems, so be it. The current volume includes a section of the chosen poets' (sometimes self-indulgent) comments on their poems, only some of which are useful or interesting, and none of which contributes much to our reading of the poems. I'd like to see them replaced with the guest editor's arguments. The series editor would need to bar the door to book-jacket-blurb puffery and pseudo-intellectual mumbo-jumbo, and demand well-chosen evidence and clear reasoning. But if every year this project turned one of our best poets, the guest editor, into a better and more prolific critic, it would be wonderful. And his or her critical responses, if well-written, would be invaluable in themselves.

The following was published as a letter to the editor of the Literary Review of Canada. *It is my reply to Fraser Sutherland's essay entitled 'A Response to James Pollock's "Choosing the Best Canadian Poetry"'.*

My thanks to Fraser Sutherland for his genial response, but I take issue with three points.

He blames the poor state of poetry criticism in Canada, in part, on the 'dismal landscape' of our institutional literary culture — blogs, prizes, journals, workshops, subsidies, public readings, poetry organizations — but I'm impatient with this familiar line of complaint. The form the institutions take doesn't matter. What matters is that well-read, energetic, honest critics, who write well, devote themselves to writing criticism. We're not talking about producing operas here. True, critics need venues, and fortunately they've got some. But otherwise, all they need is a bit of time, a few review copies, and a laptop. Let our best potential critics stop making excuses and get to work.

I'm more sympathetic when Sutherland blames literary theory, especially post-structuralism, for the decline of evaluative criticism; on this subject I refer interested readers to Ronan McDonald's useful recent book, *The Death of the Critic*. But let's not get carried away. Sutherland attacks the supposedly destructive influence of Frye and Atwood, but Frye, besides being a great theorist and interpreter, and therefore extraordinarily helpful to interpretive and evaluative critics, was the finest reviewer of Canadian poetry we had in the 1950s. See his collected reviews in *The Bush Garden*. As for Atwood, I do not agree that *Survival* is deplorable. It has nothing to do with evaluative criticism, but as cultural theory it's brilliant. The problem is not that Frye's or Atwood's influence was too strong. It is that, in the last half of the twentieth century, no other critic in Canada was strong enough.

Finally, to answer Sutherland's question about my disappointment with so many of the poets of Atwood's generation: I'm dismayed, in reading Purdy, Newlove and MacEwen, among others, by their poverty of technique. I'm with him when he writes that 'craftsmanship is no guarantee of good poetry'. I've never heard anyone say it is. But surely it's a prerequisite. Against craftsmanship Sutherland cites Whitman of all poets, that master of rhetoric and free-verse prosody, so he's apparently confusing craftsmanship with traditional formalism here. To say my 'critical tastes lean toward the formalist' is therefore incorrect; I value technical mastery, whether avant-garde, formalist or in between, because it is indispensable to good poetry. Of course, I value other things too — imagination, intelligence, emotion, sensuousness, moral force, spiritual insight, innovation, engagement with tradition — but if the technique is weak, I'm just not interested.

☆

Long Time Coming

On the rare occasions when my American literary friends ask me, as an expatriate Canadian, to recommend some poets from my country, the first thing I do is steer them away from the anthologies. Let me make you a list, I say, and whip out my pen. If I see an old disused copy of *The New Oxford Book of Canadian Verse in English* or *15 Canadian Poets X 3* on someone's bookshelf, however, I know it's already too late; that reader won't be taking a stab at Canadian poetry again until something drastic happens. 'No, really,' I splutter, 'We do have good poets in Canada,' but I can see what my friend, with her quizzical look, is thinking: 'If you guys can't get your act together to produce a decent anthology, I'm not wasting my time.' And so, when I stumbled upon the English critic Michael Schmidt's dismissive remark, in his 1998 book *Lives of the Poets*, that Canadian poetry is a 'short street', I understood exactly what had happened: he'd been reading our anthologies. It was going to take a lot to change his mind.

Fortunately, Evan Jones and Todd Swift, two Canadian poets living in the U.K., have taken Schmidt's dismissal as a challenge. Schmidt is editorial director at Carcanet in the U.K.; and Jones and Swift persuaded him to publish, and let them edit, the first anthology of Canadian poetry to appear in Britain in fifty years, a book entitled *Modern Canadian Poets*. Any editors with that kind of spirit deserve a considered read.

And I am, I'm happy to report, delighted by the editors' stated principles of selection: 'We offer poets with an interest in the wider cosmopolitan tradition and history of poetry: poets of sophistication, style, and eloquence; poets who are informed by the great poetry that came before them.' I can't tell you what a thrill it was to read these words. After slogging through so many anthologies designed to explore national themes and draw lines of national continuity, it's just tremendously exciting to find editors who are actually interested in Canadian poetry as poetry. Moreover, the editors make just the right diagnosis: that Canadian poetry has been isolated from the world by an inward-looking nationalism, which, they say, is exactly what their anthology is designed to help over-come.

Even better: the editors put their principles to work in their selections. They take a huge leap forward by excluding a great whack of bad and medi-ocre but endlessly-anthologized poets: the 'loud-mouthed, formless Every-man' poets, as the editors call them (let's say, Al Purdy, John Newlove and George Bowering), along with the mediocre celebrities who are 'no longer poets firstly' (presumably Margaret Atwood, Leonard Cohen and Michael Ondaatje), and, not least, though the editors don't even mention them, the usual boring representatives of the avant-garde (Fred Wah, bpNichol and Christopher Dewdney, among others). This great debunking is so long over-due, and so welcome, it fills me with joy. When a country lionizes its bad and mediocre poets and marginalizes its good ones, the effect on its younger poets, not to mention the literary culture as a whole, is devastating. At first it's confusing, then depressing, then it fills anyone with any spirit with right-eous indignation. To see someone finally, finally, point out in an anthology that the Emperor has no clothes, is just tremendous.

Moreover, I have never read a general anthology of Canadian poetry with such a sustained rate of excellent choices. Of the thirty-eight poets here, no less than two dozen are very good, among Canada's best. For com-parison, in Gary Geddes's aforementioned classroom anthology, *15 Canadian Poets X 3* (2001), just nine or ten of the forty-five poets are very good. Jones and Swift treat us to selections from A.M. Klein, John Glassco, Anne Wilkin-son, Irving Layton, George Johnston, Douglas LePan, P.K. Page, Margaret Avison, Don Coles, Richard Outram, Jay Macpherson, Daryl Hine, John Thompson, Eric Ormsby, Robert Allen, Robyn Sarah, Anne Carson, Dionne Brand, Elise Partridge, George Elliott Clarke and, among French Canadians, Emile Nelligan, Hector de Saint-Denys Garneau, Anne Hébert and Robert Melançon. (There are also five more poets whose presence here I'm merely ambivalent about, namely Joan Murray, Anne Compton, A.F. Moritz, Mary Dalton and Steven Heighton.) Given this hoard of riches, all the following caveats, however serious, are mere footnotes.

So finally I've got an anthology of Canadian poets I can recommend to my friends. But I'm afraid it could have been even better, and in several ways.

One problem has to do with the way the editors interpret their guiding principle of cosmopolitanism. In most cases it means what they say it means: sophistication, style, eloquence, an interest in the wider tradition and history of poetry, and responsiveness to the great poetry of the past. I couldn't be happier with that. However, occasionally what it seems to mean is simply that the poet has an international background; or that he or she was an early imitator, for a Canadian, of modernist technique; or that his or her subject matter is international, even if their poems are not particularly good. Thus, for example, the editors write of David McGimpsey that his poems unfold in an 'international landscape ... in terms often openly and sarcastically Canadian, even provincial'. Provincial treatment of international subject matter is not a promising recipe for good poetry — I should think, if anything, it would be the reverse — and the McGimpsey poem included here, a long and apparently earnest elegy for the actor who played the Skipper on *Gilligan's Island,* called 'In Memoriam: A.H., Jr.' — no, I'm not kidding — illustrates my point:

Jonas Grumby,
You ran straight into a palm tree & conked-out.
A severe case of *bumpinus on the nogginus....*

And so on for 250 lines. All its American material, and the superficial allusion to Tennyson in the title, can't make this poem cosmopolitan in the true sense, wanting as it is — to use the editors' words — in sophistication, eloquence and style.

Then there are the early-adopters: the good old bad poet W.W.E. Ross, and the interesting striver Alfred Bailey. (The editors call the latter 'infinitely modern', whatever that means.) Neither is any good, despite the editors' protestations. Here's Ross, flat as a piece of paper:

The reflection of the moon in the water.
It is broken by the ripples.
The silence.

And here's a bit of one of his melodramatic and incoherent prose poems:

Along the trenches of the understanding runs the electric explosive assault that ends by turning them in a new direction. The others, those that remained, were not capable of the transmutation necessary.

Doesn't this sound like a bit of dime-store science fiction from the 1930s? The editors open their book with this stuff, though not before introducing poor Ross as having 'made an impact few poets of his generation achieved'. Not an auspicious beginning for this anthology, to say the least. (If only it had started instead with, say, 'The Truant' by E. J. Pratt.) And here's Bailey, the second poet in the book, whose 'rare achievement has cemented his importance':

> We the People
> of the great North American
> societal provenience
> await with hope
> the hazard of high endeavour
> with a good deal of uncertainty,
> not to say misgiving.

And we your readers/await with hope/your learning to write/with a good deal of uncertainty,/not to say despair. It doesn't matter that these poets were ahead of their time in Canada in their imitation of modernist techniques — imagism in Ross's case, and, supposedly, the metaphysical in Bailey's. If their poems were any good, it would be a different story. But alas, they're not.

And finally, there are the multinationals: the German-American-Canadian poet Norm Sibum, and the Polish-English-Canadian expatriate poet Marius Kociejowski. I don't know their work very well, and the editors supply just one very long poem for each, so I hesitate to make any sweeping judgments; but based on the limited evidence offered here, it seems to me their inclusion has much more to do with their international pedigree than the quality of their work. And I have a similar reaction, on the given evidence, to the work of the Canadian-British-American poet David Wevill.

All three of these debased versions of cosmopolitanism — those based on subject-matter, early adoption of modernist style, and international background — are dangerous because they lose sight of the main thing: sophistication, style, eloquence and genuine responsiveness to the great poetry of the past, including the poetry of other countries. In a published interview the editors inadvertently put their finger on the problem when they refer to their cosmopolitan principle as an argument for 'a set of themes and ideas'. But choosing poets based on their themes and ideas in an anthology like this is always a mistake. International themes and ideas have no inherent superiority to national ones, and vice versa. True poetic cosmopolitanism is a matter of effective technical resources and genuine response to the larger poetic tradition, and not a matter of the poet's material or background or even technical experiments. The poetry must be good, otherwise it gives the cosmopolitan a bad name. And that is the last thing we need in this country.

The editors' cosmopolitan impulse gets them into trouble in one other way, too. To be sure, I am pleased that the editors include four French-language poets from Quebec in translation, which is something Canadian anthologists haven't done since A.J.M. Smith published *The Oxford Book of Canadian Verse: In French and English* in 1960. What's more, the poets chosen are the right ones: as I say, Emile Nelligan, Hector de Saint-Denys Garneau, Anne Hébert and Robert Melançon. Would they had included more. It is odd, however, that only Hébert is given her own discrete section in the anthology, whereas the others are included only briefly along with the original poems of their poet-translators. In such cases, both the Quebec poet and the translator get short shrift. Anne Carson's four entries include two translations of Nelligan, for example, and Glassco's five include three versions of Saint-Denys Garneau. It also means that, except for Hébert, none of the French-language poets gets properly introduced. As a result, what could have been a cosmopolitan coup feels more like an afterthought.

What's more, the quality of the translations varies considerably. I very much like Anne Carson's translations of Nelligan, which are the best I've seen, and I'm equally pleased by Glassco's versions of Saint-Denys Garneau. But Eric Ormsby's versions of Melançon are not particularly strong, and the translation of Hébert, by Alan Brown, is quite bad, despite the editors' high praise. Take, for instance, this line from Hébert's poem 'Mystère de la Parole':

Notre coeur ignorait le jour lorsque le feu nous fut ainsi remis,
    et sa lumière
creusa l'ombre de nos traits

Hébert's best translator, A. Poulin, Jr., conveys this vividly, as follows:

Our hearts ignored the day when we were given fire, and its light
carved the
shadows of our features

Brown, however, offers this stumbling, incoherent crib:

Our heart had never known the light when that first was thus
confided to us, and
its glimmer deepened the shadow of our features

If the editors really think the latter is a 'significant achievement', then I'm speechless. Hébert deserves better treatment than this.

Another serious weakness of the book — a missed opportunity, really — springs from the decision to leave out the best of the younger generation of Canadian poets, by deciding on the odd and arbitrary cut-off birth year of 1962. It is precisely the younger generation that, as the editors say themselves, is most concertedly, as a group, 'working towards a larger, more cosmopolitan audience'. And so, if cosmopolitanism is the founding principle of this anthology, why leave these younger poets out? I wish the editors had traded out Ross, Bailey, McGimpsey and so forth, for, say, Ken Babstock, Stephanie Bolster, Carmine Starnino, Tory Jollimore, Tim Bowling and Karen Solie, all born, I believe, in the 1960s, not to mention some slightly older poets like Jeffery Donaldson, Richard Sanger and Ricardo Sternberg. True, this generation has been amply anthologized in Carmine Starnino's groundbreaking anthology *The New Canon,* which likewise eschews nationalism for the sake of good poetry, and the editors assert in the aforementioned interview that they didn't want to cover the same ground twice. But the truth is, they do include four poets who are in Starnino's book. Adding eight or ten more of the best from the new generation would have made *Modern Canadian Poets* a much better, and more truly cosmopolitan, anthology.

To compensate for this neglect of the younger generation, moreover, the editors reserve four slots for some slightly older poets they say 'share elements of the four points from which poets of the current generation are derived: the post-colonial, the formal, the experimental, the pop-cultural.' (The poets they've picked to represent these odd categories are, respectively, George Elliott Clarke, Steven Heighton, Lisa Robertson and David McGimpsey.) But any arbitrary departure from their main principles of selection was bound to be a botch. Fortunately, Clarke, and perhaps Heighton, deserve to be here because their poems are good, and they're genuinely cosmopolitan. The other two — the last two poets in the book — just feel weirdly out of place.

Yet another problem involves the introductions the editors provide for most of the poets in the book. The biographical material is helpful to me in the case of poets I didn't know, but the critical opinions are often ill-considered. There are, for example, some curious omissions in the discussion of poets' influences. The editors make much of Wallace Stevens's influence on Eric Ormsby, for instance, but ignore the even more significant — and, on Ormsby's part, self-avowed — influence of Rilke. In the discussion of George Elliott Clarke, similarly, the editors mention Robinson, Masters and Shakespeare, but for some reason neglect to mention Derek Walcott and the blues. More seriously, the editors' praise is sometimes exaggerated. For instance, the editors describe Steven Heighton in grandiose terms as '[t]he beginning of a new consciousness in Canadian poetry' and 'the precursor to the current generation of more deliberately literary and formal poets'. What makes Heighton, who published his first book in 1989, more of a precursor than, say, George Johnston, Jay Macpherson, Daryl Hine or Eric Ormsby? The editors' own anthology is an argument against this claim.

Similarly, the editors' characterization of A. M. Klein as a 'major poet' is just too much. Klein is a tragic figure who wrote some fine poems, especially 'Portrait of the Poet as Landscape'. Surely he belongs here. But a major poet (like, say, Rilke, Celan or Eliot) he is not. This kind of grandiose claim only undermines the authority of the editors and makes them look provincial, which is the last thing they want to do in a book like this. In the anthology's introduction they make a much more modest claim for Klein as 'The poet who comes closest to being the great Canadian figure of the twentieth century.' But even this is over the top. At his best Klein is a fine poet; at his worst (as in *The Hitleriad*) he's awful. I don't see any reason to elevate him over Page, Hine, Ormsby & Co. At his best, he is their peer. Let's leave it at that.

I have a few minor quibbles with the book, as well. The editors make some odd choices and omissions of individual poems, particularly for Page, Layton, Hine and Ormsby; in the latter case they have reprinted one of his worst poems, 'Flamingos', apparently because it exhibits him at his most Stevensian. It's a shame not to find Page's 'Stories of Snow' or 'Deaf-Mute in a Pear Tree' or 'After Reading *Albino Pheasants*'; instead we get 'Planet Earth' (one of those *glosas* of hers I've never particularly liked), and 'Man with One Small Hand' (though I am grateful the editors included 'Arras' and 'Cry Ararat!' and 'After Rain'). With Layton, similarly, it's disappointing not to find some of his best lyrics here, such as 'The Fertile Muck' and 'The Birth of Tragedy'. These poems are common anthology pieces for a reason. And the choices in Hine's case, as so often with selections from this poet, are just odd, though particularly here given that Evan Jones edited Hine's recent volume of selected poems. With all this poet's riches to choose from, why pick 'An Adolescent' and 'Patroclus Putting on the Armor of Achilles', neither of which is first-rate Hine? Why not, say, 'Phoenix Culpa', 'The Trout', 'Noon' or 'The Copper Maple', or some of the sonnets from *Arrondissements*? And finally, there are some irritating typos in the book, as in Partridge's 'In the Barn' and Clarke's 'This Given Day'.

But I don't want to lose sight of the big picture here. It's my job to hold the editors' feet to the flames for their mistakes, which is why I've spent so much time complaining; but most of the time the experience of reading this anthology, as I said at the outset, is a pleasure. Here's a taste of what you can expect, a vivid and moving poem I hadn't read before, called 'Alexandria's Waltz', by Robert Allen:

> Blue deluxe in shadow, the big tent wobbles
> with shiny pools of rain. A summer tempest of birds
> swoops to the sagging bleachers, while beneath
> the antics of blackbirds and grackles
> grows a slow field of weeds and wild timothy.
>
> Each day another guywire snaps, leaning
> the bigtop closer to the ground. The circus
> is dispossessed, bankruptcy writs posted
> on anything that stands. And everywhere, telltale
> signs of haste: two rubber boots, different
> sizes, by themselves in the mud; a pitchfork
> and spade, planted on a knoll in the meadow.
>
> But greatest, bluest memory of the show —
> Alexandria the elephant waltzes in the weed-grown

centre ring, as if her keeper stood
goading her still, pulling her down on gnarled
knees to whisper Sanskrit keepsakes
in the cool tent of her ear.

Now, that's more like it: sophistication, eloquence and style. Just read this
poem aloud to yourself a couple of times, and you'll hear what I mean.

So, for all its imperfections, with two dozen of Canada's best poets filling its pages, this is the best general anthology of modern Canadian poetry
we have. It's been a long time coming.

PART III

On Criticism: A Self-Interview

You spend a lot of time passing judgment on other poets' work. So my first question is: Who do you think you are?
Ha. Well, look: I am, like everyone else in this line of work, a 'self-appointed critic'. But let me suggest that your question reveals a certain world view. The scientist, I suspect, is your intellectual hero.

I do admire science, but what does that have to do with judging poetry?
In science, you make an hypothesis, conduct an experiment, and prove the hypothesis objectively right or wrong. According to this view, non-scientific fields like literary criticism express only individual tastes; the critic's opinion is no more valuable than that of anyone else. Therefore, to write criticism, and especially to make value judgments, is mere arrogance. Have I got you pegged?

I suppose you have. But hasn't literary criticism become more and more scientific in the past hundred years? Hasn't it gotten over the need for subjective value judgments?
You're speaking of French structuralism? Russian formalism, Prague School semiotics? Granted, these movements have all made valuable contributions to our knowledge of literary structure. But they have limits. They have great difficulty, in particular, in getting from linguistic and structural analysis of a poem to an evaluation of its quality. And the source of this limitation is their reliance on disengaged reason, together with the idea that language — including the critic's language — is essentially an instrument for designating things.

I don't follow you. And anyway, isn't that what language is?
Let me finish. This disengaged stance of the so-called scientific critic has infected other kinds of criticism, too, especially in the academy. It's all too common for a critic, in the most unimaginative, emotionless and abstract prose imaginable, to apply certain already articulated concepts to a poem,

and — no surprise — find exactly what he's looking for, whether an ideological no-no, or some irreconcilable contradiction, or, at best, some particular idea. The critic is looking for secrets, but they are always the same secrets, known beforehand, and so he treats all poems as if they were the same. He's unwilling or unable to immerse himself in the poem, and so he remains closed off from it, and the poem itself stays hidden.

Oh, come on. Are you saying he shouldn't try to be objective?
We just can't fully experience, much less evaluate, a poem in that way. The critic has got to immerse herself in it. She needs to engage not just her reason but her emotion, sensuality and imagination. And — to answer your earlier question — she needs to recognize that language, including her own critical language, is not primarily a designating instrument. It's a medium for expressing insights and perceptions and shades of feeling. Criticism, to be good, must be a kind of passionate, imaginative and even sensuous thinking.

So criticism is an art.
No, no. That's not what I'm saying. Of course, the idea that it's an art is so widespread by now among reviewers and non-academic critics that it's almost a cliché. The critic writes, they say, to entertain the reader with his witty prose, but you can't take his judgments seriously because they're just his opinions, and opinions are merely subjective. Sound familiar?

Couldn't have said it better myself. Well, if it's not an art, and it's not a science, then what is it?
As I say, it's a kind of thinking. It has more in common with philosophy than art. It wants to convince the reader of something, whether an interpretation or evaluation or both. But, unlike philosophy, it is not mainly concerned with ideas.

What about critical theory?
That's different. Yes, criticism depends on theory, which borrows ideas from philosophy all the time. But the primary concern of criticism is poetry and the poem; the critic seeks to reveal the poem's secrets to the reader. To do this she needs to engage more faculties than reason alone. She is a guide;

she shows how the poem does what it does, and judges it according to its achievement.

But how can such guidance and such judgments be of any use to anybody else if criticism isn't objective?
Well, look, it's true: there is no absolute truth in criticism. But neither is criticism merely subjective. Not all judgments are equally valid.

I don't follow you.
Think of it this way: There is a finite number of plausible interpretations and evaluations of a poem, and of those, some are more persuasive than others. We need these plausible interpretations and judgments because the more there are, and the better they are, the closer readers can get to the truth — even if, like Achilles in Zeno's paradox, they are forever chasing the tortoise and never quite able to catch him.

But if criticism isn't a science, how can we decide which critical judgments and interpretations are more persuasive than others?
Well, it takes a lot of work. In disputing someone's thinking about a poem, it's not enough merely to say that it's wrong. You've got to make the case for a better judgment, a better interpretation. Only if your new thinking is persuasive enough that it supersedes the first in the eyes of many thoughtful and knowledgeable readers can yours be said to be closer to the truth. Granted, widespread agreement on contemporary writing in particular is often a matter for the future, and even then no judgment is ever safe from being superseded or at least refined. Still, what one wants is a healthy number of strong, highly persuasive interpretations and judgments, which may well contradict one another, but which cannot be responsibly ignored.

Ah, I see. This sounds like Nietzschean perspectivism.
Very perceptive.

Thanks. But why do we need interpretations and judgments anyway? Surely what matters is the poetry itself?
Yes, indeed. But the relationship between criticism and poetry is not parasitical, as it is so often accused of being. It's symbiotic. They need each other.

How do you mean?
You occasionally hear a well-known poet — Anne Carson, for example — complaining that, now that she's famous, critics don't really criticize her work any more. In her *Paris Review* interview, Carson acknowledges that for a long time editors dismissed her work out of hand, but she adds that, 'since then there's been what people call a paradigm shift, which means now you can't do anything wrong, but which really means people are offering equally blind judgments of the work. I don't know why that happens. I guess people are just afraid to think. They like to have a category that's ready so they can say: "Okay, now we know this is good, we can enjoy it."'

She wants an honest critic.
Exactly. Poets like her understand how important good criticism is to their work because they know that fame is no guarantee of good poetry. They want demanding readers. They want to stay good, they want to get better, but without clear-eyed, specific criticism, that can be very difficult for them to do. And in Carson's case, the lack of honest criticism has been bad for her poetry.

But she's a celebrated poet. What about someone who's just published a first book?
It's the same thing. There are some people, I realize, who think we should all just lie to each other and pretend that everything everybody publishes is good. If a book is bad, they say, we should just ignore it. They don't realize how condescending this is to the poor bad poet. They would rather let him waste his life writing godawful verse than give him a chance either to get better or go into a different line of work.

But what's the harm in encouraging him a little?
You don't seem to realize how damaging that is to the literary culture. If there are no effective standards of quality, or these standards are kept secret, then poets can't tell the difference between their good poems and their bad. Poets who might have become great start believing their own blurbs, and think they're great already. Bad or mediocre poets who might have become good stay bad. And the whole mess breeds cynicism and confusion among readers. The whole literary culture gets cut off from the outside world, until, one day, a critic or anthologist from elsewhere appears, takes a look at the bad poetry everyone says is so wonderful, recoils in horror or shrugs in

mystification, and looks elsewhere, unwilling to dig for the good stuff in a culture that doesn't seem to know what the good stuff is. The job of the critic is to prevent this from happening. Or stop it from happening.

I concede the point.
That's gracious of you.

I suppose it is. Are there other ways that criticism can help poets?
By letting them see what they're doing in their work.

Surely they know what they're doing already.
Well, yes and no. Good poets are master artists. But a lot of what they do is unconscious; the poems come special delivery from the gods. It's one reason many poets concentrate so fiercely on their technique, by the way: to get the conscious intellect out of the way of the incoming poem. And good criticism can help poets see what the gods are doing in their work. It can help them see underlying relationships among poems they didn't know were there. It can help them understand the course of their own development, and see when they've gotten off on a wrong track — often wilfully, without letting themselves be guided by the gods.

I see. Now, this is all well and good, but surely the critic isn't writing only for the benefit of poets.
No, of course, good criticism helps readers, too. By helping them find good poets, for example. So much poetry is published every year that no one could possibly read all of it, even if one were so inclined. And a lot of it is not very good. But a critic is a gold miner. He blasts his way through tons of quartz and granite to find the precious metal which, by staking his claim, he gets into circulation as quickly as possible.

A kind of Consumer's Guide to Poetry.
Well, yes. But criticism also helps readers read. They must learn how to read each new poet they encounter anyway, either laboriously, by themselves, or more quickly, guided by a teacher or a critic — and in the case of great or difficult poets, by more than one.

Anything else?

Critics can also help reader and poet alike by placing poems in the context of poetry as a whole. Poems talk to each other, we know; they move over in bed when a new one climbs in. And it helps everyone if a critic can demonstrate which poems are sleeping with which. It helps readers know how to read them. And it helps poets by making their poems more fully available to readers, by rescuing them from their illusory isolation on the page. Like people, poems left alone for too long go crazy and die. They need the company of other poems, especially their families, to survive. And every poet worth reading wants her poems to survive.

So what's in it for the critic?

Pleasure. And insight. And if the critic is also a poet, criticism can help him learn his art. It puts him on intimate terms with the work of his predecessors and contemporaries. It helps him understand how his own poetry differs from and relates to the poetry of others, helps him find new poems to respond to with his own, and teaches him a thing or two about technique. There is no end to the education of a poet.

Are there hazards?

There are. For the reader, bad criticism can be confusing, misleading, pernicious, a waste of time. For the poet, it can be maddening. Even good criticism, for the poet-critic, takes time and energy she might have spent writing poems. So one must strike a balance. And the criticism must be good.

What makes it good?

Ah. Well, first, it has got to be well-written. Bad prose is inexcusable in a critic, not only because it is unreadable, but because it totally undermines her authority. Repulsive jargon, wilful obscurity, inhuman tone, incoherence, narcissism, dullness, clichés — in short, bad style, whether barbarous, mechanical or self-absorbed, betrays a critic utterly. The critic who writes badly is no judge of others' writing; she ought to be pleaded with, then upbraided and, if she persists, ignored.

All right. So describe good critical prose, if you will.

There's no great mystery. It should be fluent, coherent and clear. It should be free of cant, though it may deploy the technical vocabulary of rhetoric and prosody when necessary in order to be precise. It should have wit, energy, vividness, figures of speech. It should be addressed to the educated common reader. It should be a pleasure to read. But good writing is not all that criticism is good for. Criticism, however pleasurable, is not an art.

So you've said.
Well, as I say, there are those who claim to read criticism purely for pleasure. They find it entertaining to see Jorie Graham roasted on William Logan's spit, but they don't take it seriously; to them, it's just an opinion. They have no conception of the crucial role criticism plays in preventing the corruption of literary culture.

Hence the need for honest judges.
You took the words out of my mouth.

But what has criticism got to do to fulfill that role?
It has got to make definite interpretations and judgments, and support them with cogent arguments. It should offer insights, and choose its evidence carefully. It should put the shoulder of persuasive rhetoric to the wheel. And above all, criticism should be fully, humanly, engaged. The attempt to turn it into a science in the past hundred years has been, on balance, disastrous.

Harping on that again.
Look, the critic is not a scientist. She's a philologist, in its root sense: a lover of words. She loves words enough to serve them in her own writing. She loves them enough to immerse herself in poems.

You've used that word before: 'immerse'. What do you mean?
I mean the critic has got to get inside the poem. She can't stand on the outside looking at it from a distance through her ideological telescope.

And how does she get inside the poem?
Well, first, the critic must set up camp in the great dictionaries. Show me a good critic, and I'll show you a man with a dog-eared OED.

Or carpal tunnel.
Nowadays, yes. It's an occupational hazard. But a dictionary habit makes a critic discerning, sensitive to tone and shades of connotation. It gives him insight into etymology, lets him see images in words that to others are blank abstractions, makes him able to catch puns both serious and amusing, and in general, makes him aware of what is going on beneath the surface of a poet's words.

What else?
Second, the critic ought to cultivate a poet's sensitivity to grammar. Grammar — and in English, syntax in particular — is the source of energy in language. Far from being a code of laws, grammar is to the true poet and critic an extraordinarily flexible, subtle and powerful *techné* — part technology, part magic — for making meaning, creating rhythm, and affecting readers in a great variety of ways, from seduction to hypnosis. If you cannot understand why a well-written periodic sentence, for example, is erotic, turn in your critic's licence at the door.

Hands off.
I'm just saying. Third, the critic needs a sure command of rhetoric — not necessarily an encyclopedic knowledge of every twenty-five-dollar Greek term in the handbook....

Anacoluthon.
... what I'm saying is, he's got to have a thorough grasp of the major categories of tropes and schemes, not to mention the major elements of rhetoric writ large, from *logos, pathos* and *ethos* to the rhetoric of genres.

Why?
Because there are three great benefits of this knowledge to the critic: it makes her sensitive to the huge variety of ways a poem can operate, the technical sources of its magic; it gives her the conceptual clarity and technical vocabulary she needs to account for these things precisely; and, not least, it makes her a better writer. It's not just a matter of identifying tropes like rare birds ('look, a synecdoche!'); rather, it's about grasping the significance of all manner of artistic choices. In short, a critic without rhetoric is like a judge who never studied law.

You sound like George Steiner.
Why, thank you. Where was I?

Fourth.
Ah. Fourth, the critic needs to understand prosody on her pulses. This is an area of tremendous weakness in the criticism of poetry, because, even if critics have a basic grasp of prosodic terminology — they can tell the difference between blank verse and terza rima — many have little or no experience writing verse, and only a superficial understanding of what it's for, and so they have great difficulty knowing what to say about it. The most common approach, besides ignoring it altogether, is to attribute to the verse some significance or effect which is in fact a quality of the rhetoric, syntax, or diction. This sort of thing is just painful to read.

Easy for you to say.
Well, it's true. Poet-critics are at a distinct advantage here, as long as they have experience writing verse and a good command of the technical vocabulary. (It is possible to write competent verse without knowing how to describe your prosody, by the way, just as a musician may play an instrument by ear without being able to read music.) What one really wants in a critic in this regard is what one always wants in criticism: sensitivity to what is happening in the poem. A critic should be able to hear, in particular, the way a poem's syntax operates in counterpoint to the verse. He should be able to describe the subtle or powerful effects of prosodic choices on the sound of a poem the way a good music critic describes the performance of a string quartet. He should study prosody. He should try his hand at verse. He should make a habit of memorizing poems, and reading them aloud.

Finally — well, not *finally*, because there is no end to the education of a critic, either — critics ought to be very well read, not just in the poetry of their own time and place, but world poetry from antiquity to the present.

Easier said than done.
Well, yes. And the great impediment to this in our time is the balkanization of academic literary studies into departments based on language, ethnicity and era — English, Slavic studies, Classics — together with an implacable institutional bias against reading poetry in translation. But nevertheless: it

is the task of a lifetime, and it is, fortunately, impossible to graduate from this university. But the critic must never stop going to his classes.

What does wide reading like this do for the critic?
The more one reads the more one realizes no poem is an island. It is impossible to understand what a poem is really doing without the context of other poems. It's like listening to someone in the same room talking on a telephone, engaged in a conference call with fifteen other people, without your being able to hear what anyone else on the line is saying. Wide reading puts the whole thing on speakerphone. You catch the echoes and allusions, the parodies and arguments, the homages and jokes and lines of influence, and can tell the difference between mawkish imitation and creative engagement with tradition. Wide reading improves your grasp of rhetoric and prosody, gives you an understanding of the place of modern poetry in literary history, and gives you both a clear view of, and a healthy sense of detachment from, the politics of aesthetic faction. And in general, it teaches you the virtues of good critical reading: openness, attentiveness, patience, critical intelligence — and love.

Does the critic have an ethical responsibility?
The critic must be honest. He must say what he thinks. He must ignore the poet's reputation, her relationship to himself or his friends, the prizes and honours she has won, her status in the literary establishment, not to mention his own career advancement, and anything else that threatens to dissuade him, and tell the truth about the poems. He has a responsibility to his readers, to the poet, to his self-respect, to the field of criticism and the art of poetry, to be an honest judge. Otherwise, he deceives his readers and the poet both, corrupts himself, and damages criticism and poetry within publishing range of his words. It is no trivial transgression. If he hasn't the courage to be honest he should give up now before anyone else gets hurt.

So there is room for objectivity, after all?
Detachment, yes. But from the world, not from the poem. A critic has got to meet the poet on the poet's terms. He has got to free himself from prior judgment, from literary faction, enmity, prior aesthetic disagreement with the poet, and read with a mind open to the poet's words. He must be prepared to dine on crow; he must be willing to change his mind about a poet

and even about his own aesthetic principles if the work in front of him persuades him he must do so. He must judge the poems' success or failure according to what they are evidently trying to achieve, not some other goal he would have preferred. And if he cannot do this, he should refrain from publishing his review.

And what about the way the critic writes? Is there an ethical dimension there?
Whatever his judgments and interpretations, he owes it to the poet and his readers to offer an argument. A judgment without an argument, including well-chosen evidence, is worthless, and a sign of a lazy critic. The kind of review that is four-fifths description and one-fifth unsupported evaluation isn't criticism, it's a blurb. It's advertising. Editors who publish such reviews should be corrected and, in case of recidivism, replaced. It is best, moreover, if a critic, in giving evidence, quotes entire poems. This ensures that he doesn't take quotations out of context, and helps his readers make up their own minds.

Anything else?
A critic ought to show the poet some respect. If the poetry is bad, he should say so; but he should never attack the poet personally. Casting aspersions on a poet's nationality, profession, religion or social class, not to mention age, race, gender, sexuality, disabilities, illnesses, addictions or anything else not directly relevant to the quality of the work, is foolish and wrong. Keats was not, despite Shelley's mythologizing, killed by the review that dismissed him as a cockney; but surely the reviewer's honour was.

☆

The Art of Poetry

Over the past twenty years, an exciting new generation of Canadian poets, many of whose predecessors once wandered around lost in the forest of nationalist ideology, has been making a bee-line for the clearing, the wider international context, of the art of poetry. Our younger poet-critics have been finding their way out too, albeit mostly on the practical level, in response to particular poets. What they haven't done yet is to think about and articulate anew their fundamental ideas about poetry and poetic value; they've been neglecting the wider intellectual context of the art.

Such neglect is not new. Except for one or two Marxist theoreticians of the avant-garde, like Steve McCaffery, and a few other borderline cases — poets with an interest in philosophy, such as Dennis Lee and Jan Zwicky — we've never really had a tradition in Canada of poet-critics who think about poetry on this level. Even in the wider English-speaking world, much of the basic thinking about poetry over the past half century has been done not by poets but by literary theorists and philosophers, too many of whom think of poetry as an ideological weapon. And the results have often been disastrous for poetry and criticism alike.

In the context of literary history, this is an aberration. For centuries it was the poet-critics — Sidney, Johnson, Coleridge, Arnold, Eliot — who did most of the important thinking about poetry, and in each case their thinking played no small role in the flourishing of the art in their time. Today, especially in Canada, there is an urgent need to renew this tradition — not so as to publish vainglorious manifestoes, but to build a foundation for our critical responses, and to spur our fellow poets on to greater achievements in the art. Unless we do so, and do so persuasively, our newly liberated poetry will remain vulnerable to powerful ideologies — not just nationalism and Marxism, but every other dogma that snarls and bares its teeth.

In what follows, I intend to think my way through some of the most influential ideas about poetry, extract the most persuasive elements of each, and combine them into a coherent and flexible theory of the art. In doing so I hope to shed some urgently needed light on our current moment in literary history.

The Art of Pleasure

In the introduction to her *New Oxford Book of Canadian Verse in English,* published in 1982, Margaret Atwood remarks that, among the younger poets in her anthology, 'there is a renewed interest ... in the intricacies of rhetoric, and an emphasis on the poem as consciously crafted.' When I first came across this passage as a student twenty years ago, I was perplexed; she might as well have said that among the new generation of hockey players there was a renewed interest in skating, and a sudden emphasis on scoring goals. What had they been interested in before, I wanted to know. And the young poets she mentions in this connection — Susan Musgrave, Marilyn Bowering, and so on — didn't exactly strike me as virtuosi, anyway. Yet, as it turned out, Atwood's larger point was prophetic: the basic change in Canadian poetry in the past twenty or thirty years has in fact been a renewed focus on good technique, which is to say, on poetry as an art.

This change has corresponded to a new attitude of aestheticism among our new Canadian poet-critics, including, for example, Eric Ormsby, Robyn Sarah, Jason Guriel and Carmine Starnino. The essence of this attitude is the idea that poetry is basically an autonomous technology for producing aesthetic pleasure, as opposed to offering moral lessons or revealing human truths.

Aestheticism began more or less with Keats and Poe, and found advocates among French Symbolists like Verlaine and Mallarmé, English aesthetes like Wilde and Rossetti, and certain American Modernists, including Eliot and Stevens. It had some considerable influence among Canadian Modernists, too, particularly the criticism of A.J.M. Smith, and, in various degrees, the poetry of P.K. Page, Irving Layton, A.M. Klein, Anne Wilkinson and Jay Macpherson, among others. Since the 1950s, however, aestheticism has not been very influential in Canada (that is, until recently). Among Canadian poets the purest exemplars in the twentieth century were perhaps John Glassco and Daryl Hine; the latter, for example, in the introduction to his 2007 *Recollected Poems,* compares a poem to 'a painting or sculpture', and defines it as 'a verbal object capable of giving a specific kind of aesthetic pleasure in itself'. Neither Glassco nor Hine wrote much criticism, however — though Glassco has plenty to say off the cuff in his

Memoirs of Montparnasse — and in any case, until recently, their influence on Canadian poetry was almost nil.

The essential aestheticist idea — poetic autonomy — was developed by the Modernists into something much larger. They realized that it isn't really the individual poem that is autonomous, since poems are in fact constantly echoing and alluding to other poems. Rather, autonomy belongs to poetry as a whole — the whole of world poetry from antiquity to the present. The classic statement of this insight is Eliot's description, in his eponymous 1919 essay, of the relationship between tradition and the individual talent: 'What happens when a new work of art is created is something that happens simultaneously to all the works of art that preceded it. The existing monuments form an ideal order among themselves, which is modified by the introduction of the new (the really new) work of art among them.' From this perspective, to value the aesthetic autonomy of poetic art — to be an aesthete — is to value not only technical mastery in individual poems, but also the creative engagement of those poems with the poetry of the past.

Why is this engagement so important? For one thing, the poetry of the past requires this engagement to stay vital, to remain a living tradition. As Charles Taylor puts it in a recent essay called 'Celan and the Recovery of Language', 'The canon of great poetry, in order to resonate again, needs a new context, a range of contemporary voices ... with which it can resonate'; otherwise, the canon 'loses its force'. But those same contemporary voices depend, in turn, upon the poems of the past, especially if they aspire to greatness and true originality. As Eliot puts it, 'not only the best, but the most individual parts of [a fully mature poet's] work may be those in which the dead poets, his ancestors, assert their immortality most vigorously.' Moreover, such creative engagement with the canon is often an important source of a poem's aesthetic pleasure: the pleasure of recognition, certainly, but also the pleasure of transformation, the alteration of the old by the introduction of the new. For these reasons, among others, any literary nationalism which seeks to avoid the influence of 'foreign' poetry and poetics — especially in a country that as yet lacks a great national canon of its own — can only be self-destructive in the extreme.

Another benefit of the new aestheticism in Canada is the value it places on good rhetoric and prosody. This has helped produce a new crop of excellent poets, from George Elliott Clarke and Elise Partridge to Ken Babstock and Jeffery Donaldson. And in criticism, the new aestheticism has led, among other things, to a revaluation of the poetry of the past. The celebrated poets of earlier generations — Al Purdy, George Bowering, John Newlove, Dorothy Livesay and so on — were notably poor writers, and consequently their work has not worn well. Their neglected contemporaries — Wilkinson, Hine, Richard Outram, Don Coles and others — are, in the eyes of the new poet-critics, vastly superior, not least because their rhetorical and prosodic technique is so much better.

I number myself among these new aesthetes; as a critic, I too stand for aesthetic pleasure, and like my fellow critics I focus on poetry as an art, particularly its rhetoric and prosody. I avidly search out poems that engage creatively with other poems, including the great poetry of the past. I believe in the primacy of art, which must remain at the heart of any good theory of poetry. I insist that, unless a poem succeeds as a work of art per se, it is not a successful poem, no matter how much I may sympathize with its other values.

The Art of Teaching How to Live

I acknowledge, however, that to ignore all other values besides the aesthetic would be to miss a great deal of what a lot of poetry does. Some poets, like Glassco and Hine, are exclusively concerned with giving pleasure. But many other poets have additional aims in mind.

Take Horace, for instance. For him, nearly as much as for any aesthete, the main purpose of poetry is to give pleasure. He apparently saw even the teaching of moral lessons in poems as important largely as a way of pleasing older readers. However, if you read his advice in the epistolary poem known as the 'Art of Poetry' about how to please, instruct and move an audience, you realize that he thought of poetry primarily in its rhetorical relationship to the reader or listener, with rhetoric understood as the art of persuasion. This explains why so many of his poems — including the 'Art of Poetry' itself — are not only addressed to particular readers, but frankly didactic in their rhetoric. Thus, for Horace, the poem is not autonomous; it gives pleasure by engaging persuasively with the reader, and specifically by teaching the reader how to live.

It isn't much of a stretch from this to the inverse, pragmatic idea that the main purpose of poetry is moral education, with pleasure merely the means to that end. For Sir Philip Sidney, for instance, poetry is a great teacher of virtue precisely because the pleasure it gives and the emotions it evokes combine to make its moral lessons more persuasive. Poetry is, as he puts it, a 'medicine of Cherries'.

John Dryden, on the other hand, like Horace, still thought that pleasure was the ultimate purpose of poetry; nevertheless, even he considered a poem trivial if it was without moral profit. He implied that the poetry that gives the deepest and strongest pleasure does so precisely by virtue of its moral lessons.

But in any case, whether they favoured virtue or pleasure, pragmatic poet-critics like these saw no contradiction between aesthetic and ethical values. And Yvor Winters, in particular, took this way of thinking to its logical conclusion. Winters was concerned with the morality of technique itself, with poetic art as 'a moral discipline'. In fact, for Winters, technique and morality are identical, and together form the single criterion of excellence in poetry. As he puts it, 'the poem will be the most valuable, which ... represents the most difficult victory [over experience]'; and 'the ability to control and shape one's experience' is 'identical with ... formal control'.

As an aesthete, I have a lot of sympathy for this version of pragmatism, because it offers a way to acknowledge ethical value in poetry without abandoning the principle that poetry is an art. The problem is that Winters basically reduces aesthetic value to ethical value, giving the latter all the critical prestige, and thus he appears to deny that poetry is or ought to be pleasurable at all. Which is just too puritanical for an aesthete like me. Not to mention that it contradicts my experience.

Still, there remains something valuable in Winters, which I would formulate this way: it is not merely that the pleasure of reading poetry makes its ethical lessons more persuasive (Sidney), or even simply that the poetry that gives the deepest and strongest pleasure does so by virtue of its moral lessons (Dryden). It is rather that masterful technique enables a poet to achieve a deeper and stronger contemplation of moral experience in poems (Winters), a richness and subtlety of comprehension that defies one's drawing a simple Aesopian moral; and (borrowing from Dryden) that this contemplation in turn produces a deep aesthetic pleasure.

But there is still one serious weakness even in this more sophisticated pragmatism. When we judge poems primarily according to ethical values, eventually we encounter one whose ethics are antithetical to our own. For a pragmatic critic, to paraphrase Winters, there are undesirable moral attitudes. It doesn't take long, moreover, for all of this to turn political. Indeed, the first pragmatic critic in Western poetics is Plato, who, in one of the most infuriating passages in *The Republic,* has Socrates advocate the wholesale censorship and re-writing of Greek mythology and poetry to conform to his moral code. We can see this sort of thing played out in all kinds of actual totalitarian systems too, from Hitler to Mao. So the question inevitably arises: if we are going to give any weight at all to ethical value in judging poetry, according to whose moral values (or political ideology) are we to judge the value of a poem?

Clearly, pragmatism as a theory of poetic value needs some additional correction before an aesthete like me can really take it seriously. For this, we may turn with gratitude to Northrop Frye. Frye was a pragmatic critic because he thought that the purpose of literary study is to strengthen and educate the imagination, train the mind, and encourage social and moral development. (He adds that for writers it has the added purpose of teaching them how to write.) But he differs from other pragmatists in that for him the moral teaching isn't direct; we don't really expect to learn moral lessons by reading poems. Rather, it is the study of literature as a whole that educates our moral imaginations. Such study turns our attention to human concerns and the authentic myths that embody them, and away from the demonic forms of those myths we call ideologies. Moreover, for Frye, any work of literature has a provisional, hypothetical status, and is part of a much greater literary universe. This is why we can value 'immoral' literature, that is, works whose moral and political values we dislike, and therefore why we should resist calls for its censorship. Rather than imprisoning us in some narrow ideology or moral code, the study of literature liberates us from both.

But the question remains: how can we value the ethical dimensions of any particular poem without falling into the trap of straitened moral or ideological judgments? There are many ideological critics today who think of criticism as a political critique of poetry. And, to some extent, I sympathize with them; sometimes political critique can utterly change the way we read a poem. Such criticism is especially helpful with regard to long surviving classics, about whose aesthetic value there is little dispute. As long as an ideological reading doesn't blind us to the mythic human concerns in the poem in question — *The Aeneid,* for example — then getting clear about its (in this case) imperialist political dimensions can be very enlightening, especially if we don't lose sight of the poem as a work of art.

When it comes to new poetry, however, such criticism is often pernicious in its effects, if not its intentions. It tends to confuse readers and poets
alike whenever it praises a poem whose ethical or political attractiveness far
outweighs its aesthetic value. In a country like Canada, which lacks a great
home-grown tradition of long-surviving classic poetry whose aesthetic
value is widely acknowledged, such criticism often overvalues aesthetically
weak verse for moral or especially political reasons. It also sometimes
undervalues aesthetically strong poetry that may be distasteful to the
critic's moral or political views, whatever they may be. This is why pragmatic and ideological critics alike need to keep their ethical and political
evaluations in perspective. Aesthetic value should always have priority.

And in any case, before we can fairly judge a poem's ethical value, it
seems to me this whole business of the ethical in poetry needs to be understood in a new way. For this purpose we may turn again to Charles Taylor,
who, in *Sources of the Self*, writes about poetry in the context of a search for
moral sources. He argues for the crucial importance to modernity of what
he calls 'the exploration of order through personal resonance,' as in, for
example, Rilke's thing-poems. In such poems, the moral sources include 'a
more deeply resonant human environment', and 'affiliations with some
depth in time and commitment'. Taylor makes the case that 'we need new
languages of personal resonance to make crucial human goods alive to us
again', and suggests that the ethical value of poetry, its real moral strength,
is its power to offer us such a language.

To see what Taylor is talking about here, let's consider Rilke's sonnet
'Archaic Torso of Apollo', in the Stephen Mitchell translation:

We cannot know his legendary head
with eyes like ripening fruit. And yet his torso
is still suffused with brilliance from inside,
like a lamp, in which his gaze, now turned to low,

gleams in all its power. Otherwise
the curved breast could not dazzle you so, nor could
a smile run through the placid hips and thighs
to that dark center where procreation flared.

Otherwise this stone would seem defaced
beneath the translucent cascade of the shoulders
and would not glisten like a wild beast's fur:

would not, from all the borders of itself,
burst like a star: for here there is no place
that does not see you. You must change your life.

This poem does not tell you how to change your life. It doesn't offer to teach you any particular virtue. What it does do is involve you in an extraordinary encounter with a work of art. The encounter is extraordinary because it is not only aesthetic. It *is* aesthetic; it involves looking closely at the damaged statue, being dazzled by it, and responding to it imaginatively, with metaphor. But the encounter is also spiritual; the poem gradually discloses, or creates, through its metaphors, the presence of the sun god in the statue, 'burst[ing] like a star'. One is reminded that for the ancient Greeks, *theos* was essentially an event; and the pressure of this spiritual event, this manifestation of the god that 'see[s] you', turns it into an ethical event, namely the realization that 'You must change your life.' In Taylor's terms, 'you' resonate profoundly with this encountered thing, this old damaged work of art, which never resonated with those who so defaced it. In your encounter with it, it comes alive for you again, it becomes a moral source for you again, a source of the good, producing in you an affiliation with some depth in time and commitment. Moreover, this distinction I'm making here among the aesthetic, spiritual and ethical elements of the encounter is not there in the poem; in the poem they are the same event.

In fact, it is really in the poem that this event occurs, that is, in the reading of it, and not in some actual encounter with a statue. It occurs in the crafty grammar, all those negative conditionals that tell us indirectly that there is far more there than a defaced statue. It occurs in the series of light metaphors which disclose or create the presence of the god. It occurs as well in the incongruous images of 'ripening fruit' and 'a wild beast's fur', which allude not to Apollo but Dionysus — as though both of the gods Nietzsche thought were necessary for great art are present here. And finally, it happens in this sonnet's breathtaking *volta* in the final line, the astonishing leap of electricity by means of which the aesthetic and spiritual event becomes an ethical one. It is, in short, the technical (that is, rhetorical and prosodic) elements of the poem that produce this effect on the reader, an event which is both aesthetic and ethical at the same time.

According to this new, more refined pragmatism, then, the ethical value of the individual poem does not derive from the moral or ideological lesson it teaches, but rather its strength as a moral source, its power to make crucial human goods resonate and come alive to us again. Such power is inseparable from, and in fact depends upon, aesthetic power, and therefore prosodic and rhetorical technique. Such a notion of pragmatism is closely related to our corrected insight from Winters: that masterful technique enables a poet to achieve a deeper and stronger contemplation of moral and political experience in poems; and that this in turn can produce a profound aesthetic pleasure in the reader.

The Art of Telling the Truth

So far I have been arguing for a synthesis of aestheticism and pragmatism which keeps art at its centre. As such, my theory engages with the poem both in itself and in relationship with the reader.

But what about the poem's relationship to a wider reality? In what sense may a poem be said to have access to the truth about the world? And assuming it does, how much value, if any, should we give to this truth-telling capacity of poetry?

Plato thought that poetry had no claim to truth at all. In *The Republic* he derides the art as third-rate *mimesis*, mere representation of the world, which is itself just a bad imitation of the Ideal Forms.

Aristotle's *Poetics*, however, revalued this notion of *mimesis*. For him, poetry is a dignified and natural representation of reality. In presenting actions, he says, a poem represents not what happened once, but the sort of thing that happens all the time. In other words, it embodies a kind of general truth about the world.

Thus, in judging the truth of a poem, the question isn't 'Did it really happen?' — the favourite inquiry of naive readers everywhere — but 'Is this what happens?' According to this view, as elaborated by Frye, the ultimate source of general truths about human concerns is therefore not history but myth. The good poet selectively frames some part of reality that corresponds to some myth, and leaves out what is irrelevant to the truth in this sense. And it is technique that enables this act of framing, which is why Aristotle devotes his treatise to analyzing the technical elements of tragic drama. Plot, for example, is the technical means by which a poet represents action, and the shape of the plot is the selective frame whereby it excludes what is irrelevant to general or mythic truth.

Later critics recognized that truth of this kind in poetry can be a major source of pleasure for the reader. Samuel Johnson, for example, says that Shakespeare's works have survived because they give pleasure, and give pleasure because they are true to human nature. And Frye in turn demonstrates how much our sense of the human truth of Shakespeare's plays depends upon the art of using displaced mythic frames.

For these reasons, an aesthete such as myself ought to have no trouble including mimeticism in a synthesis of poetic values that keeps art at its centre.

Expressivism: The Anti-Art

But the problem is that many poets and critics in the second half of the twentieth century forgot Aristotle's crucial distinction between what happened once and what happens all the time.

Ever since the eighteenth century, poetry in English has become, with some notable exceptions, ever more naturalistic and autobiographical, and ever less connected to mythology. Compare Spenser, Milton and Blake, for example, to, say, Wordsworth, Frost and Larkin. Even in these latter poets, the mythical element is still clear, however; we are still dealing with autobiography made representative of human nature by means of displaced mythical frames. But with many more recent poets working in an autobiographical mode, including unfortunately a lot of Canadian poets since the 1950s, the mimetic impulse seems to be dissolving into something else: a concern not so much with the kind of thing that happens, but, simply, with making an authentic record of what occurred.

Adam Kirsch, the American poet-critic, calls this dissolving mimetic impulse the poetics of Authenticity. It insists, as he puts it, on 'poetry as a faithful record of experience, with a puritanical distrust of artfulness as interfering with the authentic recording of that experience'. Poets in this line, he argues, include such mid-twentieth-century Americans as Frank O'Hara, Charles Olson, Denise Levertov and Muriel Rukeyser. Canadian poets of Authenticity, let me suggest, would include George Bowering, Al Purdy, John Newlove and Tom Wayman, among others.

As if this development were not bad enough, the poetics of

Authenticity produced a reaction in the next generation that was even worse, on the part of poet-critics of the so-called Language school, like Charles Bernstein and Ron Silliman in the United States, and Steve McCaffery and bpNichol in Canada. These writers mounted an ideological — and specifically Marxist — attack, not just on the recording of authentic experience, but on representation per se, because, as they saw it, the language of poetic representation merely reproduces and therefore reinforces the oppressive capitalist system. They argued, therefore, that avoiding all representation of reality altogether is an act of political resistance. This injunction against representation has been very influential, contributing to the rise of a style of indeterminacy and disjunctiveness even among poets who don't share the Language poets' revolutionary ideology.

But the Language school critique doesn't make any sense as a theory of poetic value. For one thing, it abandons all interest in aesthetic pleasure; for another, it gives up on telling the truth about the world. All it has left, as far as I can tell, is a bizarre obsession with the process of writing. And precisely for these reasons, it has no real political or ethical value.

Fortunately, by now the theorists of Language poetry seem to have at least partially grasped their mistake. Steve McCaffery, for example, admits in a recently published interview that 'This utopian belief that linguistic change is the necessary prelude to social-political change led me into conceiving my poetics as a critique of language under capitalism. That belief and optimism is [sic] now gone.' And as for that old Marxist, Ron Silliman: according to his own Web site, he now 'works as a market analyst in the computer industry'. Apparently, *la révolution, c'est mort*.

There is, however, much more to the story than this. To really understand where we are now in literary history, we need to take the Language poets seriously on one point: namely, that because language is the medium of poetry, the fundamental question facing any poetic theory is the question of the nature of language.

There are two main lines of thinking on this question. According to most Enlightenment philosophers — John Locke, for example — language is essentially an instrument for designating and describing things. Such a view lends itself naturally to mimeticism in poetics.

But for thinkers of the Counter-Enlightenment tradition — like Charles Taylor — language is essentially a medium we use to express thoughts and emotions, and thus to create social relationships and the self. According to this quite different view, designation, while certainly useful, is just one rather specialized use of language.

The latter, Counter-Enlightenment, view of language leads to two very different branches of poetics, depending on whether one puts the emphasis on language as expressive of thoughts and feelings or creative of social relationships and the self. Unfortunately, both branches have historically gone by the name of Romanticism, and this has caused untold confusion.

The kind of poetics most people associate with Romanticism in the English-speaking world is known as expressivism. For Wordsworth (as critic), poetry comes from the spontaneous overflow of powerful feelings. For Coleridge, poetry is an imaginative synthesis of the poet's feelings and thoughts. But in both cases, it is essentially the internal made external, that is, expression.

The major criterion of quality for the expressivist critic is therefore whether a poem is sincere and spontaneous in thought and feeling, or, on the contrary, merely the result of the conscious use of poetic convention. The good poem, by this view, should not be written so as to have a rhetorical effect on a reader; rather, it should convey the authentic state of mind and feelings of the poet.

We've already seen what expressivism leads to in the second half of the twentieth century: it's the second major source, together with a dissolving mimeticism, of the poetics of Authenticity. Many of the influential American poets in the 1950s and '60s, and their Canadian followers, advocated the new idea of the poem as an authentic record of experience; but they had differing views of language. Those with an implicitly Enlightenment view of language, like Frank O'Hara and Al Purdy, tended to describe things they did or that happened to them. Those with an implicitly Counter-Enlightenment view, like Denise Levertov and Dorothy Livesay, tended to express their thoughts and feelings. In practice, of course, the distinction was often a matter of emphasis; for such poets, as Adam Kirsch puts it, 'Not to falsify one's personal experience, even or especially in the name of art, is their great principle,' and this applies to the poet's feelings and state of mind just as much as to events in his or her life.

Authenticity in this sense remains a widespread ideal even today, after sixty years. As I write this, I open the current issue of *Poetry* more or less at random and stumble upon a review of Susan Howe by Daisy Fried. The latter writes that Howe's 'clichés seem the more authentic and compelling for being sentimental.'

How (the aesthete splutters) can sentimental clichés be compelling? The answer is that, for Fried and Howe, as for their predecessors, sincere feeling and authentic experience trump even the most basic principles of rhetoric. You see, such poets are not particularly interested in giving aesthetic pleasure to their readers. To them, rhetoric and prosody are not so much elements of their art as impediments to authentic representation and sincere expression. Which is why many poets of Authenticity, especially in Canada, have favoured a rough-hewn, plain-spoken style; they confuse it with an absence of rhetoric. In truth, you may have bad rhetoric or good, and you may choose from an enormous range of rhetorical techniques, the plain style included. But what you may not have, if you use the language for any purpose at all, is an absence of rhetoric. In any case, once the rough-hewn plain style becomes the dominant fashion in poetry, the result is a general narrowing of rhetorical range.

The same may be said of the widespread abandonment of metrical verse among the poets of Authenticity. They tend to see it as just another impediment to the accurate representation of experience. Of course, free verse has its own prosodic resources. In the hands of a great poet like Whitman or Eliot it can be very powerful indeed. But the thing about free verse is that it needs an expanded range of rhetorical schemes, that is, techniques for patterning words, like anaphora and syntactical parallelism, to make up rhythmically for the loss of metre; otherwise the verse goes slack. But unfortunately, as I say, many free verse poets of Authenticity consider rhetoric an impediment to expression.

Therefore, given this self-destructive antipathy to art in expressivist poetics, I can find very little of merit in it to salvage, let alone incorporate into my working theory of poetry — which seems strange, because I am a great lover of Romantic poetry. To account for this apparent contradiction, I need to return to the question of language, and consider the second kind of Romantic poetics.

The Art of World-Making

This other version of Romanticism is much more central to poetics in continental Europe than in the English-speaking world (with some notable exceptions, like William Blake), and consequently it is less well-known here.

In fact, this theory has become so dominant in Europe in the past two hundred years that Charles Taylor calls it simply 'modern poetics'. The key point is that it emphasizes the creative or performative power of language. Like expressivism, performative poetics begins with the insight that, rather than primarily designating or representing things, language mainly expresses thoughts and feelings. But instead of stopping there and making a fetish out of sincerity, it focuses on the powerful effects of that expression on the world.

Charles Taylor argues — borrowing from his predecessors in the Counter-Enlightenment tradition, from Hamann to Heidegger — that by the very act of expressing thoughts and emotions in language, we come to have new thoughts and emotions. Indeed, language makes new purposes possible for us, and new levels of behaviour, not to mention new meanings, values, and kinds of consciousness. Far from being a mere instrument of designation or even expression, language is a prodigious creator of the self.

And in fact, a performative poetics derived from this view of language makes much more sense of English Romantic poetry — Wordsworth's *Prelude,* for instance, that great epic on 'the growth of a poet's mind' — than Wordsworth's own expressivist doctrine of the spontaneous overflow of powerful feelings.

Moreover, this creative power of language also extends to social life, by making possible new kinds of relations between people. Consider, for example, what happens when someone says 'Will you marry me?' and his beloved replies, 'Yes'; or when a police officer says to someone, 'You're under arrest.' Language, in such cases, does not primarily represent; rather, it creates and transforms social relationships. It continually makes and re-makes our social world.

The major criterion of quality in performative poetics, as one would expect, is the creative or performative power of a poem. Ordinary language — 'You're my sweetheart' — is performative in the ways I have outlined above, but the problem is that its power is always threatened by cliché. It soon becomes routine, a tissue of dead metaphors. It loses its force and ceases to resonate with us; that is, unless it is resurrected by poetry. The latter is what Mallarmé means when he speaks of the poet as 'purifying the language of the tribe'.

But how exactly does the poet do this? According to performative poetics, he or she does it by opening up or renewing contact with something higher or deeper than the self, some otherwise inaccessible reality or possibility of being. What this transcendent thing is depends on the poet; for some, like Hopkins or Eliot, it's God. For others, like the Surrealists, it's erotic desire, or the unconscious, or, in the case of the Futurists, the Will to Power. For Hölderlin it's the gods, for Rilke angels, for Lorca *duende*. In performative poetics, the poem is, in Taylor's words, 'an event with performative force' in which 'something that transcends language is manifested or set free'.

To understand how this happens, and exactly where this performative power comes from, I need to return again to the theory of language. You recall that both expressivism and performative theory agree that the essential activity of language isn't designation or representation but expression. The two theories differ, however, on the key question of who or what does the expressing. In expressivism, language is essentially a vehicle of self-expression, and thus, in expressivist poetics, it is the poet who expresses.

But performative poetics, on the contrary, proposes three quite different answers to this question.

One possibility is that no one expresses, or, to use Derrida's term, it is *différance* which expresses, that is, the differences among words considered as mere 'signs'. Some such theory of language seems implied by the poetics of Language poetry. It would explain why such poetry is devoid of real emotion or strong value, since, according to this view of language, there *is* no self either to express in, or be transformed by, language. Language poetry is thus the opposite of self-expression, and, in this way, too, a radical reaction to the poetics of Authenticity.

A second, much more promising possibility is that expression arises out of conversation, and takes place in a community of speech. This idea is important to English Romantic poetry, with its preference for apostrophe and direct address, as in, for example, 'Tintern Abbey' and Coleridge's conversation poems, not to mention all the great Romantic poems of invocation, from 'Ode to the West Wind' to 'Ode to a Nightingale'. This notion is also central to dramatic monologues and dialogues, not to mention poetic drama. And it's crucial to twentieth-century European poetry, too; think of how many poems by Rilke and Celan, for example, are addressed to 'you'.

A third possibility, equally promising, is that something beyond the self expresses itself through the poet: God, Nature, Spirit, the gods, the Ideal, the unconscious, the Will to Power, *duende,* and so on. This idea clearly underlies Symbolism, and much of English Romantic poetry, too, where it is embodied in the image of the poet as an Aeolian harp: 'Not I, but the wind that blows through me', in the words of D.H. Lawrence. But it is also an ancient idea in Western poetry and poetics. Consider the invocation of the Muse in Homer and Virgil, and of the Holy Spirit in Milton; consider the insistence in Plato that the poet is possessed by a god.

What is not so clear in Western poetics, ancient or otherwise, is the precise relationship between these transcendent sources of expression and the conscious art of the poet. In fact, the dispute over poetics between Plato and Aristotle seems to have divided these two ideas from one another right at the beginning of our critical tradition, with enormous consequences for our literary history. For Plato, the poet is possessed by a god, and doesn't even know what she is saying, let alone how she is saying it. For Aristotle, on the contrary, the poet is an artist who must make all kinds of conscious technical decisions while composing poems. The aestheticist and mimetic-pragmatic traditions in poetics have both sided with Aristotle on this question — hence their emphasis on rhetorical and prosodic technique — whereas Plato's influence can be seen in the Romantic disdain for technique, at least in theory, a disdain put into practice later, as we've seen, under the auspices of the poetics of Authenticity. But Plato's influence can also be seen in the insistence of many poets — Lawrence, Rilke, Lorca — that the source of their poetic expression is higher or deeper than the self. Nevertheless, even for these poets, technique and inspiration merely complement each another; there is no technique of poetic inspiration.

The exception that proves the rule is the set of methods devised by the Surrealists to gain access to the unconscious: automatic writing, trance writing, dream analysis, and so on. Of course, there are certain poets, such as Yeats and Merrill, who have used esoteric magical techniques to make contact with spirits and angels. And of course all kinds of poets have used various other means to find inspiration, from prayer and meditation to absinthe and LSD. But this is all marginal to Western poetics per se; these techniques of inspiration, such as they are, seem to us to have little to do with the techniques of art, and rhetoric and prosody in particular.

This distinction between poetic technique and inspiration did not obtain, however, in ancient India. For example, as Roberto Calasso explains in his astonishing little book *Literature and the Gods,* the ancient Indians considered poetic metre to be a yoga, that is, a mental discipline or yoke, without which one's mind would not be powerful enough to take an offering to the gods. Consider this origin myth from the *Satapatha Brāhmana*:

> Prajāpati [the mind] constructed the fire; it was keen-edged as a razor; terrified, the gods would not come near; then, wrapping themselves in the meters, they came near, and that is how the meters got their name. The meters are sacred power; the skin of the black antelope is the form of sacred power; he puts on shoes of antelope skin; not to be hurt, he wraps himself in meters before approaching the fire.

Metre, like a shamanic animal skin, has a sacred power; before the gods will come near to the fire of the mind, they must wrap themselves in the metres for protection. Metre, then, is essentially a technique for bringing the gods close to the mind, for opening up contact with these transcendent sources of poetic expression.

As it happens, I find this corresponds well to my own experience in writing metrical verse. I want to write something, a phrase or sentence, but the words that come to mind do not fit the metre; so I must word it differently, or write something else, something I had not quite intended to say. In the white heat of composition, I find myself saying all kinds of surprising things, often with more vividness and auditory resonance than I am conscious of coming up with on my own. It feels like I'm writing with someone else — a much better poet — leaning over my shoulder, making little suggestions quietly in my ear. But without the difficult yoga or mental discipline of the metre, I would not have needed these suggestions, and chances are the poem would have been the worse for it. For me, this is what it means in practice to say that metre brings the gods closer to the mind, or that it opens up contact with a transcendent source of poetic expression higher or deeper than the self.

I hasten to add that such an experience is not to be immediately expected by beginners, any more than transcendental meditative experiences should be expected by newcomers in the yoga studio. Metre is a discipline; it takes practice. Moreover, just as you can become very proficient in the physical techniques of yoga without engaging its spiritual dimensions, so one may become perfectly adept at versifying without hearing any transcendent suggestions; in such a case, everything one thinks of to write, one is aware of thinking of oneself. This is related to the problem of too much facility that sometimes afflicts experienced poets. Writing the kind of thing they write grows too easy for them, and unless they move on to something more difficult, the god can hardly get a word in edgewise.

So now we can begin to see how the sources of performative power in poetry may be related to poetic art, or at least to prosodic technique. A good critic should be able to tell the difference between skilful prosody — witty light verse, for instance — and inspired prosody, writing in which the very difficulty of the verse seems to have given the poet access to some transcendent source of performative power, however that transcendent source may be conceived.

Now let's consider another element of poetic art: diction. Any sensitive reader of Rilke or Celan will notice how often a poem of theirs will seem to detonate in a single concentrated word. As Charles Taylor points out in his aforementioned essay on Celan, everything else in the poem, its whole rhetorical effort, prepares us for this explosion of power; but there is often some particular word — in the later poems of Celan, often a neologism — that suddenly takes on a profound resonance. Performative poetics, the tradition which both Rilke and Celan emerge out of and renew, insists that the source of this explosive power is something beyond the self of the poet. This much we know. But how exactly does the poet open up access to this power?

Both Taylor and Northrop Frye, in writing about poetic language, provide a partial answer to this question, though from very different points of view. Much of Frye's late book *Words with Power* consists of essays on four words — mountain, garden, cave, and furnace — in which he demonstrates the massive power these great biblical symbols have in Western literature. For Frye — that radical Protestant — literary language, the language of metaphor and myth, originates in the Logos or Word understood as 'kerygma', that is, voice, proclamation, revelation, apocalypse and divine breath. At its source is God, speaking, proclaiming, revealing, unveiling and incarnating himself, not as the 'I am that I am', but rather the 'I will be what I will be'. In this regard Frye is a card-carrying adherent of performative poetics, since for him the source of power in poetry transcends the poet. But it is up to the poet to deploy the powerful words. And to do so effectively, Frye argues, a poet must go to school in the Bible, the 'Great Code of Art' in Blake's phrase, together with the great body of Western literature that largely springs from it. For Frye, a poet opens up contact with the Word in part by deploying these words of power and others like them in a poem, with full imaginative awareness of their mythical and symbolic resonance in the Bible and literary tradition.

Taylor, a Catholic philosopher in the Counter-Enlightenment tradition, uses the similar expression 'words of power'. But he uses it to express a different idea, derived more or less from Heidegger. Heidegger argued that the source of expression isn't the Word, exactly, but language; as he puts it, 'Language speaks'. The job of the thinker or poet is, to paraphrase Heidegger, to remain attentive to a call emanating from a silence in which there are not yet the right words for things, to allow language itself to push us to find the right, unprecedented words, and draw them out of silence. These words, whose sacred or spiritual meanings are thereby disclosed, are what Taylor calls words of power. It is these words which, for Heidegger, enable authentic thinking and poetry. (He discusses a number of examples, borrowing many of them from a poem by Georg Trakl: house, threshold, window, tree, jug.) They seem to be merely ordinary words. But as Heidegger puts it, 'Poetry proper is never merely a higher mode of everyday language. It is rather the reverse: everyday language is a forgotten and therefore used-up poem, from which there no longer resounds a call.' The poet's job is to make these ordinary words resonate for us again, by disrupting our insensitivity to them caused by habituation. Thus for Heidegger and Taylor, a word of power can be any dead word resurrected by the poet and restored to its original glory.

In his essay 'Building Dwelling Thinking', Heidegger shows precisely how this may be done: namely, by revealing anew the fullness of the relationship between a thing — say, a jug — and the world, with the latter including the earth and sky, divinities and mortals. He reminds us, for example, that the jug is made of earth (clay), holds rainwater that fell from the sky, and is used by mortals both to pour water for drinking to keep alive, and to pour out libations to the gods (or, he might have added, communion wine for the Mass). When he's finished with it, the word 'jug' is no longer merely an empty sign designating a dead object, but once again a nexus of powerful natural and spiritual forces: a word of power.

A critic trying to form a judgment about the performative power of a poet's diction should keep both of these contexts in mind: namely, the textual context of myth, symbol and literary tradition, as in Frye, and the context of language and the world in Heidegger's sense. In both cases, the poet opens up contact with a source of power beyond the self, bringing the gods closer to the mind by a variety of precise rhetorical means. In the textual context, such techniques include allusion, echo, myth, metaphor, symbol, displacement, and so on. In the context of language and the world, the poet lays down a rhetorical landmine, using invocations, questions, images, structure, and so on to uncover beforehand the hidden natural and spiritual forces buried in a powerful word, and thereby prepare it for its culminating detonation. A critic who bears all this in mind can keep his or her discussion of performative power in poetry from dissolving into vague impressionistic or mystical speculations; the critic must carefully respond to the poet's art, and demonstrate precisely what technical means the poet uses to open up contact with a transcendent source, whatever that source may be.

Conclusion

The theory of poetry I have been uncovering in this essay places poetic art at its centre, and establishes the intimate connection between the art of poetry and five poetic values: aesthetic pleasure, moral sources, human truth, performative power, and contact with something higher or deeper than the self. My theory engages, in various ways, with the poem, poetic tradition, the poet, the reader, the world and the gods. And thus I believe it is a more comprehensive and flexible theory than any one of the major theories of poetry I have considered on its own.

The test of any theory of poetry, of course, is whether or not it helps critics understand and describe what poets are doing, and make persuasive judgments about the quality of their work. The theory I have laid out in this essay has three virtues. It has great flexibility to respond to poems according to what they are trying to achieve. It shows why critics should ultimately base their judgments of relative success or failure on the quality of the art, rather than, say, what is represented, or the ethical or political values embodied in the poem. And most importantly, it shows *how* critics may do so, even when it comes to such apparently non-aesthetic values as moral sources, truth, and contact with transcendent sources of performative power.

Throughout this essay I have called myself an aesthete. But of course, particular aesthetic values change over time: some eras and readers will especially value classical clarity and restraint, others romantic passion or intellectual challenge; but in our time it should be possible to value a wide range of aesthetic qualities, because we have the benefit of a vast literary history. I can love Lorca's fierce rhetorical passion and surreal imagery, and also Cavafy's classical restraint and clarity; nevertheless I can also value Lorca over some minor French surrealist and Cavafy over some dull author of versified history. It is not the poet's particular aesthetic values that should determine the critic's estimation of the poem, but the quality of the art.

Another test of a theory is whether it spurs poets on to greater achievements in their work. My hope is that the theory I've laid out here clarifies two things to my readers who are poets: first, that masterful technique ought to be indispensable to all poets, not just aesthetes and pragmatists; and second, that while aesthetic value is crucial to any poet who wishes his or her poems to survive, it is in fact intimately bound to poetry's other values as well. Indeed, poets who aspire to greatness would do well — even from a purely aesthetic perspective — to incorporate those other values into their art.

I said at the outset that, in the past twenty years, a generation of Canadian poets has appeared that, as a group, has a more certain grasp of the technical resources of the art of poetry than previous generations. At the same time, there are fine poets among them who I wish were more ambitious. I hope that, as this new generation develops and matures, its best poets will aspire to great things, and, more to the point, achieve them.

Truly great poetry is one of the most powerful of all manifestations of language. Its object is ultimately the formation, and transformation, of the human self and community. Its power to do these things is not different in kind from the power of ordinary language to do them; it's just greater in degree. This is because great poetry is a fusion of reason, emotion, sensuality and imagination, bringing to bear all these powers of the human soul at once, whereas other uses of language are usually more specialized: rational but cold, passionate but stupid, beautiful but shallow, effective but ultimately meaningless.

A lot of people — let's call them Philistines — say this is all nonsense, that poetry is a marginal and specialized kind of playing with words, a strange kind of niche entertainment, of no interest to serious people, and certainly with no real power to make or transform anything. 'Poetry makes nothing happen', in the words of W.H. Auden, who, while not otherwise a Philistine, was channelling one, I'm afraid, when he wrote these words.

In response, I can only appeal to my own experience as a reader. Great poetry gives me pleasure. It stimulates my intellectual, emotional and imaginative powers. It deepens my understanding of myself and other people, and helps me pay closer attention to my life. It gives me the power to perceive things more clearly, to feel not only more intensely but more subtly and precisely. It resurrects the dead world I live in, and the dead words I use, and makes the sources of strong value in my life resonate again.

I know from experience, however, what it means to be part of a community without a great poetry of its own. Whitman and Dickinson are not quite the central figures in American culture that Shakespeare is in British culture, or Homer in Greek, or Dante in Italian; but as a Canadian I feel the absence of such a major poetic figure in my own country most exquisitely. Because of this absence, the community of Canada, and therefore the self of every Canadian, has not been fully formed. Now, everyone knows achieving that level of poetic power is extremely difficult. But we also know it's not impossible.

I want our poets to try.

☆

About the Author

James Pollock is the author of *Sailing to Babylon* (Able Muse Press, 2012), a finalist for the Governor General's Award. His poetry has appeared in *The Paris Review, Maisonneuve, Poetry Daily, The Fiddlehead, AGNI, Canadian Literature,* and other journals, and has been listed in *Best Canadian Poetry 2010*. His critical essays and reviews have been published in *Contemporary Poetry Review, Canadian Notes & Queries, Arc Poetry Magazine, The New Quarterly,* and elsewhere. He earned an Honours B.A. in English literature and creative writing from York University in Toronto, and an M.A. and Ph.D. in creative writing and literature from the University of Houston, where he held several fellowships in poetry. He was a John Woods Scholar in poetry at the Prague Summer Program at Charles University in Prague, and a work-study scholar in poetry at the Bread Loaf Writers' Conference at Middlebury College in Vermont. He is an associate professor at Loras College in Dubuque, Iowa, where he teaches poetry in the creative writing program. He lives with his wife and son in Madison, Wisconsin.